COLLINS
CHEERFUL
COOKING

TEATIME COOKERY

First published 1973
ISBN 0 00 435267 X

Devised, edited and designed by Youé & Spooner Ltd.

Printed in Great Britain by Collins Clear-Type Press

COLLINS
CHEERFUL
COOKING

TEATIME COOKERY

PHYLLIS POWELL

COLLINS
LONDON & GLASGOW

Useful weights and measures

WEIGHT EQUIVALENTS

Avoirdupois		*Metric*
1 ounce	=	28·35 grammes
1 pound	=	453·6 grammes
2·3 pounds	=	1 kilogram

LIQUID MEASUREMENTS

$\frac{1}{4}$ pint	=	$1\frac{1}{2}$ decilitres
$\frac{1}{2}$ pint	=	$\frac{1}{4}$ litre
scant 1 pint	=	$\frac{1}{2}$ litre
$1\frac{3}{4}$ pints	=	1 litre
1 gallon	=	4·5 litres

HANDY LIQUID MEASURES

1 pint	=	20 fluid ounces	=	32 tablespoons
$\frac{1}{2}$ pint	=	10 fluid ounces	=	16 tablespoons
$\frac{1}{4}$ pint	=	5 fluid ounces	=	8 tablespoons
$\frac{1}{8}$ pint	=	$2\frac{1}{2}$ fluid ounces	=	4 tablespoons
$\frac{1}{16}$ pint	=	$1\frac{1}{4}$ fluid ounces	=	2 tablespoons

HANDY SOLID MEASURES

			Approximate
Almonds, ground	1 oz.	=	$3\frac{3}{4}$ level tablespoons
Arrowroot	1 oz.	=	4 level tablespoons
Breadcrumbs fresh	1 oz.	=	7 level tablespoons
dried	1 oz.	=	$3\frac{1}{4}$ level tablespoons
Butter and Lard	1 oz.	=	2 level tablespoons
Cheese, grated	1 oz.	=	$3\frac{1}{2}$ level tablespoons
Chocolate, grated	1 oz.	=	3 level tablespoons
Cocoa	1 oz.	=	$2\frac{3}{4}$ level tablespoons
Desiccated Coconut	1 oz.	=	$4\frac{1}{2}$ tablespoons
Coffee—Instant	1 oz.	=	4 level tablespoons
Ground	1 oz.	=	4 tablespoons
Cornflour	1 oz.	=	$2\frac{1}{2}$ tablespoons
Custard powder	1 oz.	=	$2\frac{1}{2}$ tablespoons
Curry Powder and Spices	1 oz.	=	5 tablespoons
Flour	1 oz.	=	2 level tablespoons
Gelatine, powdered	1 oz.	=	$2\frac{1}{2}$ tablespoons
Rice, uncooked	1 oz.	=	$1\frac{1}{2}$ tablespoons
Sugar, caster and granulated	1 oz.	=	2 tablespoons
Icing sugar	1 oz.	=	$2\frac{1}{2}$ tablespoons
Syrup	1 oz.	=	1 tablespoon
Yeast, granulated	1 oz.	=	1 level tablespoon

AMERICAN MEASURES

16 fluid ounces	=	1 American pint
8 fluid ounces	=	1 American standard cup
0·50 fluid ounces	=	1 American tablespoon *(slightly smaller than British Standards Institute tablespoon)*
0·16 fluid ounces	=	1 American teaspoon

AUSTRALIAN MEASURES
(Cup, Spoon and Liquid Measures)

These are the measures in everyday use in the Australian family kitchen. The spoon measures listed below are from the ordinary household cutlery set.

CUP MEASURES

(Using the 8-liquid-ounce cup measure)

1 cup flour	4 oz.
1 cup sugar *(crystal or caster)*	8 oz.
1 cup icing sugar *(free from lumps)*	5 oz.
1 cup shortening *(butter, margarine, etc.)*	8 oz.
1 cup honey, golden syrup, treacle	10 oz.
1 cup brown sugar *(lightly packed)*	4 oz.
1 cup brown sugar *(tightly packed)*	5 oz.
1 cup soft breadcrumbs	2 oz.
1 cup dry breadcrumbs *(made from fresh breadcrumbs)*	3 oz.
1 cup packet dry breadcrumbs	4 oz.
1 cup rice *(uncooked)*	6 oz.
1 cup rice *(cooked)*	5 oz.
1 cup mixed fruit or individual fruit such as sultanas, etc.	4 oz.
1 cup grated cheese	4 oz.
1 cup nuts *(chopped)*	4 oz.
1 cup coconut	$2\frac{1}{2}$ oz.

SPOON MEASURES

	Level Tablespoon
1 oz. flour	2
1 oz. sugar *(crystal or caster)*	$1\frac{1}{2}$
1 oz. icing sugar *(free from lumps)*	2
1 oz. shortening	1
1 oz. honey	1
1 oz. gelatine	2
1 oz. cocoa	3
1 oz. cornflour	$2\frac{1}{2}$
1 oz. custard powder	$2\frac{1}{2}$

LIQUID MEASURES

(Using 8-liquid-ounce cup)

1 cup liquid	8 oz
$2\frac{1}{2}$ cups liquid	20 oz. (1 pint)
2 tablespoons liquid	1 oz.
1 gill liquid	5 oz. ($\frac{1}{4}$ pint)

Metric equivalents and oven temperatures are not listed here as they are included in all the recipes throughout the book.

When using the metric measures, in some cases it may be necessary to cut down the amount of liquid used. This is in order to achieve a balanced recipe and the correct consistency, as 1oz equals, in fact, 28·35gm.

Introduction

If you have a family or like to entertain, why not be your own baker? It's fun, will save you money and there is nothing to compare with the taste of home-baked bread and cakes. Most of the recipes are simple and self-explanatory but, to help you further, I have listed a few tips as overall guide-lines.

Although I have suggested using fresh yeast in all my recipes, dried yeast is just as simple to use. Make sure you buy the right kind, baker's dried yeast, sold usually in grocers and supermarkets. Use exactly half the amount of fresh yeast where stated. Simply sprinkle dried yeast on the measured tepid liquid required for the recipe, leave for 15 minutes or until mixture becomes thick and frothy, then add to the flour. And remember that one of the secrets of yeast cookery is to turn on the oven while the dough is proving (rising) for the second time. This way, the oven will be really hot when the bread or buns go in.

You will see that I have used margarine for economy, but do use butter if you prefer and likewise fresh cream instead of powdered creamy topping and canned cream.

To make party cakes look even more glamorous and to pipe really professional looking biscuits and meringues, invest in a large, nylon, washable piping bag and two or three shell nozzles of varying sizes.

I have advised lining cake tins in most recipes, but naturally if you have non-stick tins there is no need to do this.

You will find in this book recipes of all types, traditional ones and new ones, all tried and tested. So try them yourself – I hope they will give you hours and even years of happy baking.

Phyllis Powell

Large cakes

There are cakes for every occasion in this chapter – everyday teas, packed lunches, family birthdays and even some which you can serve as puddings at dinner parties.

VICTORIA SANDWICH

(Illustrated on page 17)
Gives 6 portions

4oz (100gm) margarine
4oz (100gm) caster sugar, plus a little extra to sprinkle top of cooked cake
2 standard eggs
4oz (100gm) self-raising flour, sifted
2 heaped tablespoons red jam

1. Preheat oven to moderate to moderately hot, 375 deg F or gas 5 (190 deg C).
2. Grease two 7-inch (18cm) round cake tins. Line bases of tins with greaseproof paper and then grease the paper.
3. Beat the margarine with 4oz (100gm) caster sugar until light and fluffy.
4. Beat the eggs together then beat into the mixture.
5. Using a metal spoon, fold in the sifted flour.
6. Divide the mixture between the cake tins.
7. Bake the cakes in the centre of the preheated oven for 20–30 minutes, or until firm to the touch.
8. Turn out to cool on a wire rack.
9. Sandwich cakes with jam then lightly dust top of cake with caster sugar.

MADEIRA CAKE

Gives 6 portions

8oz (200gm) self-raising flour
pinch of salt
6oz (150gm) margarine
6oz (150gm) caster sugar
3 large eggs
finely grated rind of half a small lemon
2 large pieces of citron peel for decoration

1. Preheat oven to moderate to moderately hot, 375 deg F or gas 5 (190 deg C).
2. Line a deep, round 7-inch (18cm) cake tin with greaseproof paper, then grease the paper.
3. Sift the flour and salt into a basin.
4. Cream the margarine with the caster sugar until very light and fluffy.
5. Beat the eggs together then add, gradually, to creamed mixture, beating well.
6. Using a metal spoon, fold in the flour and the lemon rind.
7. Spoon mixture into the prepared tin.
8. Bake in centre of preheated oven for 45 minutes, then open the oven door and quickly place the citron peel in the centre of the cake. Shut oven door.
9. Reduce oven heat to moderate 350 deg F or gas 4 (180 deg C) and cook for 30 minutes.
10. Leave cake to cool in tin for 5 minutes then turn out to complete cooling on a wire rack. (This cake keeps well if stored in an airtight tin.)

NUT TRIANGLE CAKE

Gives 4 to 8 portions

4oz (100gm) margarine
4oz (100gm) caster sugar
2 standard eggs
4oz (100gm) self-raising flour, sifted
3 heaped tablespoons raspberry jam
3oz (75gm) walnuts, finely chopped

1. Preheat oven to moderate to moderately hot, 375 deg F or gas 5 (190 deg C).
2. Grease two 7-inch (18cm) round shallow cake tins. Line bases of tins with greaseproof paper and grease the paper.
3. Beat margarine with caster sugar until light and fluffy.
4. Beat the eggs together then beat gradually into creamed mixture.
5. Using a metal spoon, fold in the sifted flour.
6. Divide the mixture between the cake tins.
7. Bake the cakes in centre of preheated oven for 20–30 minutes or until firm to the touch.
8. Turn out to cool. Cut one cake into four triangles. Brush two triangles with warmed jam, then sprinkle these with nuts. Leave other two triangles plain.
9. Spread rest of jam on complete cake. Place triangles on top, plain ones and nutty ones alternating.

STRAWBERRY SPONGE

Gives 6 portions

For a delicious extra to this cake add some hard-frozen ice cream to the jam just before you serve it.

6oz (150gm) margarine
6oz (150gm) caster sugar
3 large eggs
6oz (150gm) self-raising flour
3 heaped tablespoons strawberry jam
3 heaped tablespoons desiccated coconut

1. Preheat oven to moderate to moderately hot, 375 deg F or gas 5 (190 deg C).
2. Grease and flour two 7½-inch (19cm) sandwich tins.
3. Beat the margarine with the caster sugar until light and fluffy.
4. Beat the eggs together. Add beaten egg very gradually to sugar mixture, beating well after each addition.
5. Sift flour, then fold into beaten mixture using a metal spoon.
6. Divide the mixture between the prepared tins and smooth the tops.
7. Bake cakes in centre of preheated oven for 25 minutes, or until well risen and firm to the touch.
8. Turn out cakes to cool on a wire rack.
9. Pick out all the strawberries from the jam and put to one side.
10. Spread 1 tablespoon of jam on top of one cake and round its sides.
11. Cut the centre out of the other cake to make a circle about 2½ inches in diameter. Put this circle to one side.
12. Coat the remaining ring with jam on the top and sides.
13. Sprinkle coconut on the ring.
14. Place the cake ring on top of the whole cake.
15. Put the reserved strawberries in the centre of the ring. Add the ice cream if used.
16. Coat the reserved piece of cake with jam and coconut and position on top of the strawberries.

BATTENBURG CAKE

Gives 5 portions

6oz (150gm) self-raising flour
pinch of salt
6oz (150gm) margarine
9oz (225gm) caster sugar
3 standard eggs, beaten
few drops pink colouring
4oz (100gm) apricot jam
3oz (75gm) ground almonds
3oz (75gm) icing sugar, sifted
almond essence
1 small egg, beaten

1. Preheat oven to moderate to moderately hot, 375 deg F or gas 5 (190 deg C).
2. Grease two 1-lb (½ kilo) loaf tins.
3. Sift flour and salt.
4. Cream margarine and 6oz (150gm) caster sugar until light and fluffy.
5. Add the standard eggs one by one, beating well.
6. Fold sifted flour into mixture, using metal spoon.
7. Put half mixture into one tin and smooth top. Colour rest pale pink. Put into other tin and smooth top. Bake both in centre of preheated oven for 25 minutes, or until golden and firm. Leave to cool.
8. Trim top off each cake to make them level. Cut each cake into two neat strips.
9. Warm jam in a small pan. Brush sides of strips. Sandwich into an oblong so you have alternate colours, making typical 'chequerboard' Battenburg Cake pattern with strips.
10. Mix ground almonds with rest of caster sugar, icing sugar and almond essence. Add small egg and knead.
11. Roll into oblong large enough to wrap around cake.
12. Brush cake with jam except the two short sides. Wrap paste around cake, leaving short ends exposed to show the pattern of pink and white squares. Crimp paste edges with fingers.

COFFEE GATEAU

(Illustrated on page 17)

Gives 6 portions

If you haven't got a piping bag, simply cover the whole cake with icing and then rough it up with a knife. You will need to make extra icing if you are doing this.

4oz (100gm) plain flour
1½ level teaspoons baking powder
6oz (150gm) margarine
4oz (100gm) caster sugar
2 large eggs
1 level dessertspoon, plus 1 level teaspoon instant coffee powder
4oz (100gm) icing sugar
1 tablespoon red jam

1. Preheat oven to moderate to moderately hot, 375 deg F or gas 5 (190 deg C).
2. Grease two 7-inch (18cm) round sandwich tins. Line with greaseproof paper.
3. Sift the flour and baking powder.
4. Cream 4oz (100gm) margarine with the caster sugar.
5. Add the eggs, one at a time, beating well after each addition.
6. Fold in the flour using a metal spoon.
7. Mix the dessertspoon of coffee with a dessertspoon of boiling water. Beat into the cake mixture.
8. Divide the mixture between the prepared cake tins. Smooth the tops.
9. Bake in the centre of the preheated oven for 20–25 minutes or until golden and firm.
10. Turn out cakes to cool on a wire rack.
11. Sift the icing sugar.
12. Cream rest of margarine with icing sugar and the teaspoon of coffee until light and fluffy.
13. When the cakes are cool, sandwich them together with the jam.
14. Spread a little icing on top and round the sides of the cake and make a stippled pattern with a fork.
15. Put the rest of the icing in a piping bag with a medium-sized star nozzle. Pipe lattice pattern across the top of the cake, and stars round edge and base.

CHOCOLATE GATEAU
Gives 6 portions

5oz (125gm) self-raising flour
pinch of salt
1oz (25gm) cocoa
1½ level teaspoons baking powder
2oz (50gm) soft margarine
6oz (150gm) soft brown sugar
3 large eggs
1 tablespoon milk
8oz (200gm) icing sugar
1 small orange

1. Preheat oven to moderate, 350 deg F or gas 4 (180 deg C).
2. Grease two 7-inch (18cm) round cake tins. Line bases of tins with greaseproof paper and grease the paper.
3. Sift the flour with the salt, cocoa and baking powder into a bowl.
4. Add 6oz (150gm) margarine to sifted mixture with the brown sugar, eggs and milk. Beat the mixture with a wooden spoon for 3 minutes, or until smooth.
5. Divide the mixture between prepared cake tins.
6. Bake cakes in centre of the preheated oven for 25 minutes, or until golden and well risen.
7. Turn out to cool on a wire rack.
8. Sift the icing sugar.
9. Cut orange in half. Squeeze out and strain juice from half of the orange. Grate the rind of this half.
10. Cream rest of margarine with icing sugar and orange juice. Stir in one teaspoon of grated orange rind.
11. Level off the top of one of the cakes.
12. Sieve or liquidize the cake trimmings to make crumbs.
13. Sandwich the cakes with a little of the icing, putting the levelled-off piece on top.
14. Smear a little icing round sides of cake.
15. Using a knife with a large blade, press cake crumbs on to sides of cake.
16. Coat top of cake with icing.
17. Put the rest of the icing in a piping bag fitted with a medium star nozzle and pipe stars round edge of cake.
18. Cut the other piece of orange into slices. Cut each slice from outer edge almost to centre, then twist each slice.
19. Decorate the centre of the cake with orange twists.

SUNDAY GATEAU
Gives 6 portions

6oz (150gm) margarine
6oz (150gm) caster sugar
3 large eggs
6oz (150gm) self-raising flour
half a 6oz (150gm) can cream
1 can (8oz or 200gm) pear halves
3oz (75gm) plain chocolate

1. Preheat oven to moderate to moderately hot, 375 deg F or gas 5 (190 deg C).
2. Grease and flour two 7½-inch (19cm) sandwich tins.
3. Cream the margarine with the caster sugar until light and fluffy.
4. Beat the eggs together. Gradually add to creamed mixture, beating well.
5. Sift the flour then fold into creamed mixture, using a metal spoon.
6. Divide mixture between the prepared cake tins and bake in centre of preheated oven for 25 minutes, or until golden and firm to the touch.
7. Turn out cakes to cool on a wire rack.
8. Sandwich the cakes with half the cream.
9. Drain the pears – juice is not needed.
10. Put the pears, rounded sides up, on a wire rack with a plate underneath.
11. Put the chocolate in a bowl over a pan of gently simmering water and leave until chocolate has melted.
12. Spoon melted chocolate over the pears to coat completely.
13. Leave to set.
14. Position the pears on top of the cake and gently spoon the rest of the cream into spaces left on top of cake. Serve the same day.

HEDGEHOG CAKE
Gives 5 to 6 portions

10oz (250gm) margarine
4oz (100gm) caster sugar
2 large eggs
4oz (100gm) self-raising flour
6oz (150gm) icing sugar
orange squash, to taste
14 tiny chocolate buttons

1. Preheat oven to moderate, 350 deg F or gas 4 (180 deg C).
2. Grease a 2-pint (1 litre) pudding basin.
3. Cream 4oz (100gm) margarine with caster sugar until fluffy.
4. Beat eggs. Gradually add to creamed mixture, beating well.
5. Using a metal spoon, fold in sifted flour.
6. Spoon into prepared basin.
7. Bake in centre of preheated oven for 1 hour, or until well risen and firm to the touch.
8. Turn out to cool.
9. Beat rest of margarine with sifted icing sugar until creamy. Flavour with orange squash.
10. Spread icing all over the cake and peak with a knife.
11. Spike the cake with the chocolate buttons.

SPIKY ALMOND CAKE
Gives 5 to 6 portions

10oz (250gm) margarine
4oz (100gm) caster sugar
2 large eggs
4oz (100gm) self-raising flour, sifted
6oz (150gm) icing sugar, sifted
strong liquid black coffee (unsweetened) to taste
1½oz (37gm) whole almonds, skinned, split and toasted

1. Preheat oven to moderate, 350 deg F or gas 4 (180 deg C).
2. Grease a 2-pint (1 litre) pudding basin.
3. Cream 4oz (100gm) margarine with caster sugar until fluffy.
4. Beat eggs. Gradually add to creamed mixture, beating well.
5. Using a metal spoon, fold in the flour.
6. Spoon into prepared basin.
7. Bake in centre of preheated oven for 1 hour, or until well risen and firm to the touch.
8. Turn out to cool.
9. Beat rest of margarine with icing sugar until light and fluffy. Flavour with coffee. Spread all over cake. Rough up with blade of knife and spike with almonds.

CHOCOLATE PARTY CAKE

Gives 5 to 6 portions

3oz (75gm) self-raising flour
1oz (25gm) cocoa powder
½ level teaspoon baking powder
4oz (100gm) margarine
4oz (100gm) caster sugar
2 large eggs
small sachet powdered creamy topping
milk to mix

1. Preheat oven to moderate, 350 deg F or gas 4 (180 deg C).
2. Grease a 2-pint (1 litre) pudding basin.
3. Sift the flour with the cocoa and baking powder. Do this three times.
4. Cream margarine with caster sugar until very light and fluffy.
5. Beat eggs. Gradually add them to creamed mixture, beating well.
6. Using a metal spoon, fold in the flour mixture.
7. Spoon into prepared basin.
8. Bake in centre of preheated oven for 1 hour, or until well risen and firm to the touch.
9. Turn out to cool.
10. Make up topping as directed on the packet.
11. Put topping in a large piping bag fitted with a large star nozzle.
12. Pipe four lines of stars up the sides of the cake to meet at the centre. Pipe a large star on top. Serve within 3 hours.

SPONGE FLAN

(Illustrated on page 18)

Gives about 6 portions

The sponge base can be made the day before and stored in an airtight tin.

3oz (75gm) self-raising flour
4oz (100gm) margarine
3oz (75gm) caster sugar
2 standard eggs
1 tablespoon warm water
1 can (1lb or ½ kilo) red plums
arrowroot, to thicken
2oz (50gm) icing sugar

1. Preheat oven to moderate, 350 deg F or gas 4 (180 deg C).
2. Grease and lightly flour an 8-inch (20cm) sponge flan tin.
3. Sift the flour into a bowl.
4. In another bowl, cream 3oz (75gm) margarine with the caster sugar until light and fluffy.
5. Beat in one egg. Separate the other egg and beat yolk into mixture. (The egg white is not needed, so use it for making meringues, see pages 41, 56–59, 68.)
6. Using a metal spoon, fold the flour and warm water into the mixture.
7. Spoon mixture into prepared tin; smooth the top.
8. Bake in centre of preheated oven for 25 minutes or until firm to the touch.
9. Leave the cake to cool in tin for 3 minutes then turn out to cool on a wire rack.
10. Drain the fruit and reserve the juice.
11. Arrange the fruit in the flan case.
12. Following the instructions on the packet, thicken the fruit juice with arrowroot. When mixture is nearly cold, spoon it on top of the fruit.
13. Beat the rest of the margarine with the icing sugar until light and fluffy.
14. Put this mixture in a piping bag fitted with a small star nozzle and pipe neat stars round top edge and base of flan.

WALNUT AND BANANA SPONGE

Gives 6 portions

4oz (100gm) margarine
4oz (100gm) caster sugar
2 standard eggs
4oz (100gm) self-raising flour, sifted
2 large ripe bananas
1oz (25gm) walnuts, chopped

1. Preheat oven to moderate to moderately hot, 375 deg F or gas 5 (190 deg C).
2. Grease two 7-inch (18cm) round, shallow cake tins. Line bases with greaseproof paper and grease the paper.
3. Beat margarine with caster sugar until light and fluffy.
4. Beat the eggs together, then beat lightly into the mixture.
5. Using a metal spoon, fold in the sifted flour.
6. Divide the mixture between the cake tins.
7. Bake the cakes in centre of preheated oven for 20–30 minutes or until firm to the touch.
8. Turn out to cool on wire rack. Fill cake not sooner than 30 minutes before serving.
9. Mash or liquidize bananas. Mix with nuts. Use to sandwich the cakes together. Serve at once.

SUGAR-FROSTED PLUM CAKE
Gives 6 portions

6oz (150gm) margarine
6oz (150gm) caster sugar
4 large eggs
6oz (150gm) self-raising flour
almond essence
6 red plums
3oz (75gm) granulated sugar
2 heaped tablespoons red plum jam

1. Preheat oven to moderate to moderately hot, 375 deg F or gas 5 (190 deg C).
2. Grease and flour two 7½-inch (19cm) sandwich tins.
3. Cream the margarine with the caster sugar until light and fluffy.
4. Separate one egg. Beat the other eggs with the egg yolk. Reserve egg white. Very gradually beat into the creamed mixture.
5. Sift the flour. Using a metal spoon, fold into the creamed mixture.
6. Flavour, to taste, with almond essence.
7. Divide mixture between the prepared tins and bake in centre of preheated oven for 25 minutes, or until well risen and firm to the touch.
8. Turn out cakes to cool on a wire cooling rack.
9. Wash the plums and dry well.
10. Coat plums with egg white then toss in sugar to coat. Leave for 2 hours to dry in a cool place.
11. Use most of jam to sandwich cakes together. Spread rest on top of cake.
12. Arrange the plums in a heap in the centre of the cake.

MOUNTAIN CAKE
Gives 5 to 6 portions

Strawberries, when they are in season, would be a delicious alternative filling.

4oz (100gm) self-raising flour
4oz (100gm) margarine
4oz (100gm) caster sugar
2 large eggs
1 can (10oz or 250gm) cream or fresh cream
1 can (8oz or 200gm) fruit cocktail

1. Preheat oven to moderate to moderately hot, 375 deg F or gas 5 (190 deg C).
2. Grease two 7-inch (18cm) round sandwich tins. Line bases with greaseproof paper and grease the paper.
3. Sift the flour.
4. Cream the margarine with the caster sugar until light and fluffy.
5. Beat the eggs together, then add them gradually to the creamed mixture, beating well.
6. Using a metal spoon, fold in the flour.
7. Divide the mixture between the prepared tins and smooth the tops.
8. Bake in the centre of the preheated oven for 25–30 minutes, or until golden and firm to the touch.
9. Turn out to cool on a wire cooling rack.
10. Spread a little cream around the sides of one sponge and put it on a plate.
11. Cut out a circle from the centre of the other sponge, about 4 inches in diameter, using a saucer as a guide.
12. Chop up the ring shape left behind.
13. Coat the 4-inch round with cream on the top and sides.
14. Drain the fruit and reserve the juice.
15. Put the chopped cake on top of the whole sponge. Sprinkle 5 tablespoons of the fruit juice on to it.
16. Pile the fruit on top of the chopped cake and then put the 4-inch circle on top.
17. Serve within an hour of making.

GRAPEFRUIT GATEAU
Gives 6 portions

6oz (150gm) margarine
6oz (150gm) caster sugar
3 large eggs
6oz (150gm) self-raising flour
1 can (8oz or 200gm) grapefruit segments
3 tablespoons lemon marmalade

1. Preheat oven to moderate to moderately hot, 375 deg F or gas 5 (190 deg C).
2. Grease and flour two 7½-inch (19cm) sandwich tins.
3. Cream margarine with caster sugar until light and fluffy.
4. Beat the eggs together, then gradually add to creamed mixture.
5. Sift the flour, then fold into creamed mixture using a metal spoon.
6. Divide mixture between the prepared tins. Smooth the tops.
7. Bake in centre of preheated oven for 25 minutes, or until well risen and firm.
8. Turn out cakes to cool.
9. Drain fruit and then chop a third of it and mix with 1 tablespoon marmalade.
10. Sandwich cakes with marmalade mixture, then spoon rest of the fruit on top.
11. Coat with rest of marmalade.

PLUM BASKET

Gives 4 to 6 portions

4oz (100gm) self-raising flour
10oz (250gm) margarine
4oz (100gm) caster sugar
2 large eggs
1 can (1lb or ½ kilo) red plums
arrowroot, to thicken
almond essence, to taste
6oz (150gm) icing sugar, sifted
strong liquid black instant coffee, to taste

1. Preheat oven to moderate to moderately hot, 375 deg F or gas 5 (190 deg C).
2. Grease two round 7-inch (18cm) sandwich tins.
3. Sift the flour into a bowl.
4. Cream 4oz (100gm) margarine with caster sugar until light and fluffy.
5. Beat the eggs together, then gradually add them to the mixture, beating well.
6. Using a metal spoon, fold in the flour.
7. Divide the mixture between the prepared tins and smooth the tops.
8. Bake in the centre of the preheated oven for 25–30 minutes, or until golden and firm to the touch.
9. Turn out cakes to cool on a wire rack.
10. Drain the juice off the fruit. Thicken the juice with arrowroot, following instructions on the packet.
11. Stir the fruit into the thickened juice and flavour with a tiny amount of almond essence.
12. Beat the icing sugar with the rest of the margarine until creamy. Add coffee, to taste.
13. Put most of the icing into a piping bag fitted with a plain, medium nozzle.
14. Spread the rest of the icing round the sides of one of the sponges.
15. Pipe straight lines, close together, on top of the other sponge. Then pipe more lines, across the first ones, to give a basket weave effect.
16. Carefully spread a little icing on sides of the 'basket' sponge and cut it in half to make two semi-circles.
17. Spoon the fruit on to the sponge with the plain top.
18. Place the two semi-circles on top of the fruit, so they tilt upwards slightly at the sides.

BLACKCURRANT DELIGHT

Gives 5 to 6 portions

6oz (150gm) margarine
6oz (150gm) caster sugar
3 large eggs
6oz (150gm) self-raising flour
half a 14½oz (362gm) can blackcurrant pie filling
half a 6oz (150gm) can cream

1. Preheat oven to moderate to moderately hot, 375 deg F or gas 5 (190 deg C).
2. Grease and flour two 7½-inch (19cm) sandwich tins.
3. Beat margarine with caster sugar until light and fluffy.
4. Beat the eggs together. Very gradually add them to creamed mixture, beating well.
5. Sift the flour, then, using a metal sooon, fold into creamed mixture.
6. Divide mixture between the prepared tins and smooth the tops.
7. Bake cakes in centre of preheated oven for 25 minutes, or until well risen and firm to the touch.
8. Turn out cakes to cool on a wire rack.
9. Cut each cake into two layers.
10. Spread pie filling then cream on each layer. Sandwich all the layers together and serve within 2 hours.

RUM AND ORANGE OBLONG

Gives 5 to 6 portions

6oz (150gm) margarine
4oz (100gm) caster sugar
2 standard eggs
4oz (100gm) self-raising flour
1 tablespoon tepid water
6oz (150gm) icing sugar
rum essence, to taste
1 can (11oz or 275gm) mandarin oranges
1 small fresh orange

1. Preheat oven to moderate, 350 deg F or gas 4 (180 deg C).
2. Grease a square 9-inch (23cm) cake tin. Line tin with greaseproof paper and grease the paper.
3. Cream 4oz (100gm) margarine with caster sugar until light and fluffy.
4. Beat the eggs together and add them gradually to the mixture, beating well.
5. Using a metal spoon, fold in the sifted flour and water.
6. Spoon mixture into prepared tin and smooth the top.
7. Bake in centre of the preheated oven for 35 minutes, or until well risen and firm to the touch.
8. Turn out to cool on a wire cooling rack.
9. Cut the cake, downwards, into two pieces.
10. Beat the rest of the margarine with 4oz (100gm) sifted icing sugar until creamy. Flavour with rum essence.
11. Mince or liquidize the drained fruit and stir it into the icing.
12. Use to sandwich the two pieces of cake together to make an oblong shape.
13. Mix the rest of the icing sugar with enough cold water to give a mixture that will coat the back of a spoon.
14. Spoon mixture on top of cake. Leave to set.
15. Decorate iced top with slices of fresh orange.

MIXED FRUIT CAKE

Gives 5 to 6 portions

12oz (300gm) plain flour
pinch of salt
1 level teaspoon baking powder
8oz (200gm) margarine
8oz (200gm) caster sugar
4 large eggs
4oz (100gm) dates, finely chopped
2oz (50gm) glacé cherries, chopped
4oz (100gm) currants
4oz (100gm) sultanas

1. Preheat oven to moderate, 350 deg F or gas 4 (180 deg C).
2. Grease a round, deep 8-inch (20cm) cake tin. Line base and sides with greaseproof paper and grease the paper.
3. Sift flour, salt and baking powder into a basin.
4. Cream the margarine with the caster sugar until light and fluffy.
5. Beat the eggs together, then gradually add to the creamed mixture, beating well.
6. Using a metal spoon, fold in the flour.
7. Mix all the fruit together, then, lightly but thoroughly, fold into the mixture.
8. Spoon mixture into the prepared tin. Smooth the top.
9. Bake in the centre of the preheated oven for 45 minutes, then reduce oven to very moderate, 325 deg F or gas 3 (170 deg C), and cook for a further $1\frac{1}{4}$ hours, or until firm to the touch.
10. Turn out to cool completely before storing in an airtight tin. Eat within a week.

DUNDEE CAKE

Gives 6 portions

2oz (50gm) whole almonds
12oz (300gm) plain flour
pinch of salt
1 level teaspoon baking powder
8oz (200gm) margarine
8oz (200gm) caster sugar
4 large eggs
1lb ($\frac{1}{2}$ kilo) mixed dried fruit (sultanas, raisins and currants)

1. Preheat oven to moderate, 350 deg F or gas 4 (180 deg C).
2. Grease a round, deep 8-inch (20cm) cake tin. Line with greaseproof paper and grease the paper.
3. Put almonds into a small pan. Cover with water. Boil then drain. Skin nuts and split each in half.
4. Sift flour, salt and baking powder.
5. Cream margarine and caster sugar until light and fluffy.
6. Beat eggs together and add, a little at a time, to creamed mixture, beating well. Fold sifted flour into creamed mixture, using metal spoon.
7. Add fruit and mix well.
8. Turn mixture into prepared tin and make slight hollow in centre. Arrange almonds over top of cake.
9. Cook, in centre of preheated oven for 45 minutes, then reduce heat to very moderate, 325 deg F or gas 3 (170 deg C), and cook for $1\frac{3}{4}$ hours or until firm to the touch.

HIT RECORD CAKE

Gives 6 to 8 portions

This is a good idea for a child's or teenager's birthday cake.

6oz (150gm) self-raising flour
12oz (300gm) margarine
4oz (100gm) caster sugar
1 large egg
3 tablespoons milk
8oz (200gm) icing sugar.
2oz (50gm) plain chocolate

1. Preheat oven to moderate to moderately hot, 375 deg F or gas 5 (190 deg C).
2. Grease two round 7-inch (18cm) sandwich tins. Line with greaseproof paper and grease the paper.
3. Sift the flour into a bowl.
4. Cream 4oz (100gm) margarine with the caster sugar until light and fluffy.
5. Gradually beat in the egg, then fold in flour.
6. Stir in the milk to give a soft mixture which will drop easily from a spoon when shaken.
7. Divide the mixture between the prepared tins.
8. Bake in the centre of the preheated oven for 25–30 minutes, or until golden brown and firm to the touch.
9. Leave cakes to cool.
10. Put the icing sugar in a bowl and beat with the rest of the margarine until creamy.
11. Put the chocolate in a basin over a pan of gently simmering water and leave until melted, then stir into the icing. Use a little to sandwich the cakes together.
12. Spread the icing round top and sides of cake.
13. Using a knitting needle, or skewer, and working quickly, make circles all round the top of the cake just like the grooves on a gramophone record.
14. Cut out a thick paper circle. Using a coloured crayon, or felt-tipped pen, print the name of the child's favourite pop star on the paper, then place in the centre of the cake.

FARMHOUSE ALMOND AND CHERRY CAKE
Gives 4 to 6 portions

8oz (200gm) self-raising flour
pinch of salt
6oz (150gm) margarine
6oz (150gm) caster sugar
3 standard eggs
3oz (75gm) glacé cherries, chopped and lightly floured
1½oz (37gm) whole almonds, skinned and chopped
2 tablespoons milk

1. Preheat oven to moderate, 350 deg F or gas 4 (180 deg C).
2. Line a deep, round 6-inch (15cm) cake tin with greaseproof paper. Grease the paper.
3. Sift the flour with the salt.
4. Cream the margarine with the sugar until light and fluffy.
5. Beat the eggs and add gradually to creamed mixture, beating all the time.
6. Mix cherries with nuts.
7. Fold flour, fruit, nuts and milk into creamed mixture.
8. Spoon into prepared tin and smooth top.
9. Bake in centre of preheated oven for 1¾–2 hours, or until firm to the touch.

LEMON MARBLE CAKE
Gives 6 portions

8oz (200gm) margarine
8oz (200gm) caster sugar
4 large eggs
7oz (175gm) self-raising flour
1oz (25gm) cocoa powder
½ level teaspoon baking powder
strained juice of a medium-sized lemon
12oz (300gm) icing sugar

1. Preheat oven to moderate, 350 deg F or gas 4 (180 deg C).
2. Grease a deep round 8-inch (20cm) cake tin. Line with greaseproof paper. Grease the paper.
3. Cream margarine with caster sugar until light and fluffy.
4. Beat the eggs. Very gradually add to creamed mixture, beating well.
5. Divide the mixture between two bowls.
6. To one bowl add 4oz (100gm) sifted flour. Fold it in, using metal spoon.
7. Sift rest of flour with the cocoa powder and baking powder. Add to the other bowl. Fold in, using a metal spoon.
8. Put dessertspoons of the mixtures, alternately, into the prepared tin. Stir gently with a skewer to mix slightly.
9. Bake in centre of preheated oven for 1 hour 40 minutes to 2 hours, or until golden and firm to the touch.
10. Turn out to cool.
11. Level off top of cake to make it as flat as possible.
12. Put on a wire rack with a plate underneath.
13. Add enough lemon juice to the icing sugar to give a mixture which will coat the back of a wooden spoon.
14. Pour icing over cake, all in one go, to coat top and sides. Leave to set.

WALNUT SPONGE
Gives 6 portions

4oz (100gm) margarine
4oz (100gm) caster sugar
2 standard eggs
4oz (100gm) self-raising flour, sifted
half a small can cream
2oz (50gm) icing sugar, sifted
10 walnut halves

1. Preheat oven to moderate to moderately hot, 375 deg F or gas 5 (190 deg C).
2. Grease two 7-inch (18cm) round, shallow cake tins. Line bases of tins with greaseproof paper and grease the paper.
3. Beat margarine with caster sugar until light and fluffy.
4. Beat the eggs together, then beat lightly into the mixture.
5. Using a metal spoon, fold in the sifted flour.
6. Divide the mixture between the cake tins.
7. Bake the cakes in centre of preheated oven for 20–30 minutes, or until firm to the touch.
8. Turn out to cool on a wire rack.
9. Sandwich cakes with cream.
10. Mix icing sugar with water to give mixture which will coat back of wooden spoon. Spoon on to cake top. Arrange nuts all round top edge. Allow to set.

PLAIN CAKE
Gives 6 portions

The extra raising agent is added because of the large amount of cornflour used.

6oz (150gm) margarine
6oz (150gm) caster sugar
3 standard eggs
4oz (100gm) cornflour
4oz (100gm) self-raising flour
pinch of salt
1 heaped teaspoon baking powder
vanilla essence, to taste

1. Preheat oven to moderate, 350 deg F or gas 4 (180 deg C).
2. Grease a deep, round 6-inch (15cm) cake tin. Line tin with greaseproof paper. Grease the paper.
3. Cream margarine with caster sugar until light and fluffy.
4. Beat the eggs together, then gradually add to mixture, beating all the time.
5. Sift the cornflour with the self-raising flour, salt and baking powder.
6. Fold flour into mixture with a metal spoon.
7. Flavour, to taste, with vanilla essence.
8. Turn into prepared tin and bake in centre of preheated oven for 1½–2 hours, or until firm to the touch.
9. Turn cake out to cool on a wire cooling rack.

PINEAPPLE COFFEE CAKE
Gives 6 portions

4oz (100gm) self-raising flour
7oz (175gm) margarine
4oz (100gm) caster sugar
2 standard eggs
milk to mix
3oz (75gm) icing sugar, sifted
1 level teaspoon instant coffee powder
1 can (8oz or 200gm) pineapple pieces, well drained

1. Preheat oven to moderate to moderately hot, 375 deg F or gas 5 (190 deg C).
2. Grease an 8-inch (20cm) square, fairly deep cake tin. Line tin with greaseproof paper, then grease the paper.
3. Sift the flour.
4. Cream 4oz (100gm) margarine with caster sugar until light and fluffy.
5. Beat in the eggs gradually.
6. Using a metal spoon, fold in the flour.
7. Add enough milk to give a mixture which will drop easily from a spoon when shaken.
8. Spoon mixture into prepared cake tin; smooth top.
9. Bake cake in centre of the preheated oven for 25–30 minutes, or until golden brown and firm to the touch.
10. Put the cake to cool on a wire cooling rack.
11. Beat the rest of the margarine with the icing sugar and the coffee.
12. Cut the cooled cake into four layers.
13. Spread icing on one layer then add some pineapple. Repeat until all the layers are sandwiched together, leaving the top plain.
14. Serve within 4 hours.

BANANA AND TREACLE CAKE
Gives 4 to 5 portions

8oz (200gm) plain flour
pinch of salt
½ level teaspoon mixed spice
6oz (150gm) margarine
3oz (75gm) caster sugar
3oz (75gm) soft brown sugar
2 standard eggs
1 large ripe banana, peeled and mashed
1 tablespoon black treacle

1. Preheat oven to very moderate, 325 deg F or gas 3 (170 deg C).
2. Grease a 2-lb (1 kilo) loaf tin. Line base with greaseproof paper. Grease the paper.
3. Sift the flour with salt and spice into a bowl.
4. Cream margarine with sugars until light and fluffy.
5. Beat the eggs. Add gradually to creamed mixture, beating well.
6. Stir in banana and treacle.
7. Using a metal spoon, fold in the flour.
8. Put in prepared tin and smooth the top.
9. Bake in centre of preheated oven for 2½ hours, or until golden brown and firm to the touch.
10. Cool in tin for 5 minutes, then turn out to complete cooling on a wire cooling rack.

CREAM LATTICE
Gives 6 portions

6oz (150gm) margarine
6oz (150gm) caster sugar
3 large eggs
6oz (150gm) self-raising flour
small sachet powdered creamy topping
milk to mix
3 heaped tablespoons raspberry jam

1. Preheat oven to moderate to moderately hot, 375 deg F or gas 5 (190 deg C).
2. Grease and flour two 7½-inch (19cm) sponge sandwich tins.
3. Cream the margarine with the caster sugar until light and fluffy.
4. Beat the eggs together then very gradually beat into the creamed mixture.
5. Sift the flour, then, using a metal spoon, fold into creamed mixture.
6. Divide mixture between the prepared tins and smooth the tops.
7. Bake cakes in centre of the preheated oven for 25 minutes or until well risen and firm to the touch.
8. Turn out cakes to cool on a wire rack.
9. Make up the creamy topping following directions on the packet.
10. Spread one tablespoon of jam on one of the cakes, then put one tablespoon of creamy topping on top of the jam.
11. Place the other cake on top.
12. Put the rest of the jam in a small pan and heat gently with two tablespoons cold water until runny. Sieve jam.
13. Put the rest of the topping in a piping bag fitted with a medium star nozzle. Pipe a lattice pattern on top of the cake, leaving large square spaces.
14. Carefully fill the spaces with the jam. Leave to cool. Serve within 3 hours.

PEEL CAKE
Gives 6 portions

8oz (200gm) self-raising flour
6oz (150gm) margarine
6oz (150gm) caster sugar
3 standard eggs
2 heaped teaspoons chopped mixed peel
1 heaped teaspoon grated lemon rind

1. Preheat oven to moderate, 350 deg F or gas 4 (180 deg C).
2. Grease a round 8-inch (20cm) cake tin. Line base and sides of tin with greaseproof paper, then grease the paper.
3. Sift the flour into a basin.
4. Cream the margarine with the caster sugar until light and fluffy.
5. Beat the eggs together, then add them, little by little, to the creamed mixture, beating all the time.
6. Using a metal spoon, fold in the flour.
7. Fold in the peel and grated lemon rind.
8. Spoon cake into prepared tin and smooth the top.
9. Bake cake in centre of the preheated oven for 1½ hours, or until firm.
10. Cool in tin for 5 minutes, then turn out to complete cooling on a wire rack.

PINEAPPLE CAKE
Gives 8 portions

8oz (200gm) self-raising flour
1 can (8½oz or 212gm) pineapple pieces
6oz (150gm) margarine
6oz (150gm) caster sugar
3 standard eggs

1. Preheat oven to moderate, 350 deg F or gas 4 (180 deg C).
2. Grease an 8-inch (20cm) round cake tin. Line with greaseproof paper. Grease the paper.
3. Sift the flour into a bowl.
4. Drain pineapple (juice is not needed) and mince the fruit.
5. Cream the margarine with the caster sugar until light and fluffy.
6. Separate the eggs.
7. Beat the egg yolks into creamed mixture.
8. Whisk egg whites until stiff and snowy.
9. Using a metal spoon, fold minced pineapple into mixture. Then fold in flour.
10. Gently fold in egg whites.
11. Turn mixture into prepared tin.
12. Bake in centre of preheated oven for 1 hour 5 minutes or until golden brown and firm to the touch.
13. Turn out cake to cool on a wire rack and eat within three days.

BLUE MOON CAKE
Gives 5 to 6 portions

4oz (100gm) self-raising flour
pinch of salt
4oz (100gm) margarine
4oz (100gm) caster sugar
2 large eggs
4 rounded tablespoons blackcurrant jam
6oz (150gm) sifted icing sugar
2oz (50gm) small mauve-coloured sweets

1. Preheat oven to moderate to moderately hot, 375 deg F or gas 5 (190 deg C).
2. Grease two round 7-inch (18cm) sandwich tins.
3. Sift the flour and salt into a basin.
4. Cream the margarine with the caster sugar until light and fluffy.
5. Beat the eggs together, then gradually add them to the creamed mixture, beating well.
6. Using a metal spoon, fold in the flour.
7. Bake the cakes in the centre of the preheated oven for 25–30 minutes, or until golden and firm to the touch.
8. Turn out cakes to cool on a wire cooling rack.
9. Sandwich the cakes with a third of the jam, then cut in half to make two semi-circles.
10. Use the rest of the jam to sandwich the semi-circles together to make one thick semi-circle.
11. Add enough cold water to the icing sugar to give a mixture that will coat the back of a wooden spoon.
12. Put the cake on a wire rack with a plate underneath. Pour the icing sugar on to the cake, all in one go, to coat top and sides of the cake.
13. Place the sweets, close together, all round top edge of cake to accentuate half moon shape. Leave to set. Store in an airtight tin and eat within three days.

PINEAPPLE AND CHERRY CAKE
Gives 6 portions

6oz (150gm) margarine
6oz (150gm) caster sugar
3 large eggs
6oz (150gm) self-raising flour
1 tablespoon milk
1 can (8oz or 200gm) pineapple pieces
1 can (8oz or 200gm) red cherries
icing sugar, for sifting

1. Preheat oven to moderate to moderately hot, 375 deg F or gas 5 (190 deg C).
2. Grease and flour two 7½-inch (19cm) sandwich tins.
3. Cream margarine with caster sugar until mixture is light and fluffy.
4. Beat the eggs together then gradually beat into creamed mixture.
5. Sift the flour then fold into creamed mixture, with milk, using a metal spoon.
6. Divide mixture between the prepared tins and smooth tops.
7. Bake cakes in centre of preheated oven for 25 minutes, or until well risen and golden.
8. Turn out cakes to cool on a wire cooling rack.
9. Drain juice off fruit – juice is not needed.
10. Mix pineapple and cherries together.
11. Hollow out a little from the centre of one cake. Pound the crumbs. Mix the fruit with the crumbs and put on the cake.
12. Cut the other cake into four pieces.
13. Sift icing over the cake pieces and arrange them on top of the fruit. Serve within 2 hours.

LEMON AND APPLE CAKE
Gives 4 portions

3oz (75gm) margarine
3oz (75gm) caster sugar
1 large egg
1 large egg yolk
3oz (75gm) self-raising flour
1 large cooking apple
2oz (50gm) soft brown sugar
2 tablespoons lemon curd
1 small red apple
3 tablespoons orange squash

1. Preheat oven to moderate to moderately hot, 375 deg F or gas 5 (190 deg C).
2. Grease and flour an 8-inch (20cm) sandwich tin.
3. Cream margarine with caster sugar until light and fluffy.
4. Beat egg and yolk together, then gradually beat into creamed mixture.
5. Sift the flour and fold into the mixture with a metal spoon.
6. Spoon mixture into tin and smooth the top.
7. Bake in centre of preheated oven for 25 minutes, or until golden and firm to the touch.
8. Turn out to cool on a wire cooling rack.
9. Peel and core the cooking apple. Cut into slices and stew with the brown sugar and 2 tablespoons water until tender.
10. Sieve the cooked apple and mix with lemon curd.
11. Spread mixture on top of the cake.
12. Decorate with slices of unpeeled red apple tossed in orange squash and serve immediately.

PEAR GATEAU
Gives 4 to 5 portions

Use fresh pears instead of canned, when in season. Simply peel, halve and core them, then stew them in sugar syrup until tender.

4oz (100gm) self-raising flour
large pinch of salt
6oz (150gm) margarine
4oz (100gm) caster sugar
2 large eggs
vanilla essence
2oz (50gm) icing sugar, sifted
1 can (1lb or ½ kilo) pear halves
4 glacé cherries
edible pink food colouring

1. Preheat oven to moderate to moderately hot, 375 deg F or gas 5 (190 deg C).
2. Grease and lightly flour two round 7-inch (18cm) sandwich tins. Line bases with greaseproof paper and grease paper.
3. Sift the flour and salt.
4. Cream 4oz (100gm) margarine with the caster sugar until light and fluffy.
5. Beat the eggs, then add them gradually to the creamed mixture, beating well.
6. Using a metal spoon, fold in the flour.
7. Flavour to taste with vanilla essence.
8. Divide the mixture between the prepared tins and bake in the centre of the preheated oven for 25–30 minutes, or until firm to the touch.
9. Turn out to cool on a wire cooling rack.
10. Beat the rest of the margarine with sifted icing sugar until creamy, then add a little vanilla essence.
11. Chop one pear half finely and mix into icing.
12. Sandwich cakes with the icing.
13. Drain juice off pears and reserve juice.
14. Put the pear halves, hollow sides up, on top of the cake.
15. Fill the hollows with finely chopped cherries.
16. Boil the pear juice until thick.
17. When juice is nearly cool, colour it pink and spoon it over the pears.
18. Serve within an hour.

STICKY ORANGE CAKE
Gives 4 to 6 portions

8oz (200gm) self-raising flour
large pinch of salt
6oz (150gm) margarine
8oz (200gm) caster sugar
3 standard eggs
1 tablespoon orange squash
1 medium-sized orange

1. Preheat oven to moderate, 350 deg F or gas 4 (180 deg C).
2. Grease an 8-inch (20cm) round, deep cake tin. Line base with greaseproof paper and grease the paper.
3. Sift the flour and salt into a bowl.
4. Cream the margarine with 6oz (150gm) caster sugar until light and fluffy.
5. Beat the eggs together, then gradually add to creamed mixture, beating well.
6. Using a metal spoon, fold in flour.
7. Stir in orange squash.
8. Spoon mixture into the prepared cake tin.
9. Bake in the centre of the preheated oven for 1¼–1½ hours or until firm to the touch.
10. Turn out to cool on a wire cooling rack.
11. Wash the orange; do not peel it. Cut into thin slices.
12. Put the rest of the sugar in a pan with 6 tablespoons cold water. Heat slowly until sugar is dissolved, then boil until syrupy. Add the orange slices and cook for 2 minutes. Leave in pan to cool.
13. Lift orange slices out of pan and put, overlapping, on top of cake, then spoon the syrup over them. Eat within two days.

Victoria sandwich (see page 6)

Coffee gateau (see page 7)

Dripping cake (see page 27)

Cherry cake (see page 21)

Saint Clement's cake (see page 39)

Sponge flan (see page 9)

Banana shortcake (see page 30)

Peach meringue surprise (see page 41)

NUT AND ORANGE BLOCK CAKE
Gives 5 to 6 portions

4oz (100gm) margarine
4oz (100gm) caster sugar
2 standard eggs
4oz (100gm) self-raising flour, sifted
1 tablespoon tepid water
1 can (11oz or 275gm) mandarin oranges, well drained
1 small can cream
3oz (75gm) walnuts, finely chopped

1. Preheat oven to moderate, 350 deg F or gas 4 (180 deg C).
2. Grease a square, 9-inch (23cm) cake tin. Line tin with greaseproof paper and grease the paper.
3. Cream margarine with caster sugar until light and fluffy.
4. Beat eggs together and add them gradually to mixture.
5. Using a metal spoon, fold in flour and water.
6. Spoon mixture into prepared tin and smooth the top.
7. Bake in centre of preheated oven for 35 minutes or until well risen and firm to the touch.
8. Turn out to cool. Arrange fruit in rows on top of cake.
9. Smear cream around the sides. Mark into pattern with fork on two opposite sides of cake only. Press nuts on to other sides.

CHOCOLATE RASPBERRY CAKE
Gives 4 to 5 portions

3oz (75gm) self-raising flour
3oz (75gm) margarine
3oz (75gm) caster sugar
2 standard eggs
1 tablespoon warm water
2oz (50gm) plain chocolate
2 individual portions frozen raspberry mousse (not thawed)

1. Preheat oven to moderate, 350 deg F or gas 4 (180 deg C).
2. Grease and lightly flour an 8-inch (20cm) sponge flan tin.
3. Sift the flour into a bowl.
4. Cream margarine with the caster sugar until light and fluffy.
5. Beat in one egg. Separate the other egg and beat the yolk into the mixture. (The white is not needed, so save it for making meringues, see pages 41, 56–59, 68.)
6. Using a metal spoon, fold flour and water into the mixture.
7. Spoon into prepared cake tin and smooth the top.
8. Bake in the centre of the preheated oven for 25 minutes, or until firm to the touch.
9. Leave to cool in the tin for 5 minutes, then turn out to complete cooling on a wire rack.
10. Put the chocolate in a bowl over a pan of gently simmering water. Leave until chocolate has melted.
11. Carefully spoon the melted chocolate over the inside of the sponge flan, to coat it. Leave to set.
12. Cut the frozen mousse into chunks. Put in centre of flan and serve at once.

COCONUT MOUSSE CAKE
Gives 5 to 6 portions

6oz (150gm) margarine
6oz (150gm) caster sugar
3 large eggs
6oz (150gm) self-raising flour
4oz (100gm) marshmallows
2 heaped tablespoons desiccated coconut
3 tablespoons evaporated milk

1. Preheat oven to moderate to moderately hot, 375 deg F or gas 5 (190 deg C).
2. Grease and flour two 7½-inch (19cm) sandwich tins.
3. Cream margarine with caster sugar until light and fluffy.
4. Beat the eggs together. Very gradually add to creamed mixture, beating well.
5. Sift the flour. Using a metal spoon, fold into creamed mixture.
6. Divide mixture between the prepared tins and smooth the tops.
7. Bake in centre of preheated oven for 25 minutes, or until well risen and firm to the touch.
8. Turn out cakes to cool on a wire cooling rack.
9. Put marshmallows in a bowl over a pan of gently simmering water and leave until melted.
10. Stir coconut and milk into melted marshmallows.
11. Cut each cake into two layers. Sandwich all the layers with the warm marshmallow mixture, then spread a little on the top. Leave for 45 minutes before serving and eat within 3 hours of adding the filling.

ICE CREAM SURPRISE
Gives 4 portions

Keep ice cream in freezing compartment of refrigerator until just before adding to cake.

3oz (75gm) margarine
3oz (75gm) caster sugar
1 large egg
1 large egg yolk
3oz (75gm) self-raising flour
half a 1lb (½ kilo) jar mincemeat
5 tablespoons fresh orange juice
3 small individual brickettes vanilla ice cream
1 rounded teaspoon grated orange rind

1. Preheat oven to moderate to moderately hot, 375 deg F or gas 5 (190 deg C).
2. Grease and flour a 7½-inch (19cm) sandwich tin.
3. Cream margarine with caster sugar until light and fluffy.
4. Beat the egg with the egg yolk, then gradually beat them into creamed mixture.
5. Sift the flour, then fold it in using a metal spoon.
6. Spoon mixture into tin and smooth the top.
7. Bake in centre of preheated oven for 25 minutes, or until firm and golden.
8. Turn out to cool on a wire cooling rack.
9. Mix mincemeat with orange juice.
10. Hollow out a little of the centre of the cake.
11. Mix these cake crumbs with the mincemeat and spoon into the cake.
12. Top with pieces of ice cream.
13. Sprinkle orange rind on top.

GINGER TOP CAKE

Gives 4 to 6 portions

If you have some stem ginger in the house use a little, chopped up, in place of the marmalade. Thicken a little of the syrup from the jar with arrowroot.

3oz (75gm) self-raising flour
1oz (25gm) cocoa
1 level teaspoon baking powder
4oz (100gm) margarine
4oz (100gm) caster sugar
2 large eggs
2 tablespoons ginger marmalade
half a 6oz (150gm) can cream or fresh cream
4 bought gingernut biscuits

1. Preheat oven to moderate to moderately hot, 375 deg F or gas 5 (190 deg C).
2. Grease two round 7-inch (18cm) sandwich tins. Line bases with greaseproof paper and grease the paper.
3. Sift the flour with the cocoa and baking powder into a bowl. Do this twice.
4. Cream the margarine with the caster sugar until light and fluffy.
5. Beat the eggs, then gradually add to creamed mixture, beating well.
6. Using a metal spoon, fold in the sifted flour.
7. Divide the mixture between the prepared tins and smooth the tops.
8. Bake in the centre of the preheated oven for 25–30 minutes or until firm to the touch.
9. Turn out to cool on a wire cooling rack.
10. Sandwich cakes with the ginger marmalade.
11. Spread the cream on top.
12. Crush the biscuits, not too finely, and sprinkle on top of the cake. Serve within 2 hours of adding cream.

CHOCOLATE CUSTARD GATEAU

Gives 5 to 6 portions

6oz (150gm) margarine
6oz (150gm) caster sugar
3 large eggs
6oz (150gm) self-raising flour
1 cup cold thick custard, chilled
4 tablespoons evaporated milk
2oz (50gm) plain chocolate, grated
1oz (25gm) milk chocolate, grated

1. Preheat oven to moderate to moderately hot, 375 deg F or gas 5 (190 deg C).
2. Grease and flour two 7½-inch (19cm) sandwich tins.
3. Cream margarine with caster sugar until light and fluffy.
4. Beat the eggs together. Very gradually add eggs to creamed mixture, beating well.
5. Sift the flour, then fold into creamed mixture.
6. Divide mixture between the prepared tins and smooth the tops.
7. Bake in centre of preheated oven for 25 minutes, or until well risen and firm to the touch.
8. Turn out cakes to cool on a wire rack.
9. Mix custard with milk then stir in 1oz (25gm) plain chocolate and the milk chocolate.
10. Sandwich cakes with most of the filling.
11. Spread rest of filling on top of cake. Sprinkle rest of grated chocolate on top and serve within an hour.

LACY CAKE

Gives 4 to 5 portions

This cake is best kept in an airtight tin for two days before adding the decoration.

1oz (25gm) cocoa
3oz (75gm) self-raising flour
1 level teaspoon baking powder
6oz (150gm) margarine
4oz (100gm) caster sugar
2 large eggs
3oz (75gm) icing sugar
1oz (25gm) plain chocolate, grated

1. Preheat oven to moderate to moderately hot, 375 deg F or gas 5 (190 deg C).
2. Grease two round 7-inch (18cm) sponge flan tins. Line bases with greaseproof paper and grease the paper.
3. Sift the cocoa with the flour and baking powder into a bowl. Do this three times.
4. Cream 4oz (100gm) margarine with the caster sugar until light and fluffy.
5. Beat the eggs, then gradually add them to the creamed mixture, beating well.
6. Using a metal spoon, fold in the flour.
7. Divide the mixture between the prepared tins and bake in the centre of the preheated oven for 25–30 minutes, or until firm to touch.
8. Turn out cakes to cool on a wire cooling rack.
9. Beat the rest of the margarine with 2oz (50gm) sifted icing sugar until creamy. Stir in the chocolate.
10. Sandwich the cakes with the chocolate mixture.
11. Place a paper doily with a lacy pattern on top of the cake. Sift the rest of the icing sugar over the doily. The sugar will sift through the holes in the doily to make a pretty pattern. Carefully remove the doily.

CHERRY CAKE
(Illustrated on page 17)
Gives 6 portions

8oz (200gm) plain flour
2 level teaspoons baking powder
pinch of salt
6oz (150gm) margarine
6oz (150gm) caster sugar
3 standard eggs
3oz (75gm) glacé cherries
1 tablespoon milk

1. Preheat oven to moderate, 350 deg F or gas 4 (180 deg C).
2. Line a deep 8-inch (20cm) square cake tin with greaseproof paper. Grease the paper.
3. Sift the flour with the baking powder and salt.
4. Cream the margarine with the sugar until light and fluffy.
5. Beat the eggs, then add them very gradually to the creamed mixture, beating all the time.
6. Wash the cherries in very hot water; dry thoroughly. Cut each cherry into four and toss them in a little flour.
7. Fold flour and milk into the creamed mixture.
8. Fold in the cherries so they are evenly distributed.
9. Spoon mixture into prepared tin and smooth top.
10. Bake in centre of preheated oven for 1¾–2 hours, or until firm to the touch.
11. Turn out to cool on a wire cooling rack. This cake will keep for a week if stored in an airtight tin.

TWO-TONE CAKE
Gives 5 to 6 portions

6oz (150gm) margarine
6oz (150gm) caster sugar
3 large eggs
5oz (125gm) self-raising flour
1oz (25gm) cocoa
½ level teaspoon baking powder
1 can (6oz or 150gm) cream or fresh cream

1. Preheat oven to moderate to moderately hot, 375 deg F or gas 5 (190 deg C).
2. Grease and flour two 7½-inch (19cm) sandwich tins.
3. Cream margarine with caster sugar until light and fluffy.
4. Beat the eggs together, then gradually add to creamed mixture, beating well.
5. Put half the creamed mixture in another bowl.
6. Sift 3oz (75gm) flour and fold into one lot of mixture.
7. Sift rest of flour with cocoa and baking powder and fold into mixture in the other bowl.
8. Put the brown mixture into one of the prepared tins and smooth the top. Put the white mixture into the other tin and smooth the top.
9. Bake in centre of preheated oven for 25 minutes or until well risen and firm to the touch.
10. Turn out to cool on a wire rack.
11. Spread the cream on top of the white cake and put the brown cake on the top.

COFFEE LOAF
Gives 4 to 5 portions

8oz (200gm) plain flour
pinch of salt
½ level teaspoon mixed spice
1oz (25gm) semolina
6oz (150gm) margarine
3oz (75gm) caster sugar
3oz (75gm) soft brown sugar
2 standard eggs
3 tablespoons strong liquid black coffee, unsweetened
1 tablespoon black treacle
12oz (300gm) mixed dried fruit (sultanas, currants and raisins)

1. Preheat oven to very moderate, 325 deg F or gas 3 (170 deg C).
2. Grease a 2-lb (1 kilo) loaf tin. Line base with greaseproof paper. Grease the paper.
3. Sift flour with salt, spice and semolina into a bowl.
4. Cream margarine and sugars until light and fluffy.
5. Beat in the eggs, a little at a time.
6. Stir in coffee and treacle.
7. Using a metal spoon, fold in sifted flour and fruit.
8. Put in prepared tin and smooth the top.
9. Bake in centre of preheated oven for 2½ hours, or until firm to the touch and golden.
10. Leave to cool in tin for 5 minutes, then turn out to complete cooling on a wire rack. Serve sliced and spread with butter.

APRICOT ICE CREAM SURPRISE
Gives 4 to 5 portions

Keep ice cream in the freezer compartment of the refrigerator until you are ready to serve the cake.

3oz (75gm) self-raising flour
3oz (75gm) margarine
3oz (75gm) caster sugar
2 standard eggs
1 tablespoon warm water
half an 8oz (200gm) can apricot halves
2 individual brickettes vanilla ice cream

1. Preheat oven to moderate, 350 deg F or gas 4 (180 deg C).
2. Grease and lightly flour an 8-inch (20cm) sponge flan tin.
3. Sift the flour into a bowl.
4. In another bowl, cream the margarine and caster sugar until light and fluffy.
5. Beat in one egg. Separate the other egg and beat the yolk into the mixture. (The white is not needed, so save it for meringues, see pages 41, 56–59, 68.)
6. Using a metal spoon, fold in the sifted flour and warm water.
7. Spoon the mixture into the prepared tin and smooth the top.
8. Bake in the centre of the preheated oven for 25 minutes, or until firm to the touch.
9. Leave cake to cool in the tin for 5 minutes then turn out to complete cooling on a wire rack.
10. Drain the fruit – juice is not needed.
11. Chop the fruit and put into centre of cake.
12. Quickly chop the ice cream and put into centre of cake. Serve at once.

TRAFFIC LIGHT CAKE
Gives 4 to 5 portions

4oz (100gm) margarine
4oz (100gm) caster sugar
2 large eggs
4oz (100gm) self-raising flour
3 heaped tablespoons apricot jam
1 heaped tablespoon greengage jam
1 heaped tablespoon raspberry jam

1. Preheat oven to moderate, 350 deg F or gas 4 (180 deg C).
2. Grease a 9-inch (23cm) square, fairly deep cake tin. Line the base and sides with greaseproof paper. Grease the paper.
3. Cream the margarine with the caster sugar until light and fluffy.
4. Beat the eggs together, then add them gradually to the creamed mixture, beating well.
5. Using a metal spoon, fold in the sifted flour.
6. Spoon mixture into prepared cake tin and smooth the top.
7. Bake in the centre of the preheated oven for 25–30 minutes, or until golden and firm to the touch.
8. Turn out cake to cool on a wire cooling rack.
9. Cut the cake in half, downwards, so you have two oblongs.
10. Sandwich the oblongs with 2 tablespoons apricot jam.
11. Using a small metal cutter (or using an egg cup and cutting round it with a sharp knife) make three small circles on the top of the cake, to look like a set of traffic lights.
12. Fill each hollow with a different colour of jam.

BUTTERSCOTCH FLAN
Gives 5 portions

3oz (75gm) self-raising flour
4½oz (112gm) margarine
5oz (125gm) caster sugar
2 standard eggs
1 tablespoon warm water
½ pint (250ml) milk, less 4 tablespoons
1 heaped tablespoon cornflour
1oz plain chocolate, grated

1. Preheat oven to moderate, 350 deg F or gas 4 (180 deg C).
2. Grease and lightly flour an 8-inch (20cm) sponge flan tin.
3. Sift the flour into a bowl.
4. Cream 3oz (75gm) margarine with 3oz (75gm) caster sugar until light and fluffy.
5. Beat in one egg. Separate the other egg and beat the yolk into the mixture. (The white is not needed, so save this to use for meringues, see pages 41, 56–59, 68.)
6. Using a metal spoon, fold in the self-raising flour and the warm water.
7. Spoon mixture into the prepared tin and smooth the top.
8. Bake in the centre of the preheated oven for 25 minutes, or until firm to the touch.
9. Leave flan to cool in the tin for 3 minutes then turn out to cool on a wire rack.
10. Melt the rest of the margarine.
11. Add rest of the sugar to the melted margarine and cook gently until golden brown.
12. Add the milk and bring to the boil.
13. Blend the cornflour with 2 tablespoons cold water. Stir into milk.
14. Bring mixture to boil.
15. Cook for 2 minutes stirring all the time until mixture thickens.
16. Cover the top of the mixture with wetted greaseproof paper and leave until nearly cold.
17. Pour mixture into flan. Leave to become completely cold.
18. Decorate top of flan with grated chocolate and serve within an hour of adding the filling.

FRUIT SALAD FLAN
Gives 4 to 5 portions

3oz (75gm) self-raising flour
3oz (75gm) margarine
3oz (75gm) caster sugar
2 standard eggs
1 tablespoon warm water
1 small banana
1 glacé cherry
1 ring canned pineapple
2 slices fresh orange
a few small green grapes
1 cup cold thick custard, chilled
2 heaped tablespoons apricot jam

1. Preheat oven to moderate, 350 deg F or gas 4 (180 deg C).
2. Grease and lightly flour an 8-inch (20cm) sponge flan tin.
3. Sift flour into a bowl.
4. Cream margarine with caster sugar until light and fluffy.
5. Beat in one egg. Separate the other egg and beat in the yolk. (The white is not needed, so save it for making meringues, see pages 41, 56–59, 68.)
6. Using a metal spoon, fold in flour and warm water.
7. Spoon mixture into prepared tin and smooth the top.
8. Bake in centre of preheated oven for 25 minutes, or until firm to the touch.
9. Leave cake to cool in tin for 3 minutes then turn out to complete cooling on a wire rack.
10. Peel banana and leave whole.
11. Put cherry in centre of pineapple ring.
12. Remove rind from orange.
13. Wash the grapes.
14. Put custard in the flan and arrange fruit attractively on the top.
15. Gently heat jam with 2 tablespoons water. Spoon over the fruit. Leave to cool and eat within 2 hours of decorating.

FROSTED GRAPE GATEAU
Gives 5 portions

4oz (100gm) self-raising flour
large pinch of salt
4oz (100gm) caster sugar, plus a little extra for grapes
6oz (150gm) margarine
1 small egg
2 large eggs
2oz (50gm) icing sugar
vanilla essence
6oz (150gm) small green grapes

1. Preheat oven to moderate, 350 deg F or gas 4 (180 deg C).
2. Grease two 7-inch (18cm) sandwich tins. Line the bases with greaseproof paper and grease the paper.
3. Sift the flour and salt into a bowl.
4. Cream 4oz (100gm) caster sugar with 4oz (100gm) margarine until light and fluffy.
5. Separate the small egg. Beat the two eggs with the egg yolk, then gradually add them to the creamed mixture, beating all the time.
6. Using a metal spoon, fold in the flour.
7. Divide the mixture between the tins and smooth the tops.
8. Bake in centre of the preheated oven for 25–30 minutes, or until golden and firm to the touch.
9. Leave cakes to cool on a wire rack.
10. Cream the rest of the margarine with the icing sugar until very creamy.
11. Flavour to taste with vanilla essence.
12. Use icing to sandwich the cakes together.
13. Wash and dry the grapes.
14. Brush the grapes with egg white and toss them in the extra sugar to completely coat the fruit. Leave for 1 hour to dry in a cool place.
15. Decorate top of cake with tiny bunches of sugared grapes. Serve within 3 hours of decorating.

RICE CAKE
Gives 4 portions

3oz (75gm) margarine
3oz (75gm) caster sugar
1 large egg
1 large egg yolk
3oz self-raising flour
1 can (11oz or 275gm) mandarin oranges
1oz (25gm) plain chocolate
1 can (6oz or 150gm) creamed rice pudding

1. Preheat oven to moderate to moderately hot, 375 deg F or gas 5 (190 deg C).
2. Grease and flour a 7½-inch (19cm) sandwich tin.
3. Cream margarine with caster sugar until light and fluffy.
4. Beat the egg with the yolk, then gradually beat into the creamed mixture.
5. Using a metal spoon, fold in the sifted flour.
6. Bake in centre of preheated oven for 25 minutes, or until golden and firm to the touch.
7. Turn out to cool on a wire cooling rack.
8. Carefully hollow out a little of the centre of the cake.
9. Drain juice off fruit.
10. Chop half the fruit and mix with the crumbs which you have hollowed out from cake. Put into centre of cake.
11. Put the chocolate in a bowl over a pan of gently simmering water. Leave until melted.
12. Stir rice into melted chocolate and put in refrigerator for 10 minutes.
13. Spoon rice on top of cake. Top with rest of fruit and serve within the hour.

GRAPE AND BANANA FLAN
Gives 6 portions

3oz (75gm) self-raising flour
3oz (75gm) margarine
3oz (75gm) caster sugar
2 standard eggs
1 tablespoon warm water
6oz (150gm) small green grapes
1 large banana
half a packet of orange jelly, made up and left to set
2 tablespoons apricot jam

1. Preheat oven to moderate, 350 deg F or gas 4 (180 deg C).
2. Grease and lightly flour an 8-inch (20cm) sponge flan tin.
3. Sift the flour into a bowl.
4. Cream margarine with the caster sugar until light and fluffy.
5. Beat one egg into the mixture, then separate the other egg and beat the yolk into mixture. (The white is not needed, so save it for making meringues see pages 41, 56–59, 68.)
6. Using a metal spoon, fold the flour and warm water into the mixture.
7. Spoon mixture into prepared tin and smooth top.
8. Bake flan in centre of the preheated oven for 25 minutes or until firm to the touch.
9. Leave the flan to cool in tin for 5 minutes, then turn it out to complete cooling on a wire rack.
10. Remove pips from grapes and, if you like, skin them.
11. Peel and slice the banana, then mix with the grapes.
12. Chop the jelly and put it in the base of the flan. Top with fruit.
13. Heat the jam in a small pan with 1 teaspoon cold water. Sieve and then spoon it over fruit.
14. Leave to cool then serve within 3 hours.

HAZELNUT CAKE
Gives 4 to 6 portions

1lb (½ kilo) cooking apples
2½oz (62gm) very soft margarine
8oz (200gm) caster sugar
12oz (300gm) self-raising flour
pinch of salt
grated rind of very small orange
8oz (200gm) currants
1½oz (37gm) hazelnuts
2 teaspoons golden syrup

1. Preheat oven to very moderate, 325 deg F or gas 3 (170 deg C).
2. Grease a round, deep 7-inch (18cm) cake tin. Line base with greaseproof paper and grease the paper.
3. Peel apples and cut them up roughly. Discard cores.
4. Stew the apples with 1 tablespoon cold water for 10 minutes. Sieve or liquidize, then leave to cool.
5. Cream margarine and sugar.
6. Beat apples into creamed mixture.
7. Sift flour, salt and orange rind.
8. Fold into creamed mixture.
9. Fold in the currants. Then turn mixture into prepared tin.
10. Bake in centre of preheated oven for 1½ hours or until firm to the touch.
11. Meanwhile toast hazelnuts to make outer skins brittle. Remove outer skins. Mix nuts with syrup and spoon on to turned-out cake.

RHUBARB CAKE
Gives 6 portions

Use fresh rhubarb, stewed with sugar, when in season.

6oz (150gm) margarine
6oz (150gm) caster sugar
3 large eggs
6oz (150gm) self-raising flour
½ level teaspoon cinnamon
half an 8oz (200gm) can rhubarb
half an 8oz (200gm) can raspberries
1 teacup cold thick custard

1. Preheat oven to moderate to moderately hot, 375 deg F or gas 5 (190 deg C).
2. Grease and flour two 7½-inch (19cm) sandwich tins.
3. Beat the margarine with the caster sugar until light and fluffy.
4. Beat the eggs together, then very gradually add to creamed mixture, beating well.
5. Sift the flour and cinnamon. Using a metal spoon, fold into the creamed mixture.
6. Divide mixture between the tins and smooth the tops.
7. Bake cakes in centre of the preheated oven for 25 minutes, or until well risen and golden.
8. Turn cakes out to cool on a wire cooling rack.
9. Cut each cake into two layers.
10. Mix the well-drained fruits together and sieve them.
11. Mix custard with sieved fruit.
12. Sandwich the cake with this mixture and serve within an hour.

SULTANA AND APPLE CAKE
Gives 6 portions

1lb (½ kilo) cooking apples
2½oz (62gm) soft, white cooking fat
8oz (200gm) caster sugar
12oz (300gm) self-raising flour
pinch of salt
1 level teaspoon mixed spice
8oz (200gm) sultanas

1. Preheat oven to very moderate, 325 deg F or gas 3 (170 deg C).
2. Grease a round deep 7-inch (18cm) cake tin. Line base with greaseproof paper and grease the paper.
3. Peel apples, then cut them up roughly, discarding the cores.
4. Stew the apples with one tablespoon cold water for 10 minutes. Sieve or liquidize them, then leave to cool.
5. Cream the fat and sugar.
6. Beat apple into creamed mixture.
7. Sift flour, salt and mixed spice.
8. Fold into creamed mixture with a metal spoon.
9. Fold in the sultanas.
10. Turn mixture into prepared tin and bake in centre of the preheated oven for 1½ hours or until a warmed knife blade inserted into the centre is clean when withdrawn.
11. Turn out to cool on a wire cooling rack.
12. Store in an airtight tin and eat cake within three days.

NUT AND CHERRY CAKE
Gives 6 portions

6oz (150gm) margarine
6oz (150gm) caster sugar
3 large eggs
6oz (150gm) self-raising flour
1 tablespoon milk
1 can (4oz or 100gm) pineapple cubes, drained and minced
4oz (100gm) glacé cherries, chopped and lightly floured
1½oz (37gm) whole almonds, skinned and chopped
1 small can cream or ¼ pint (125ml) fresh double cream, whipped

1. Preheat oven to moderate to moderately hot, 375 deg F or gas 5 (190 deg C).
2. Grease and flour two 7½-inch (19cm) sandwich tins.
3. Cream margarine with caster sugar until light and fluffy.
4. Beat the eggs together, then gradually beat into creamed mixture.
5. Sift the flour, then fold into creamed mixture with milk, using a metal spoon.
6. Divide mixture between the prepared tins and smooth tops.
7. Bake cakes in centre of preheated oven for 25 minutes or until well risen and golden.
8. Turn out cakes to cool on a wire cooling rack.
9. Drain any juice off minced fruit. Mix with cherries, nuts and cream. Sandwich cakes with fruit and nut mixture. Serve the same day.

AMERICAN ICED LOAF
Gives 5 to 6 portions

9oz (225gm) self-raising flour
pinch of salt
4oz (100gm) caster sugar
4oz (100gm) raisins
2 dessertspoons black treacle
½ pint (250ml) milk
1 standard egg
2 medium egg whites
12oz (300gm) granulated sugar
pinch of cream of tartar

1. Preheat oven to cool, 300 deg F or gas 2 (150 deg C).
2. Grease a 2-lb (1 kilo) loaf tin.
3. Sift the flour and salt into a bowl.
4. Stir in caster sugar and raisins.
5. Mix in the treacle, milk and whole egg. Mix well.
6. Put in prepared tin and smooth the top.
7. Bake in centre of preheated oven for 1½ hours, or until firm to the touch.
8. Turn out to cool.
9. Put 4 tablespoons plus 1 dessertspoon water in a pan.
10. Add granulated sugar and cream of tartar. Stir over a low heat until sugar has completely dissolved. Bring to the boil and boil for 2½ minutes, or until a little of the syrup forms a soft ball when dropped in a cup of cold water.
11. Whisk egg whites until stiff and snowy.
12. Slowly pour sugar syrup on to egg whites whisking – icing should start to peak.
13. Spread over the cake and leave to set. Cut the same day.

SUPER COFFEE SPONGE
Gives 6 portions

6oz (150gm) margarine
6oz (150gm) caster sugar
3 large eggs
5½oz (137gm) self-raising flour
1 level dessertspoon instant coffee powder
¼ level teaspoon baking powder
1 tablespoon milk
1 can (6oz or 150gm) cream or ¼ pint (125ml) fresh double cream

1. Preheat oven to moderate to moderately hot, 375 deg F or gas 5 (190 deg C).
2. Grease and flour two 7½-inch (19cm) sandwich tins.
3. Cream margarine with caster sugar until light and fluffy.
4. Beat the eggs together. Then very gradually add eggs to creamed mixture, beating well.
5. Sift the flour with the coffee powder and baking powder. Do this three times.
6. Using a metal spoon, fold the flour mixture into the creamed mixture. Stir in milk.
7. Divide between prepared tins and smooth the tops.
8. Bake in centre of preheated oven for 25 minutes, or until golden and firm to the touch.
9. Turn out cakes to cool on a wire rack.
10. Cut each cake into two layers. Sandwich all the layers with cream. Serve that day.

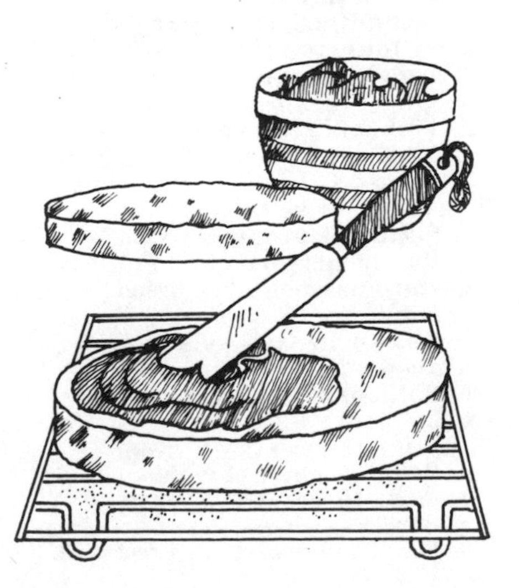

GUAVA FLAN
Gives 4 portions

4oz (100gm) plain flour
2oz (50gm) margarine
1 level tablespoon caster sugar
1 small egg yolk, beaten
1 cup cold thick custard
1 can (8oz or 200gm) guavas

1. Preheat oven to moderately hot, 400 deg F or gas 6 (200 deg C).
2. Grease a 7½-inch (19cm) flan tin or sandwich tin.
3. Sift the flour into a bowl.
4. Rub in margarine until mixture resembles fine breadcrumbs.
5. Stir in sugar.
6. Add enough of the egg yolk to mix to a stiff dough.
7. Roll out dough and fit into tin. Prick the pastry.
8. Bake in centre of preheated oven for 15 minutes, or until golden.
9. Leave to cool.
10. Put custard in the flan and top with the fruit. Eat the same day.

MARMALADE CREAM FLAN
Gives 4 portions

4oz (100gm) plain flour
2oz (50gm) margarine
1 level tablespoon caster sugar
1 small egg yolk, beaten
1 can (6oz or 150gm) cream
2 heaped tablespoons rough-cut marmalade

1. Preheat oven to moderately hot, 400 deg F or gas 6 (200 deg C).
2. Grease a 7½-inch (19cm) flan tin or sandwich tin.
3. Sift the flour into a bowl.
4. Rub in margarine until mixture resembles fine breadcrumbs.
5. Stir in the sugar.
6. Add enough egg yolk to mix to a stiff dough.
7. Roll out dough and fit into tin. Prick pastry.
8. Bake in centre of preheated oven for 15 minutes, or until golden.
9. Leave to cool.
10. Mix the cream with the marmalade and spoon into the flan. Eat within 2 hours of filling.

APRICOT WHIP FLAN
Gives 4 portions

4oz (100gm) plain flour
2oz (50gm) margarine
1 small egg yolk, beaten
1 can (8oz or 200gm) apricots
2 large egg yolks
1oz (25gm) caster sugar
½ pint (250ml) milk
rum essence, to taste

1. Preheat oven to moderately hot, 400 deg F or gas 6 (200 deg C).
2. Grease a 7½-inch (19cm) flan tin or sandwich tin.
3. Sift the flour into a bowl.
4. Rub in margarine until mixture resembles fine breadcrumbs.
5. Mix in small egg yolk to make a firm dough.
6. Roll out and fit into the prepared tin.
7. Prick pastry and bake in centre of preheated oven for 15 minutes, or until golden.
8. Leave to cool.
9. Drain the fruit – juice is not needed.
10. Mince or liquidize the fruit.
11. Whisk the remaining egg yolks with sugar.
12. Heat the milk – do not let it boil.
13. Pour milk on to eggs.
14. Return to pan and cook gently, stirring all the time, until mixture is thick enough to coat back of a wooden spoon.
15. Add fruit then rum essence, to taste. Leave to cool.
16. Fill flan with cooled mixture and eat 2 hours after filling.

RASPBERRY VELVET FLAN
Gives 4 portions

4oz (100gm) plain flour
2oz (50gm) margarine
1 level tablespoon caster sugar
1 small egg yolk, beaten
1 can (8oz or 200gm) raspberries or fresh raspberries when in season
½ pint (250ml) cold raspberry blancmange

1. Preheat oven to moderately hot, 400 deg F or gas 6 (200 deg C).
2. Grease a 7½-inch (19cm) flan tin or sandwich tin.
3. Sift the flour into a bowl.
4. Rub in the margarine until mixture resembles fine breadcrumbs.
5. Stir in the sugar.
6. Add enough egg yolk to mix to a stiff dough.
7. Roll out dough and fit into the tin.
8. Prick the pastry.
9. Bake in centre of preheated oven for 15 minutes, or until golden.
10. Leave to cool.
11. Mix drained and sieved fruit with blancmange and spoon into flan. Eat the same day.

FRENCH CHOCOLATE FLAN
Gives 4 portions

4oz (100gm) plain flour
2oz (50gm) margarine
1 small egg yolk, beaten
4oz (100gm) plain chocolate
½ pint (250ml) cold water
2oz (50gm) caster sugar
cornflour, to thicken
3 large bananas

1. Preheat oven to moderately hot, 400 deg F or gas 6 (200 deg C).
2. Grease a 7½-inch (19cm) flan tin or sandwich tin.
3. Sift the flour into a bowl.
4. Rub in margarine until the mixture resembles fine bread-crumbs.
5. Add enough egg yolk to mix to a firm dough.
6. Roll out dough and fit into the tin.
7. Prick the pastry.
8. Bake in centre of preheated oven for 15 minutes, or until golden.
9. Put the chocolate in a pan with half the water and the sugar. Heat gently until dissolved, then boil for 3 minutes.
10. Add rest of water and boil again until thick and syrupy.
11. Thicken mixture with cornflour following instructions on the packet. Leave to cool.
12. Peel and slice the bananas. Layer them in the flan.
13. Pour chocolate sauce into flan and eat within an hour of adding filling.

APPLE GINGER FLAN
Gives 4 portions

4oz (100gm) plain flour
2oz (50gm) margarine
1 level tablespoon caster sugar
1 small egg yolk, beaten
2 large cooking apples
half a teacup water
2oz (50gm) granulated sugar
1 level teaspoon powdered ginger

1. Preheat oven to moderately hot, 400 deg F or gas 6 (200 deg C).
2. Grease a 7½-inch (19cm) flan tin or sandwich tin.
3. Sift the flour into a bowl.
4. Rub in margarine until mixture resembles fine breadcrumbs.
5. Stir in caster sugar
6. Add enough egg yolk to mix to a firm dough.
7. Roll out dough and fit into the tin. Prick the pastry.
8. Bake in centre of preheated oven for 15 minutes, or until golden.
9. Leave to cool.
10. Peel and core the apples. Cut into thick wedges.
11. Gently heat water and granulated sugar until sugar dissolves. Stir in the ginger and boil for 1 minute.
12. Put apples in sugar liquid and cook very gently until apples are tender but still whole. Leave to cool.
13. Spoon apple and syrup into the flan. Eat the same day.

BLACKCURRANT FLAN
Gives 4 portions

4oz (100gm) plain flour
2oz (50gm) margarine
2 level tablespoons caster sugar
1 small egg yolk, beaten
¼oz (6gm) cornflour, plus extra to thicken fruit
½ pint (250ml) milk
1 can (6oz or 150gm) cream
1 can (8oz or 200gm) blackcurrants

1. Preheat oven to moderately hot, 400 deg F or gas 6 (200 deg C).
2. Grease a 7½-inch (19cm) flan tin or sandwich tin.
3. Sift the flour into a bowl.
4. Rub in margarine until mixture resembles fine breadcrumbs.
5. Stir in half the sugar.
6. Add enough egg yolk to mix to a stiff dough.
7. Roll out dough and fit into tin. Prick the pastry.
8. Bake in centre of preheated oven for 15 minutes, or until golden.
9. Leave to cool.
10. Mix cornflour with a little milk in a bowl. Put rest of milk in pan and bring to the boil and pour on to blended mixture, stirring.
11. Bring to boil, stirring until thick. Stir in rest of sugar. Leave to cool.
12. Mix cooled mixture with the cream.
13. Drain juice off the fruit and thicken with cornflour following directions on packet.
14. Mix fruit with thickened juice.
15. Spoon cornflour mixture into flan and top with fruit. Eat the same day.

COFFEE AND ORANGE FLAN
Gives 4 portions

4oz (100gm) plain flour
2oz (50gm) margarine
2 level tablespoons caster sugar
1 small egg yolk, beaten
small sachet blancmange powder
½ pint (250ml) milk
coffee essence, to taste
1 can (11oz or 275gm) mandarin oranges

1. Preheat oven to moderately hot, 400 deg F or gas 6 (200 deg C).
2. Grease a 7½-inch (19cm) flan tin or sandwich tin.
3. Sift the flour into a bowl.
4. Rub in margarine until mixture resembles fine breadcrumbs.
5. Stir in half the sugar.
6. Add enough egg yolk to give a stiff dough.
7. Roll out dough and fit into the tin. Prick the pastry.
8. Bake in centre of preheated oven for 15 minutes, or until golden and cooked.
9. Leave to cool.
10. Make up blancmange as directed on packet, using the milk and remaining sugar. Flavour, to taste, with coffee essence. Leave to cool.
11. Fill flan with coffee mixture. Top with well-drained fruit and eat the same day.

PLUM JAM CAKE
Gives 5 to 6 portions

8oz (200gm) self-raising flour
3oz (75gm) caster sugar
3oz (75gm) margarine
3 tablespoons red plum jam
1 large egg
a little milk

1. Preheat oven to moderate to moderately hot, 375 deg F or gas 5 (190 deg C).
2. Grease a 6-inch (15cm) round, deep cake tin.
3. Sift the flour and sugar.
4. Rub in the margarine.
5. Mix in the jam, beaten egg and enough milk to mix to a fairly soft dough.
6. Put in prepared tin.
7. Bake in centre of preheated oven for 45–50 minutes, or until golden and firm to the touch.
8. Turn out to cool on a wire cooling rack.

DRIPPING CAKE
(Illustrated on page 17)
Gives about 6 portions

To clarify dripping (separate it from meat bits and juices) put it in a dish, and pour boiling water on top and leave it in the refrigerator overnight. Next day, lift layer of dripping off top. The sediment will have sunk to base of dish.

12oz (300gm) self-raising flour
pinch of salt
4oz (100gm) dripping
4½oz (112gm) caster sugar, plus a little extra
6oz (150gm) sultanas
1 large egg
5 tablespoons milk

1. Preheat oven to moderate to moderately hot, 375 deg F or gas 5 (190 deg C).
2. Grease and line the base of a 7-inch (18cm) round, deep cake tin.
3. Sift flour and salt into a bowl.
4. Cut the dripping up a little and rub it into the flour until mixture resembles fine breadcrumbs.
5. Stir in 4oz (100gm) caster sugar and the sultanas.
6. Beat the egg with the milk.
7. Stir egg and milk into rubbed-in mixture to make a stiff dough.
8. Put in prepared tin and press down lightly.
9. Sprinkle rest of sugar over top of cake.
10. Bake in centre of preheated oven for 1 hour 10 minutes, then test by inserting the warmed blade of a knife into the cake. If the cake is done the knife blade will be clean when withdrawn. If not, cook a little longer, then test again in the same way.
11. Turn out to cool on a wire rack. Sprinkle on extra sugar.
12. Store cake in an airtight tin and eat it within three days.

FIG CAKE
Gives 5 portions

8oz (200gm) self-raising flour
pinch of salt
4oz (100gm) margarine
4oz (100gm) caster sugar
2oz (50gm) currants
4oz (100gm) dried figs, finely chopped
1 standard egg
5 tablespoons milk

1. Preheat oven to moderate, 350 deg F or gas 4 (180 deg C).
2. Grease a round 6-inch (15 cm) cake tin. Line the tin with greaseproof paper. Grease the paper.
3. Sift the flour and salt into a bowl.
4. Rub in the margarine until mixture resembles fine breadcrumbs.
5. Stir in the sugar and fruit.
6. Add egg and milk.
7. Spoon into prepared tin and make a small hollow in the centre of the mixture.
8. Bake in centre of preheated oven for 1¼–1½ hours.
9. Leave to cool completely before storing in an airtight tin. Eat within four days.

AUNT EMILY'S APRICOT CAKE
Gives 5 portions

8oz (200gm) self-raising flour
pinch of salt
4oz (100gm) margarine
4oz (100gm) caster sugar
2oz (50gm) chopped mixed peel
3oz (75gm) stewed and minced dried apricots
1 standard egg
5 tablespoons milk

1. Preheat oven to moderate, 350 deg F or gas 4 (180 deg C).
2. Grease a deep, round 6-inch (15cm) cake tin. Line tin with greaseproof paper. Grease the paper.
3. Sift the flour and salt into a bowl.
4. Rub in the margarine until mixture resembles fine breadcrumbs.
5. Stir in sugar, peel and fruit.
6. Mix in egg and milk.
7. Put into prepared tin.
8. Bake in centre of preheated oven for 1¼–1½ hours.
9. Leave in tin for 10 minutes before turning out to cool.

ORANGE CAKE
Gives 6 portions

12oz (300gm) self-raising flour
large pinch of salt
6oz (150gm) caster sugar
4oz (100gm) margarine
8oz (200gm) currants
1 large egg, beaten
1 small orange
milk to mix

1. Preheat oven to moderate, 350 deg F or gas 4 (180 deg C).
2. Grease a 7-inch (18cm) cake tin. Line tin with greaseproof paper and grease the paper.
3. Sift the flour and salt into a bowl.
4. Stir in the sugar.
5. Rub in the margarine until the mixture resembles fine breadcrumbs.
6. Stir in the currants.
7. Add the egg.
8. Grate the orange rind and stir 1 heaped teaspoonful into the mixture.
9. Squeeze out the orange juice and add enough milk to make up to 12 tablespoons of liquid.
10. Add orange liquid to mixture.
11. Turn into prepared tin and bake in centre of preheated oven for 1½ hours, or until firm to the touch.
12. Turn out to cool on a wire cooling rack.

MINCEMEAT CAKE
Gives 6 portions

12oz (300gm) self-raising flour
4oz (100gm) margarine
4½oz (112gm) caster sugar
2 large eggs
4 tablespoons milk
1 jar (14½oz or 362gm) mincemeat

1. Preheat oven to moderate, 350 deg F or gas 4 (180 deg C).
2. Grease an 8-inch (20cm) round, deep cake tin. Line the tin with greaseproof paper and grease the paper.
3. Sift the flour into a bowl.
4. Rub in the margarine until the mixture looks like fine breadcrumbs.
5. Stir in 4oz (100gm) caster sugar.
6. Beat the eggs with the milk and add to the mixture.
7. Stir in the mincemeat, then beat for at least 3 minutes, using a wooden spoon.
8. Turn into prepared tin.
9. Bake in the centre of the preheated oven for 1½ hours, or until golden and firm to the touch.
10. Turn out to cool on a wire cooling rack.
11. Sprinkle rest of sugar over the top of the cake.

CUT AND COME AGAIN CAKE
Gives 5 portions

8oz (200gm) self-raising flour
6oz (150gm) margarine
4oz (100gm) caster sugar
6oz (150gm) sultanas
1 large egg, beaten
5 tablespoons milk

1. Preheat oven to moderate, 350 deg F or gas 4 (180 deg C).
2. Grease a deep, round 6-inch (15cm) cake tin. Line with greaseproof paper. Grease the paper.
3. Sift the flour into a bowl.
4. Rub in margarine with your fingertips until mixture resembles fine breadcrumbs.
5. Stir in sugar and fruit.
6. Add the beaten egg and milk.
7. Spoon into prepared tin.
8. Bake in centre of preheated oven for 1¼–1½ hours.
9. Cool completely before storing in an airtight tin. Eat within a week.

DATE CAKE
Gives 6 portions

See Dripping Cake (page 27) for method of clarifying dripping.

12oz (300gm) self-raising flour
pinch of salt
½ level teaspoon cinnamon or nutmeg
4oz (100gm) dripping, clarified
4oz (100gm) caster sugar
6oz (150gm) dates, chopped
1 large egg
5 tablespoons milk

1. Preheat oven to moderate to moderately hot, 375 deg F or gas 5 (190 deg C).
2. Grease and line the base of a 7-inch (18cm) round, deep cake tin with greaseproof paper. Lightly grease the paper.
3. Sift the flour with the salt and cinnamon or nutmeg into a bowl.
4. Cut the dripping into small pieces. Rub it into flour until the mixture resembles fine breadcrumbs.
5. Stir in the sugar, dates, egg and milk to make a stiff mixture.
6. Put it in prepared tin and press it down lightly.
7. Cook cake in centre of preheated oven for 1 hour 10 minutes. Test by inserting a warmed knife blade. If it is clean when withdrawn then the cake is ready. If not, cook a little longer and test again.
8. Turn out to cool on a wire cooling rack.
9. Store cake in an airtight tin and eat within three days.

BANANA SUGAR CAKE
Gives 4 to 5 portions

8oz (200gm) self-raising flour
4oz (100gm) margarine
4oz (100gm) caster sugar
1 standard egg
4 tablespoons milk
1 large ripe banana, mashed
1 level tablespoon soft brown sugar

1. Preheat oven to moderate, 350 deg F or gas 4 (180 deg C).
2. Grease a round, deep 6-inch (15cm) cake tin. Line with greaseproof paper. Grease the paper.
3. Sift the flour into a mixing bowl.
4. Rub in the margarine until mixture resembles fine breadcrumbs.
5. Stir in caster sugar, egg and milk.
6. Add the banana and mix well
7. Put in prepared tin and bake in centre of preheated oven for 1¼–1½ hours.
8. While the cake is still warm, sprinkle the brown sugar on the top. Leave to cool. Store in an airtight tin and eat within three days.

LEMONY CLOVE CAKE
Gives 5 to 6 portions

8oz (200gm) plain flour
pinch of salt
pinch of grated nutmeg
good pinch of powdered cloves
1 level teaspoon bicarbonate of soda
1 heaped teaspoon cream of tartar
3oz (75gm) margarine
8oz (200gm) sultanas
⅛ pint (65ml) lemon curd (measure in glass measuring jug)
3 tablespoons milk
2 standard eggs

1. Preheat oven to moderate to moderately hot, 375 deg F or gas 5 (190 deg C).
2. Well grease a deep 8-inch (20cm) cake tin. Line tin with greaseproof paper and grease the paper.
3. Sift the flour with the salt, nutmeg, cloves, bicarbonate of soda and cream of tartar into a bowl.
4. Rub in the margarine until mixture resembles fine breadcrumbs.
5. Stir in the fruit, lemon curd and milk.
6. Lightly whisk the eggs, then stir into the mixture.
7. When thoroughly mixed, put in prepared tin.
8. Bake cake in centre of the preheated oven for 1¼–1½ hours, or until firm to the touch.
9. Cool in the tin for 10 minutes, then turn out to complete cooling on a wire rack.

NO-EGG CAKE
Gives 4 portions

6oz (150gm) plain flour
large pinch of salt
3 level teaspoons baking powder
2½oz (62gm) margarine
3oz (75gm) caster sugar
3oz (75gm) sultanas
grated rind of half a small orange
milk to mix

1. Preheat oven to moderate to moderately hot, 375 deg F or gas 5 (190 deg C).
2. Grease and lightly flour a 6-inch (15cm) deep, round cake tin.
3. Sift the flour, salt and baking powder into a mixing bowl.
4. Rub in the margarine until mixture looks like fine breadcrumbs.
5. Stir in the sugar, sultanas and grated rind.
6. Add enough milk to give a rather stiff dropping consistency: the spoon should need a good shake before the mixture will fall off it.
7. Put the mixture into the prepared cake tin. Smooth the top.
8. Bake the cake in the centre of the preheated oven for 45 minutes to 1 hour, or until well risen and firm to the touch.
9. Turn cake out to cool on a wire cooling rack and serve the same day.

BANANA SHORTCAKE

(Illustrated on page 18)
Gives about 6 portions

1½oz (37gm) plain flour
pinch of salt
1 level teaspoon baking powder
8oz (200gm) medium oatmeal
1oz (25gm) caster sugar
2oz (50gm) margarine
milk to mix
2 large ripe bananas
2 tablespoons canned or fresh thick cream

1. Preheat oven to very moderate, 325 deg F or gas 3 (170 deg C).
2. Grease two baking sheets.
3. Sift the flour with the salt and baking powder in a bowl.
4. Mix in the oatmeal and sugar.
5. Cut the margarine into small pieces and rub into flour until mixture resembles fine breadcrumbs.
6. Add enough milk to mix to a stiff dough.
7. Sprinkle working surface with a little flour and oatmeal, mixed.
8. Roll out dough on working surface to about ¼-inch thick.
9. Using a large saucer as a guide, cut out three rounds from the dough.
10. Put the rounds on baking sheets.
11. Bake in the centre of the preheated oven for 35 minutes, or until golden brown and crisp.
12. Put to cool on a wire rack.
13. Peel and mash the bananas and mix them with the cream.
14. Sandwich the rounds with the banana mixture and serve the same day.

AMERICAN SHORTCAKE

Gives 6 portions

8oz (200gm) self-raising flour
6oz (150gm) margarine
6oz (150gm) caster sugar
1 large egg yolk, beaten
1 can (15oz or 375gm) peach slices or fresh strawberries when in season
1 can (6oz or 150gm) cream

1. Preheat oven to moderate, 350 deg F or gas 4 (180 deg C).
2. Grease two 7½-inch (19cm) sandwich tins.
3. Sift the flour.
4. Rub in the margarine.
5. Stir in the sugar.
6. Mix in enough egg to give a stiff dough.
7. Press into prepared tins, and smooth the tops.
8. Bake in centre of preheated oven for 25–35 minutes, or until golden.
9. Cut one round into four triangles. Leave both rounds to cool in the tins.
10. Drain the fruit very well.
11. Put fruit on whole shortcake round, then spoon on the cream.
12. Arrange triangles on the cream and serve within 2 hours.

OVERNIGHT CAKE

Gives 5 portions

If you have any brandy or sherry, add a tablespoon to the fruit.

6oz (150gm) currants and sultanas, mixed
strained juice of a small orange
1 heaped teaspoon orange rind
8oz (200gm) self-raising flour
4oz (100gm) margarine
4oz (100gm) caster sugar
1 standard egg
5 tablespoons milk

1. Put fruit with the orange juice and rind in a bowl. Leave to stand overnight.
2. Next day, preheat oven to moderate, 350 deg F or gas 4 (180 deg C).
3. Grease a round, deep 6-inch (15cm) cake tin. Line with greaseproof paper. Grease the paper.
4. Sift the flour into a mixing bowl.
5. Rub in the margarine.
6. Stir in the sugar.
7. Add the egg and milk, then mix in the fruit and its liquid.
8. Spoon into prepared tin and bake in centre of preheated oven for 1¼–1½ hours.
9. Cool in the tin for 10 minutes, then turn out to complete cooling on a wire rack.

SNOWY TOPPED CAKE

Gives 5 portions

8oz (200gm) self-raising flour
4oz (100gm) margarine
4oz (100gm) caster sugar
6oz (150gm) currants
1 standard egg
5 tablespoons milk
2oz (50gm) icing sugar, sifted

1. Preheat oven to moderate, 350 deg F or gas 4 (180 deg C).
2. Grease a deep, round 6-inch (15cm) cake tin. Line with greaseproof paper. Grease the paper.
3. Sift the flour into a bowl.
4. Rub in the margarine until mixture resembles fine breadcrumbs.
5. Stir in caster sugar and fruit.
6. Add the egg and milk and mix to a dough.
7. Spoon into prepared tin and bake in centre of preheated oven for 1¼–1½ hours, or until firm to the touch.
8. Leave to cool.
9. Mix the icing sugar with enough water to give a mixture which will coat the back of a wooden spoon.
10. Spoon the mixture on top of the cake so it dribbles down the sides. Store in an airtight tin and eat within four days.

CHOCOLATE AND COCONUT CAKE
Gives 6 portions

6oz (150gm) self-raising flour
1oz (25gm) cocoa powder
1 level teaspoon baking powder
large pinch of salt
3½oz (87gm) margarine
2oz (50gm) desiccated coconut
4oz (100gm) soft brown sugar
1 large egg
milk to mix
vanilla essence, to taste

1. Preheat oven to moderate, 350 deg F or gas 4 (180 deg C).
2. Grease a deep, round 8-inch (20cm) cake tin. Line base and sides with greaseproof paper. Grease the paper.
3. Sift the flour, cocoa, baking powder and salt into a bowl. Do this twice.
4. Rub the margarine into the flour until mixture resembles fine breadcrumbs.
5. Stir in the coconut and sugar.
6. Add the beaten egg with just enough milk to give a fairly soft mixture which will drop easily from the spoon when shaken.
7. Flavour, to taste, with vanilla essence.
8. Put into prepared tin and smooth the top.
9. Bake cake in centre of the preheated oven for 45 minutes, or until well risen and firm to the touch.
10. Turn out to cool on a wire cooling rack. Store in an airtight tin and eat within two days.

GINGER LOAF
Gives 4 to 5 portions

8oz (200gm) plain flour
4oz (100gm) margarine
4oz (100gm) caster sugar
3oz (75gm) crystallized ginger, finely chopped
1 large egg
¼ pint (125ml) milk

1. Preheat oven to moderate to moderately hot, 375 deg F or gas 5 (190 deg C).
2. Grease a 1-lb (½ kilo) loaf tin.
3. Sift the flour into a bowl.
4. Rub in margarine until mixture resembles fine breadcrumbs.
5. Stir in the sugar and ginger.
6. Add the egg and enough milk to mix to a soft dropping consistency.
7. Spoon mixture into prepared tin and smooth the top.
8. Bake in centre of preheated oven for 1¼ hours, or until firm to the touch.
9. Turn out to cool on a wire cooling rack. Store in an airtight tin and eat within four days.

RAISIN LOAF
Gives 4 to 5 portions

8oz (200gm) self-raising flour
4oz (100gm) margarine
8oz (200gm) raisins
4oz (100gm) granulated sugar
1 heaped teaspoon grated lemon rind
1 standard egg
5 tablespoons milk

1. Preheat oven to moderate, 350 deg F or gas 4 (180 deg C).
2. Grease a 1-lb (½ kilo) loaf tin. Line with greaseproof paper. Grease the paper.
3. Sift the flour into a bowl.
4. Rub in margarine until mixture resembles fine breadcrumbs.
5. Stir in raisins, sugar and lemon rind.
6. Add egg and enough milk to mix to stiff dropping consistency.
7. Put in prepared tin and smooth the top.
8. Bake in centre of preheated oven for 1¼ hours, or until firm to the touch.
9. Turn out to cool on a wire cooling rack. Store in an airtight tin and eat within three days.

CHOCOLATE LOAF
Gives 4 to 5 portions

7oz (175gm) self-raising flour
1oz (25gm) cocoa
½ level teaspoon baking powder
4oz (100gm) margarine
4oz (100gm) granulated sugar
1 standard egg
5 tablespoons milk

1. Preheat oven to moderate, 350 deg F or gas 4 (180 deg C).
2. Grease a 1-lb (½ kilo) loaf tin. Line with greaseproof paper. Grease the paper.
3. Sift flour with cocoa and baking powder into a bowl. Do this twice.
4. Rub in margarine until mixture resembles fine breadcrumbs.
5. Mix in the sugar.
6. Add egg and enough milk to give stiff dropping consistency.
7. Spoon into prepared tin and smooth the top.
8. Bake in centre of preheated oven for 1¼ hours, or until firm to the touch.
9. Turn out to cool on a wire cooling rack. Keep in an airtight tin for two days before eating, to allow it to become more moist.

ALL CHERRY LOAF
Gives 4 to 5 portions

8oz (200gm) plain flour
pinch of salt
2 level teaspoons baking powder
4oz (100gm) margarine
4oz (100gm) caster sugar
4oz (100gm) glacé cherries, chopped
1 large egg
¼ pint (125ml) milk
almond essence, to taste
1 can (8oz or 200gm) red cherries
arrowroot

1. Preheat oven to moderate to moderately hot, 375 deg F or gas 5 (190 deg C).
2. Grease a 1-lb (½ kilo) loaf tin.
3. Sift flour, salt and baking powder into a bowl.
4. Rub in margarine until mixture resembles fine breadcrumbs.
5. Stir in sugar and cherries.
6. Add egg and enough milk to give soft dropping consistency.
7. Add almond essence to taste.
8. Put in prepared tin and smooth the top.
9. Bake in centre of preheated oven for 1¼ hours, or until firm to the touch.
10. Turn out to cool on a wire cooling rack.
11. Drain juice off cherries.
12. Thicken juice with arrowroot as instructed on packet.
13. Put fruit in thickened juice and leave to cool.
14. Spoon on top of loaf and eat within 2 hours of adding decoration.

DATE LOAF

Gives 8 to 10 portions

12oz (300gm) self-raising flour
2oz (50gm) margarine
4oz (100gm) granulated sugar
6oz (150gm) dates, chopped
1 tablespoon golden syrup

1. Preheat oven to moderate, 350 deg F or gas 4 (180 deg C).
2. Grease a 2-lb (1 kilo) loaf tin.
3. Sift the flour into a bowl.
4. Rub in margarine until mixture resembles fine breadcrumbs.
5. Stir in sugar and fruit.
6. Add syrup and ¼ pint (125ml) water. Mix well.
7. Spoon mixture into prepared tin and smooth the top.
8. Bake in centre of preheated oven for 1½ hours, or until firm to the touch.
9. Turn out to cool on a wire cooling rack.

CRUMBLY ORANGE LOAF

Gives 4 to 5 portions

6oz (150gm) prunes
8oz (200gm) self-raising flour
4oz (100gm) margarine
4oz (100gm) granulated sugar
grated rind and strained juice of a medium-sized orange
1 standard egg
2 tablespoons milk

1. Soak prunes overnight in cold water. Drain, stone and chop.
2. Preheat oven to moderate, 350 deg F or gas 4 (180 deg C).
3. Grease a 1-lb (½ kilo) loaf tin. Line base and sides with greaseproof paper. Grease the paper.
4. Sift the flour into a bowl. Mix 1oz (25gm) flour with prunes.
5. Rub margarine into rest of flour until mixture resembles fine breadcrumbs.
6. Stir in sugar, orange rind, juice and prunes.
7. Add egg and enough milk to give stiff dropping consistency.
8. Put in prepared tin and smooth the top.
9. Bake in centre of preheated oven for 1¼ hours, or until firm to the touch.
10. Turn out to cool on a wire cooling rack. Store in an airtight tin and eat within three days.

CHOCOLATE-TOPPED LOAF

Gives 4 to 5 portions

8oz (200gm) plain flour
pinch of salt
2 level teaspoons baking powder
4oz (100gm) margarine
4oz (100gm) caster sugar
1 heaped teaspoon grated orange rind
1 large egg
¼ pint (125ml) milk
2oz (50gm) icing sugar
strained juice of 1 large orange
1oz (25gm) plain chocolate, grated

1. Preheat oven to moderate to moderately hot, 375 deg F or gas 5 (190 deg C).
2. Grease a 1-lb (½ kilo) loaf tin.
3. Sift the flour with salt and baking powder into a bowl.
4. Rub in margarine until mixture resembles fine breadcrumbs.
5. Stir in sugar and rind.
6. Add egg and enough milk to mix to a soft dropping consistency.
7. Put in prepared tin and smooth the top.
8. Bake in centre of preheated oven for 1¼ hours, or until firm to the touch.
9. Turn out to cool on a wire cooling rack.
10. Mix sifted icing sugar with enough orange juice to give a mixture which will coat the back of a wooden spoon.
11. Spoon on top of loaf.
12. Sprinkle grated chocolate on top of the icing. Eat the same day.

CLOSE-TEXTURED FRUIT LOAF

Gives 8 to 10 portions

12oz (300gm) self-raising flour
pinch of salt
2oz (50gm) margarine
4oz (100gm) granulated sugar
6oz (150gm) raisins
1 tablespoon golden syrup

1. Preheat oven to moderate, 350 deg F or gas 4 (180 deg C).
2. Grease a 2-lb (1 kilo) loaf tin.
3. Sift the flour and salt into a bowl.
4. Rub in margarine until mixture resembles fine breadcrumbs.
5. Stir in sugar and fruit.
6. Add syrup and ¼ pint (125ml) water. Mix well.
7. Spoon mixture into prepared tin and smooth top.
8. Bake in centre of preheated oven for 1½ hours, or until firm to the touch.
9. Turn out to cool on a wire cooling rack.

PEEL LOAF

Gives 8 to 10 portions

6oz (150gm) caster sugar
3oz (75gm) lard
½ level teaspoon cinnamon
8oz (200gm) plain flour
½ level teaspoon bicarbonate of soda
1 large egg, beaten
1 tablespoon milk
4oz (100gm) chopped mixed peel

1. Preheat oven to moderate, 350 deg F or gas 4 (180 deg C).
2. Grease a 2-lb (1 kilo) loaf tin. Line base with greaseproof paper. Grease the paper.
3. Put 8 tablespoons water in a pan. Add sugar, lard and cinnamon.
4. Bring to boil and simmer for 3 minutes. Leave to cool a little.
5. Sift flour with bicarbonate of soda into a bowl.
6. Stir in lard mixture.
7. Add the egg and milk.
8. Stir in the peel.
9. Put in prepared tin and smooth the top.
10. Bake in centre of preheated oven for 1 hour, or until firm to the touch.
11. Turn out to cool on wire rack. Store in an airtight tin.

PRUNE TEA LOAF
Gives 8 to 10 portions

8oz (200gm) prunes, stewed
6oz (150gm) caster sugar
3oz (75gm) lard
½ level teaspoon nutmeg
pinch of salt
8oz (200gm) plain flour
½ level teaspoon bicarbonate of soda
1 large egg, beaten
1 tablespoon milk

1. Preheat oven to moderate, 350 deg F or gas 4 (180 deg C).
2. Grease a 2-lb (1 kilo) loaf tin. Line base with greaseproof paper. Grease the paper.
3. Stone and chop the fruit. (Make sure it is well drained.)
4. Put 8 tablespoons water in a pan and add sugar, lard, nutmeg and salt.
5. Bring to boil and simmer for 3 minutes. Leave to cool a little.
6. Sift flour with bicarbonate of soda into a bowl, then add lard mixture.
7. Add egg and enough milk to give a fairly soft mixture.
8. Stir in prunes.
9. Put in prepared tin and smooth the top.
10. Bake in centre of preheated oven for 1 hour, or until firm to the touch.
11. Turn out to cool on a wire cooling rack. Store in an airtight tin.

SUNSHINE FRUIT LOAF
Gives 8 to 10 portions

2oz (50gm) dried apricots
2oz (50gm) prunes
4oz (100gm) raisins
8oz (200gm) self-raising flour
4oz (100gm) margarine
4oz (100gm) granulated sugar
1 large egg
milk to mix

1. Put apricots and prunes in cold water and leave to soak overnight.
2. Preheat oven to moderate, 350 deg F or gas 4 (180 deg C).
3. Grease a 2-lb (1 kilo) loaf tin.
4. Stone and chop the soaked fruit and mix with raisins.
5. Sift the flour into a bowl
6. Rub in margarine until mixture resembles fine breadcrumbs.
7. Stir in sugar and fruit.
8. Add egg and enough milk to mix to a stiff dropping consistency.
9. Put in prepared tin and smooth the top.
10. Bake in centre of preheated oven for 1¼ hours, or until firm to the touch.
11. Turn out to cool on wire rack.

PLAIN AND SPICY LOAF
Gives 4 to 5 portions

8oz (200gm) plain flour
pinch of salt
2 level teaspoons baking powder
4oz (100gm) margarine
4oz (100gm) caster sugar
1½ level teaspoons mixed spice
1 large egg
¼ pint (125ml) milk

1. Preheat oven to moderate to moderately hot, 375 deg F or gas 5 (190 deg C).
2. Grease a 1-lb (½ kilo) loaf tin.
3. Sift flour with salt and baking powder into a bowl.
4. Rub in margarine until mixture resembles fine breadcrumbs.
5. Stir in caster sugar and spice.
6. Add egg and enough milk to mix to stiff dropping consistency.
7. Put in prepared tin and smooth the top.
8. Bake in centre of preheated oven for 1¼ hours, or until golden and firm to the touch.
9. Turn out to cool on wire cooling rack. Serve with butter and apricot jam.

CINNAMON AND SUGAR LOAF
Gives 4 to 5 portions

8oz (200gm) self-raising flour
1 level teaspoon cinnamon, plus a little extra
4oz (100gm) margarine
4oz (100gm) caster sugar
1 large egg
¼ pint (125ml) milk
6 sugar lumps

1. Preheat oven to moderate to moderately hot, 375 deg F or gas 5 (190 deg C).
2. Grease a 1-lb (½ kilo) loaf tin.
3. Sift the flour with 1 level teaspoon cinnamon into a bowl.
4. Rub in margarine until mixture resembles fine breadcrumbs.
5. Stir in caster sugar.
6. Add egg and enough milk to give a soft dropping consistency. Mixture should drop from spoon as soon as it is shaken.
7. Put in prepared tin.
8. Bake in centre of preheated oven for 1¼ hours or until firm to the touch.
9. Turn out to cool on a wire cooling rack.
10. Crush the sugar lumps and mix with a little cinnamon, then sprinkle on top of cake. Store in an airtight tin and eat within three days.

FIGGY LOAF
Gives 4 to 5 portions

8oz (200gm) self-raising flour
4oz (100gm) margarine
4oz (100gm) caster sugar
4oz (100gm) dried figs, stewed, drained and chopped
2 teaspoons liquid black coffee, unsweetened
1 large egg
¼ pint (125ml) milk

1. Preheat oven to moderate to moderately hot, 375 deg F or gas 5 (190 deg C).
2. Grease a 1-lb (½ kilo) loaf tin.
3. Sift the flour into a bowl.
4. Rub in margarine until mixture resembles fine breadcrumbs.
5. Stir in the sugar, fruit and coffee.
6. Add the egg and enough milk to give a soft dropping consistency.
7. Spoon mixture into prepared tin and smooth top.
8. Bake in centre of preheated oven for 1¼ hours, or until firm to the touch.
9. Turn out to cool on a wire cooling rack. Store in an airtight tin and eat within four days.

APPLE LOAF
Gives 4 to 5 portions

8oz (200gm) self-raising flour
4oz (100gm) margarine
4oz (100gm) caster sugar
1 large egg
¼ pint (125ml) milk
2 red eating apples
2 tablespoons apricot jam

1. Preheat oven to moderate to moderately hot, 375 deg F or gas 5 (190 deg C).
2. Grease a 1-lb (½ kilo) loaf tin.
3. Sift the flour into a bowl.
4. Rub in margarine until mixture resembles fine breadcrumbs.
5. Stir in sugar.
6. Add egg and enough milk to give a soft dropping consistency.
7. Put in prepared tin and smooth the top.
8. Bake in centre of preheated oven for 1¼ hours, or until firm to the touch.
9. Turn out to cool on a wire cooling rack.
10. Core apples but do not peel. Cut them into thin wedges and arrange on top of cake, overlapping.
11. Heat the jam gently.
12. Spoon jam over apples, then leave to cool. Eat the same day.

FESTIVE LOAF
Gives 4 to 5 portions

8oz (200gm) self-raising flour
4oz (100gm) margarine
4oz (100gm) granulated sugar
1 standard egg
5 tablespoons milk
2oz (50gm) icing sugar
3 glacé cherries, halved

1. Preheat oven to moderate, 350 deg F or gas 4 (180 deg C).
2. Grease a 1-lb (½ kilo) loaf tin. Line with greaseproof paper. Grease the paper.
3. Sift the flour into a bowl.
4. Rub in margarine until mixture resembles fine breadcrumbs.
5. Stir in sugar.
6. Add egg and enough milk to give stiff dropping consistency.
7. Put in prepared tin and smooth the top.
8. Bake in centre of preheated oven for 1¼ hours, or until firm to the touch.
9. Turn out to cool on wire cooling rack.
10. Mix sifted icing sugar with enough water to give a stiff mixture. Spoon on loaf and let it dribble down sides.
11. Put cherries on top. Eat within one day of adding the icing.

LUNCH BOX CAKE
Gives 4 to 5 portions

7oz (175gm) self-raising flour
½ level teaspoon baking powder
1oz (25gm) desiccated coconut
4oz (100gm) margarine
4oz (100gm) granulated sugar
1 large egg
milk to mix

1. Preheat oven to moderate, 350 deg F or gas 4 (180 deg C).
2. Grease a 1-lb (½ kilo) loaf tin. Line with greaseproof paper. Grease the paper.
3. Sift flour with baking powder into a bowl. Mix with coconut.
4. Rub in margarine until mixture resembles fine breadcrumbs.
5. Stir in the sugar.
6. Add egg and enough milk to mix to a stiff, dropping consistency.
7. Spoon into prepared tin.
8. Bake in centre of preheated oven for 1¼ hours, or until firm to the touch.
9. Turn out to cool on a wire cooling rack. Store in an airtight tin.

Chocolate éclairs (see page 60)

Cream horns (see page 61)

Butterflies (see page 48)

Apple squares (see page 49)

Candle cup cakes (see page 49)

Ring doughnuts (see page 66)

Strawberry tartlets (see page 62)

Cream oat crisps (see page 73)

APPLE SQUARE CAKE

Gives 6 portions

1lb (½ kilo) cooking apples
5oz (125gm) soft brown sugar
4oz (100gm) golden syrup
2oz (50gm) plus 1 tablespoon black treacle
6oz (150gm) margarine
12oz (300gm) self-raising flour
2 level teaspoons ground ginger
2 standard eggs

1. Preheat oven to moderate to moderately hot, 375 deg F or gas 5 (190 deg C).
2. Grease the base of a fairly deep 8-inch (20cm) square cake tin. Line with greaseproof paper and grease the paper.
3. Wash, dry and grate the unpeeled apples. Cover and put to one side.
4. Put the sugar, syrup, 2oz (50gm) treacle and margarine in a pan. Heat slowly until the sugar has dissolved.
5. Sift the flour and ginger into a bowl.
6. Beat the eggs and add them gradually, with the melted ingredients, to the flour mixture. Beat well until smooth.
7. Stir in the apples.
8. Turn mixture at once into the prepared tin and spread it evenly.
9. Bake the cake in the centre of the preheated oven for 1 hour 15 minutes, or until firm to the touch.
10. Leave cake in tin for 10 minutes, then turn out carefully to complete cooling on a wire cooling rack.
11. Gently heat rest of treacle in a small pan and brush it over the top of the cake.
12. Store cake in an airtight tin and eat it within four days.

MARMALADE TREAT

Gives about 8 portions

8oz (200gm) self-raising flour
2 level teaspoons ground ginger
3oz (75gm) margarine
6oz (150gm) golden syrup
8oz (200gm) marmalade (not jelly marmalade)
2 tablespoons hot water
1 large egg, beaten

1. Preheat oven to very moderate, 325 deg F or gas 3 (170 deg C).
2. Grease an 8-inch (20cm) square, fairly deep cake tin. Line the base of the tin with greaseproof paper, then grease the paper.
3. Sift the flour and the ginger into a mixing bowl.
4. Put the margarine and syrup in a small pan and heat gently until the margarine melts.
5. Pour the melted mixture into the sifted ingredients.
6. Stir in the marmalade, hot water and beaten egg. Mix well.
7. Pour the mixture into the prepared tin. Bake in the centre of the preheated oven for 1 hour 10 minutes, or until firm to the touch.
8. Leave in the tin for 10 minutes before turning out to cool on a wire rack. (This cake keeps well if stored in an airtight tin.)

OATMEAL LOAF

Gives 8 to 10 portions

8oz (200gm) plain flour
1 level teaspoon cream of tartar
2 level teaspoons bicarbonate of soda
pinch of salt
2oz (50gm) oatmeal (not instant kind)
4oz (100gm) sultanas
6 tablespoons milk
2oz (50gm) soft brown sugar
3 tablespoons black treacle
1oz (25gm) margarine

1. Preheat oven to moderate, 350 deg F or gas 4 (180 deg C).
2. Grease a 2-lb (1 kilo) loaf tin.
3. Sift flour with cream of tartar, bicarbonate of soda and salt into a bowl.
4. Mix in oatmeal and fruit.
5. Put the milk in a small pan with sugar, treacle and margarine.
6. Heat gently until melted, stirring occasionally.
7. Stir melted mixture into flour mixture. Mix well.
8. Put in prepared tin.
9. Bake in centre of preheated oven for 1 hour 5 minutes, or until cooked.
10. Turn out to cool on wire rack. Serve with jam.

BLACK TREACLE LOAF

Gives 8 to 10 portions

8oz (200gm) plain flour
1 level teaspoon cream of tartar
2 level teaspoons bicarbonate of soda
1 level teaspoon salt
2oz (50gm) oatmeal (not instant kind)
4oz (100gm) raisins
6 tablespoons milk
2oz (50gm) caster sugar
3 tablespoons black treacle
1oz (25gm) margarine

1. Preheat oven to moderate, 350 deg F or gas 4 (180 deg C).
2. Grease a 2-lb (1 kilo) loaf tin.
3. Sift flour with cream of tartar, bicarbonate of soda and salt into a bowl.
4. Mix in oatmeal and fruit.
5. Put milk in a small pan with sugar, treacle and margarine.
6. Heat gently until melted, stirring occasionally.
7. Pour melted mixture into flour and mix well.
8. Put in prepared tin and smooth the top.
9. Bake in centre of preheated oven for 1 hour 5 minutes, or until cooked.
10. Turn out to cool on wire rack. Serve with butter.

SYRUP CAKE
Gives 6 portions

5oz (125gm) self-raising flour
½ level teaspoon baking powder
1oz (25gm) oatmeal (not the instant kind)
1oz (25gm) caster sugar
4oz (100gm) margarine
2 heaped tablespoons golden syrup
2 large eggs

1. Preheat oven to moderate, 350 deg F or gas 4 (180 deg C).
2. Grease a round, deep 7-inch (18cm) cake tin. Line with greaseproof paper and grease the paper.
3. Sift the flour and baking powder into a bowl.
4. Stir oatmeal and sugar into the flour.
5. Melt margarine and syrup in a pan over a gentle heat.
6. Beat the eggs in a basin.
7. Beat syrup and eggs into the flour mixture.
8. Put mixture in prepared cake tin and smooth the top.
9. Bake in centre of preheated oven for 40 minutes, or until well risen and golden.
10. Leave to cool on a wire rack.
11. Store cake in airtight tin and eat within five days.

SUGAR-TOPPED CAKE
Gives 6 portions

8oz (200gm) plain flour
4 level teaspoons baking powder
pinch of salt
8oz (200gm) currants
4oz (100gm) caster sugar
2oz (50gm) margarine
10 tablespoons milk
2 standard eggs
5 lumps of sugar

1. Preheat oven to moderate, 350 deg F or gas 4 (180 deg C).
2. Grease a deep 6-inch (15cm) cake tin. Line the base with greaseproof paper. Grease the paper.
3. Sift the flour with the baking powder and salt into a bowl.
4. Mix in the currants and the caster sugar.
5. Melt the margarine in a small pan; remove from heat and add the milk and eggs. Beat well.
6. Add to dry ingredients and beat well with a wooden spoon.
7. Put mixture in prepared cake tin. Smooth the top.
8. Cook the cake in centre of preheated oven for 1¼–1½ hours or until a warmed knife blade inserted into centre of cake is clean when withdrawn. Turn out to cool.
9. Crush the sugar lumps and sprinkle on top of cake.
10. Leave to finish cooling on wire rack.

NUT AND JAM TOPPER
Gives 4 to 6 portions

8oz (200gm) plain flour
4 level teaspoons baking powder
pinch of salt
8oz (200gm) sultanas
4oz (100gm) caster sugar
2 oz (50gm) margarine
10 tablespoons milk
2 standard eggs
1½oz (37gm) whole almonds, skinned and split
2 heaped tablespoons apricot jam

1. Preheat oven to moderate, 350 deg F or gas 4 (180 deg C).
2. Grease a deep, round 6-inch (15cm) cake tin. Line the base with greaseproof paper and grease the paper.
3. Sift the flour with the baking powder and salt.
4. Mix in the sultanas and caster sugar.
5. Melt the margarine in a small pan. Remove from heat and add milk and eggs. Beat well.
6. Add to dry ingredients and beat well with wooden spoon.
7. Put mixture in prepared cake tin. Smooth the top.
8. Cook the cake in centre of preheat oven for 1¼–1½ hours, or until firm to the touch. Turn out to cool.
9. Mix nuts with heated jam. Spoon on top of cake and leave to cool.

COFFEE ROLL
Gives 4 to 5 portions

3 standard eggs
4oz (100gm) caster sugar
3oz (75gm) self-raising flour
1 tablespoon tepid water
2 rounded tablespoons plum jam
4oz (100gm) margarine
4oz (100gm) icing sugar, sifted
4 tablespoons strong liquid instant black coffee

1. Preheat oven to hot, 450 deg F or gas 8 (230 deg C).
2. Grease a 12-inch (30cm) by 9-inch (23cm) Swiss roll tin. Line with greaseproof paper and grease the paper.
3. Put the eggs and caster sugar in a fairly large bowl and whisk until the mixture is very thick and will hold the impression of the whisk for 5 seconds.
4. Using a metal spoon, fold in the sifted flour, then the water.
5. Pour at once into the prepared tin.
6. Bake in the centre of the preheated oven for 7–10 minutes, or until firm to the touch.
7. Turn out on to greaseproof paper and roll the cake up with the paper. Leave to cool.
8. Unroll the cake and remove the paper.
9. Spread jam on the cake.
10. Cream the margarine with the icing sugar until very creamy.
11. Add coffee to the icing. Use more if you prefer a stronger taste.
12. Roll up the cake with the jam inside.
13. Spread coffee icing all over the cake and mark into a pattern with a fork. Eat the same day.

DOUBLE FILLED ROLL
Gives 4 portions

3oz (75gm) self-raising flour
3 standard eggs
4oz (100gm) caster sugar
2 heaped tablespoons chocolate spread
1 can (8oz or 200gm) raspberries
1 heaped tablespoon raspberry jam

1. Preheat oven to hot, 450 deg F or gas 8 (230 deg C).
2. Grease a Swiss roll tin about 12 inches (30cm) by 9 inches (23cm). Line with greaseproof paper. Grease the paper.
3. Sift the flour.
4. Put eggs and sugar in a bowl and whisk until very thick – the mixture should hold the impression of the whisk for 5 seconds.
5. Using a metal spoon, fold in the flour.
6. Spoon mixture into prepared tin.
7. Bake in centre of preheated oven for 7–10 minutes, or until well risen and golden.
8. Turn out on to greaseproof paper. Roll up with the paper and leave to cool.
9. Unroll and remove paper.
10. Spread chocolate on the cake.
11. Drain the fruit. Push through a sieve then mix with jam. Spread on top of chocolate and roll up the cake. Eat within 2 hours.

PEPPERMINT ROLL
Gives about 4 portions

1oz (25gm) cocoa
1 level teaspoon baking powder
2oz (50gm) self-raising flour
3 standard eggs
4oz (100gm) caster sugar
1 tablespoon tepid water
2oz (50gm) margarine
3oz (75gm) icing sugar
peppermint essence, to taste
4 flat, square chocolate-coated peppermint creams

1. Preheat oven to hot, 450 deg F or gas 8 (230 deg C).
2. Grease a 12-inch (30cm) by 9-inch (23cm) Swiss roll tin. Line the base with greaseproof paper and grease the paper.
3. Sift the cocoa with the baking powder and flour. Do this twice.
4. Put the eggs and sugar in a bowl. Whisk until the mixture is very thick and creamy and will hold the impression of the whisk for 5 seconds.
5. Using a metal spoon, fold in the flour and water.
6. Pour at once into the prepared tin.
7. Bake in the centre of the preheated oven for 7–10 minutes, or until well risen and firm to the touch.
8. Turn out cake on to sugared greaseproof paper. Roll up with the paper inside.
9. Leave to cool.
10. Beat the margarine with the sifted icing sugar until light and fluffy. Add peppermint essence, to taste.
11. Unroll the cake and remove the paper.
12. Spread icing (reserving 1 tablespoon) on the cake and roll it up.
13. Spread reserved icing on top of the roll and decorate with triangles of peppermint chocolates, letting them overlap slightly. Eat the same day.

FRUIT YOGURT ROLL
Gives 4 portions

3 standard eggs
4oz (100gm) caster sugar
3oz (75gm) self-raising flour
¼ pint (125ml) carton raspberry yogurt

1. Preheat oven to hot, 450 deg F or gas 8 (230 deg C).
2. Grease a Swiss roll tin about 12 inches (30cm) by 9 inches (23cm). Line with greaseproof paper. Grease the paper.
3. Put eggs and caster sugar in a bowl and whisk until very thick – the whisk should leave an impression on the mixture for 5 seconds after it is removed from bowl.
4. Using a metal spoon, fold in the sifted flour.
5. Put into prepared tin.
6. Bake in centre of preheated oven for 7–10 minutes, or until well risen and golden.
7. Turn out on to greaseproof paper and roll up with the paper.
8. Leave to cool.
9. Unroll the cooled cake and remove the paper.
10. Spread yogurt on the cake and roll it up again. Serve at once.

SAINT CLEMENT'S CAKE
(Illustrated on page 18)
Gives about 6 portions

4oz (100gm) self-raising flour
2oz (50gm) margarine
4 standard eggs
4oz (100gm) caster sugar
2 level tablespoons lemon curd
10oz (250gm) icing sugar
strained juice of half a medium lemon
few slices of orange and lemon crystallized sweets

1. Preheat oven to moderate, 350 deg F or gas 4 (180 deg C).
2. Grease an 8-inch (20cm) round, deep cake tin. Line base of tin with greaseproof paper.
3. Sift the flour into a bowl.
4. Melt the margarine in a small pan. Leave to cool.
5. Put the eggs and the caster sugar in a large bowl and whisk until very pale and creamy. The mixture should hold the impression of the whisk for 5 seconds.
6. Fold the flour and melted margarine into whisked mixture.
7. Pour into prepared cake tin and bake in the centre of the preheated oven for 30 minutes, or until firm to the touch.
8. Turn out cake to cool on a wire rack.
9. Cut the cake into three layers.
10. Sandwich the cake with the lemon curd.
11. Sift icing sugar.
12. Mix lemon juice and a little water into the icing sugar to make an icing stiff enough to coat the back of a wooden spoon.
13. Pour icing over cake so that top and sides are coated. (Never try to spread glacé icing.) Leave to set.
14. Cut the orange and lemon slices into strips and use to decorate top of cake.

STRAWBERRY AND LIME SPONGE

Gives 4 to 5 portions

half a packet of lime jelly
1 can (8oz or 200gm) strawberries
2 tablespoons strawberry jam
3oz (75gm) self-raising flour
3 standard eggs
4oz (100gm) caster sugar
1 tablespoon tepid water

1. Make up the jelly as instructed on the packet but discard 5 tablespoons of the water. (Remember, you need only half the jelly.)
2. Wet a very shallow small tin or dish and pour the jelly into this. Leave to set.
3. Mix the well-drained fruit with the jam.
4. Preheat oven to hot, 450 deg F or gas 8 (230 deg C).
5. Grease a 12-inch (30cm) by 9-inch (23cm) Swiss roll tin. Line base with greaseproof paper. Grease the paper.
6. Sift the flour into a bowl.
7. Put the eggs and caster sugar in another bowl and whisk until mixture is very thick and will hold the impression of the whisk for 5 seconds.
8. Using a metal spoon, fold in the flour and tepid water.
9. Pour at once into prepared tin.
10. Bake in centre of preheated oven for 7–10 minutes, or until golden and firm to the touch.
11. Turn out on to greaseproof paper, and, with the help of the paper, roll up the cake and leave to cool.
12. Unroll the cake and take away the paper.
13. Spread the fruit mixture on the cake.
14. Chop up the set jelly finely and put on top of the fruit.
15. Roll up the cake tightly. Eat within 4 hours.

CLOUD CAKE

Gives 6 portions

3 large eggs
3oz (75gm) caster sugar
3oz (75gm) self-raising flour
1 tablespoon tepid water
3oz (75gm) white marshmallows
1 can (6oz or 150gm) cream or fresh cream
1 heaped tablespoon desiccated coconut

1. Preheat oven to moderate, 375 deg F or gas 5 (190 deg C).
2. Grease a deep, square 8-inch (20cm) cake tin. Line base with greaseproof paper. Grease the paper.
3. Put eggs and sugar in the mixer and whisk until very thick and mousse-like – mixture should have almost doubled in volume.
4. Using a metal spoon, fold in flour and water.
5. Spoon very quickly into prepared tin.
6. Bake at once in centre of preheated oven for 25 minutes or until golden and firm to the touch.
7. Turn out very gently to cool on wire cooling rack.
8. Put marshmallows in a basin over a pan of hot water and leave until melted.
9. Cut cold cake into two layers.
10. Sandwich cake with the marshmallows.
11. Mix cream and coconut and put on top of the cake.

FEATHERLIGHT SPONGE

Gives 5 to 6 portions

2 large eggs
3oz (75gm) caster sugar
3oz (75gm) self-raising flour
1 tablespoon tepid water
2 heaped tablespoons bramble jelly

1. Preheat oven to hot, 425 deg F or gas 7 (220 deg C).
2. Grease two round 7-inch (18cm) sandwich tins. Line bases with greaseproof paper. Grease the paper.
3. Whisk the eggs and the caster sugar in a large bowl until the mixture is very thick and will hold the impression of the whisk for 5 seconds.
4. Using a metal spoon, fold in the sifted flour and tepid water.
5. Immediately put the mixture into the prepared tins.
6. Bake at once in centre of the preheated oven for 20–30 minutes, or until firm to the touch.
7. Very gently, turn out to cool on a wire rack.
8. Sandwich cakes with the bramble jelly. Eat the same day.

GENOESE SLICE

Gives 4 to 5 portions

You need an electric mixer to make this light-as-air sponge.

4oz (100gm) self-raising flour
2oz (50gm) margarine
4 standard eggs, separated
4oz (100gm) caster sugar
3 tablespoons apricot jam
1 can (1lb or ½ kilo) peach slices, drained

1. Preheat oven to hot, 425 deg F or gas 7 (220 deg C).
2. Grease a fairly shallow cake tin about 10 inches (25cm) by 9 inches (23cm). Line base with greaseproof paper and grease the paper.
3. Sift the flour. (If the weather is cold, warm flour for 5 minutes in a low oven.)
4. Gently melt the margarine in a small pan and put to one side.
5. Whisk the egg yolks with the caster sugar until mixture is very thick and will hold the impression of the whisk for 5 seconds.
6. Whisk the egg whites until very stiff and snowy.
7. Using a metal spoon, carefully fold whites into yolk mixture.
8. Quickly and lightly fold in flour with a metal spoon, then margarine.
9. Pour at once into prepared tin and immediately put in the centre of the preheated oven to cook for 20–30 minutes, or until golden brown and firm to the touch. Turn out to cool.
10. Cut into two oblongs. Sandwich with a third of the jam.
11. Melt the rest in a pan with 2 tablespoons of water.
12. Arrange the peach slices, overlapping, on top of the cake in rows. Spoon the jam on top and leave to cool.
13. Serve within an hour.

TWO-RING GATEAU
Gives 4 portions

3¾oz (93gm) plain flour
3oz (75gm) margarine
12 tablespoons cold water
3 standard eggs
1 can (6oz or 150gm) cream
1 can (8oz or 200gm) strawberries

1. Preheat oven to hot, 425 deg F or gas 7 (220 deg C).
2. Grease a baking sheet.
3. Sift the flour in a bowl.
4. Put the margarine and water in a pan. Heat gently until margarine melts, then bring to the boil.
5. Beat flour into mixture, all in one go.
6. Cook, beating, until mixture forms a mass in centre of pan.
7. Take off heat and then gradually beat in the eggs.
8. Put mixture in a large piping bag fitted with a large plain nozzle.
9. Pipe a ring of mixture on prepared baking sheet, using half the mixture in bag. Then pipe another ring beside it so the two rings will join up to look like a figure eight when cooked.
10. Bake in centre of preheated oven for 25 minutes, or until well risen and firm.
11. Make a long slit in side of both rings to allow steam to escape. Leave to cool.
12. Cut pastry into two layers.
13. Sandwich with a mixture of cream and drained, sieved fruit.

PEACH MERINGUE SURPRISE
(Illustrated on page 18)
Gives 5 portions

This cake must be eaten within five hours of adding the filling, but the meringue case can be made the day before.

3 large egg whites
6oz (150gm) caster sugar
1 heaped teaspoon cornflour
1 teaspoon white vinegar
a little vanilla essence
1 can (15oz or 375gm) peach halves
¼ pint (125ml) cold, thick custard

1. Preheat oven to cool, 300 deg F or gas 2 (150 deg C).
2. Grease a 12-inch (30cm) piece of foil. Put the foil on a baking sheet.
3. Whisk the egg whites until very stiff.
4. Very gradually whisk in the sugar.
5. Using a metal spoon, fold cornflour into whisked mixture with the vinegar and vanilla essence.
6. Put half of the meringue in a piping bag fitted with a large plain nozzle. Pipe a thick ring of meringue on the foil.
7. Spread half of the rest of the meringue in the centre of the circle, so you have made a basket shape. Use rest of meringue to pipe a 'wall' on basket, so making a fairly deep case.
8. Bake in the centre of the preheated oven for 45 minutes, or until firm. (The meringue should be like marshmallow under its firm top coating.)
9. Leave meringue to cool.
10. Drain the fruit. The juice will not be needed.
11. Chop or mince half the fruit and stir it into the custard.
12. Fill the cooled meringue with custard mixture, then top with the remaining pieces of fruit, rounded sides up.

CRACKLE MERINGUE CAKE
Gives 4 portions

2 standard egg whites
4oz (100gm) caster sugar
1oz (25gm) roughly crushed cornflakes
1 cup cold thick custard, chilled
2 tablespoons canned cream

1. Preheat oven to very cool, 225 deg F or gas ¼ (110 deg C).
2. Line a large baking sheet with foil.
3. Whisk egg whites until very stiff.
4. Whisk in half the sugar. Using a metal spoon, fold in the rest of the sugar and the cornflakes.
5. Put in a large piping bag fitted with a large plain nozzle.
6. Pipe a plain solid round on the foil, then pipe a ring of mixture round the edge, then another ring on top making a wall.
7. Bake in centre of preheated oven for 2 hours, or until really dry.
8. Mix custard with cream and use to fill the case. Eat within two hours.

MERINGUE OVAL
Gives 4 portions

2 standard egg whites
4oz (100gm) caster sugar
1 cup cold thick chocolate blancmange
3 heaped tablespoons canned or fresh cream
1oz (25gm) plain chocolate, grated

1. Preheat oven to very cool, 225 deg F or gas ¼ (110 deg C).
2. Line a baking sheet with foil.
3. Whisk egg whites until very stiff.
4. Whisk in half the sugar, then fold in the rest with a metal spoon.
5. Put mixture in a piping bag fitted with a medium star nozzle.
6. Pipe an oval shape, working from outside to centre.
7. Pipe a wall of stars round edge of oval.
8. Cook in centre of preheated oven for 2 hours.
9. Leave to cool.
10. Mix blancmange with cream.
11. Spoon on to meringue oval.
12. Sprinkle chocolate on top. Serve within an hour of adding the filling.

CHOUX TOWER
Gives 5 to 6 portions

3¾oz (93gm) plain flour
3oz (75gm) margarine
12 tablespoons cold water
3 standard eggs
small sachet powdered creamy topping
milk to mix
3 heaped tablespoons apricot jam

1. Preheat oven to hot, 425 deg F or gas 7 (220 deg C).
2. Grease a baking sheet.
3. Sift the flour into a bowl.
4. Put the margarine and water in a pan. Heat gently until margarine melts, then bring to the boil.
5. Beat flour into mixture all in one go.
6. Cook mixture, beating, until it forms a mass in centre of pan.
7. Take off heat and gradually beat in the eggs.
8. Put mixture in a large piping bag fitted with a plain nozzle.
9. Pipe blobs on the baking sheet with plenty of space between them.
10. Bake in centre of preheated oven for 20–25 minutes, or until well risen.
11. Make a hole in each one and leave to cool.
12. Make up topping as directed on the packet. Pipe some into each bun through the holes you have made.
13. Heat the jam and brush buns with it.
14. Pile up the buns, sticking them together with jam, so they make a tower shape. Leave to cool and eat the same day.

CHOUX GATEAU
Gives about 6 portions

5½oz (137gm) plain flour
1 level tablespoon caster sugar
3½oz (87gm) margarine
1 standard egg, beaten
2 large eggs
4oz (100gm) granulated sugar
¼ pint (125ml) thick, cold custard
3 tablespoons evaporated milk
1 can (15½oz or 387gm) fruit salad

1. Preheat oven to hot, 425 deg F or gas 7 (220 deg C).
2. Grease a large baking sheet.
3. Sift 3oz (75gm) flour and the caster sugar into a bowl.
4. Rub in 1½oz (37gm) of the margarine.
5. Mix to a stiff dough with a little of the beaten egg.
6. Roll out the dough to an 8-inch circle and put it on the baking sheet.
7. Put the rest of the margarine in a small pan with ¼ pint (125ml) cold water. Heat gently until the margarine melts, then bring to the boil.
8. Beat 2½oz (62gm) flour into the boiled mixture.
9. Cook mixture gently, beating, for one minute or until mixture forms a mass in centre of pan.
10. Take pan off heat and gradually beat in two eggs.
11. Put the mixture in a piping bag fitted with ½-inch plain nozzle.
12. Brush the pastry circle on the baking sheet with the rest of the beaten egg.
13. Pipe a ring of the mixture in the piping bag round the edge of the pastry circle.
14. Pipe 14 small pastry balls on the baking sheet.
15. Bake the pastry in the centre of the preheated oven for 25 minutes or until well risen and firm.
16. Allow the pastry to cool.
17. Put the granulated sugar in a pan with ¼ pint (125ml) water. Stir over a low heat until the sugar has dissolved, then bring to the boil and boil until golden.
18. Very carefully, using a fork and wearing oven gloves, dip each pastry ball in this toffee and stick it on to the outer ring of the pastry case. Spoon the rest of the toffee over the balls. Allow it to cool.
19. Fill the centre of the case with custard mixed with milk; top with drained fruit. Serve the same day.

CHOUX TREAT
Gives 4 to 5 portions

4¾oz (118gm) plain flour
2oz (50gm) margarine
½ pint (250ml) cold water
3 standard eggs
¼ pint (125ml) thick, cold custard
half a 6oz (150gm) can cream or fresh cream
2oz (50gm) icing sugar
edible yellow food colouring

1. Preheat oven to hot, 425 deg F or gas 7 (220 deg C).
2. Grease a baking sheet.
3. Sift the flour into a basin.
4. Put the margarine and water into a small pan and heat gently until the margarine melts.
5. Beat in the flour, all at once; keeping on a low heat, beat until mixture forms a mass in the centre of the pan.
6. Take off heat and cool for 2 minutes.
7. Beat the eggs together and add them, very gradually, to the flour, beating until the mixture is smooth and glossy.
8. Spoon mixture on to the prepared baking sheet in a rough oval about 4 inches across and at least 1 inch thick.
9. Bake in the centre of the preheated oven for 40–50 minutes, or until pastry is pale golden and feels dry to the touch.
10. Split the cake in half to make two layers. Carefully scrape away any soft pastry from the inside of the layers.
11. Leave layers to cool.
12. Mix the custard with the cream. Cover and put to chill in the refrigerator.
13. Mix the sifted icing sugar with enough cold water to make an icing which will coat the back of a wooden spoon. Colour a very delicate yellow.
14. Spoon the icing on top of one of the layers. Leave to set.
15. Spoon custard mixture on the other layer. Put iced layer on top and serve within 2 hours.

LARDY CAKE
Gives 6 portions

2lb (1 kilo) plain flour
1oz (25gm) fresh yeast
½ pint (250ml) tepid milk
½ pint (250ml) tepid water
1 level teaspoon salt
6oz (150gm) lard
7oz (175gm) caster sugar, plus a little extra for glazing

1. Sift the flour into a bowl.
2. Cream the yeast with a little of the tepid milk, then mix with rest of tepid liquids.
3. Make a well in the centre of the flour and add the yeast liquid. Beat well then knead for 5 minutes.
4. Grease or oil the inside of a large polythene bag and slip the bowl of dough inside.
5. Leave in a warm place – not near direct heat or boiler – for 1 hour, or until the dough has doubled in size.
6. Knead salt into risen dough then knead well again.
7. Roll out fairly thinly into a long oblong. Spread half the lard on the oblong, then sprinkle on half the sugar, but cover only the top two-thirds of the dough.
8. Fold the dough into three, bringing the bottom third up and the top third down. Seal the edges with a rolling pin.
9. Roll out again into an oblong and repeat the whole procedure, using up the rest of the lard and the rest of the 7oz (175gm) caster sugar. Fold into three again.
10. Roll out to 1½ inches thick.
11. Put into a large, fairly shallow tin. Leave in a warm place for 20 minutes, or until dough has risen to top of tin.
12. Preheat oven to hot, 425 deg F or gas 7 (220 deg C).
13. Bake cake in centre of the preheated oven for 45 minutes – 1 hour, or until well risen and golden. Half way through the cooking, brush the cake with a glaze made of 2 level tablespoons caster sugar and 4 tablespoons water. Eat the same day hot or cold.

ONE-MIX APRICOT LOAF
Gives 4 to 5 portions

3oz (75gm) dried apricots
8oz (200gm) self-raising flour
½ level teaspoon baking powder
4oz (100gm) soft margarine
4oz (100gm) caster sugar
2 standard eggs
2 tablespoons milk

1. Leave apricots to soak in cold water overnight.
2. Drain apricots and chop finely.
3. Preheat oven to moderate to moderately hot, 375 deg F or gas 5 (190 deg C).
4. Grease a 1lb (½ kilo) loaf tin.
5. Sift flour. Put all the ingredients in a bowl and beat for 2 minutes with a wooden spoon.
6. Spoon mixture into prepared tin and smooth top.
7. Bake in centre of preheated oven for 1½ hours, or until firm to the touch.
8. Turn out to cool on a wire cooling rack. Store in an airtight tin and eat within four days.

ONE-MIX MARMALADE CAKE
Gives 4 portions

4oz (100gm) self-raising flour
4oz (100gm) soft margarine
4oz (100gm) caster sugar
2 large eggs, well beaten
½ level teaspoon baking powder
3 heaped tablespoons thick-cut marmalade

1. Preheat oven to moderate to moderately hot, 375 deg F or gas 5 (190 deg C).
2. Grease two 7½-inch (19cm) sandwich tins. Line with greaseproof paper; grease the paper.
3. Sift flour. Put all the ingredients in a bowl, adding 1 tablespoon marmalade. Beat for 2 minutes, using a wooden spoon.
4. Divide mixture between the prepared tins and smooth tops.
5. Bake in the centre of preheated oven for 25–30 minutes, or until firm to the touch.
6. Turn out to cool on a wire cooling rack.
7. Sandwich cakes with rest of the marmalade. Store in an airtight tin and eat within a week.

ONE-MIX GINGER AND DATE CAKE
Gives 4 portions

4oz (100gm) self-raising flour
4oz (100gm) soft margarine
4oz (100gm) caster sugar
2 large eggs, well beaten
½ level teaspoon baking powder
1 level teaspoon powdered ginger
3oz (75gm) dates, finely chopped
½ cup thick, cold custard

1. Preheat oven to moderate to moderately hot, 375 deg F or gas 5 (190 deg C).
2. Grease two 7½-inch (19cm) sandwich tins. Line with greaseproof paper. Grease the paper.
3. Sift flour. Put all ingredients, except the custard, in a bowl. Beat for 2 minutes, using a wooden spoon.
4. Divide mixture between the prepared tins.
5. Bake in centre of preheated oven for 25–30 minutes, or until firm to the touch.
6. Turn out to cool on a wire cooling rack.
7. Sandwich with cold custard. Store in an airtight tin and eat within two days.

ONE-MIX COCONUT CAKE
Gives 4 portions

3oz (75gm) self-raising flour
1½oz (37gm) desiccated coconut
1 level teaspoon baking powder
4oz (100gm) soft margarine
4oz (100gm) caster sugar
2 large eggs, well beaten
2 tablespoons milk
1 can (6oz or 150gm) cream

1. Preheat oven to moderate to moderately hot, 375 deg F or gas 5 (190 deg C).
2. Grease two 7½-inch (19cm) sandwich tins. Line bases with greaseproof paper. Grease the paper.
3. Sift flour. Put all the ingredients, except ½oz (12gm) coconut and the cream, in a bowl. Beat for 2 minutes, using a wooden spoon.
4. Divide between prepared tins.
5. Bake in centre of preheated oven for 25–30 minutes, or until firm to the touch.
6. Turn out to cool on wire cooling rack.
7. Sandwich with cream and extra coconut.
8. Store in an airtight tin and eat within two days.

EXTRA QUICK CHERRY CAKE
Gives 4 portions

4oz (100gm) self-raising flour
4oz (100gm) soft margarine
4oz (100gm) caster sugar
2 large eggs
½ level teaspoon baking powder
3oz (75gm) glacé cherries

1. Preheat oven to moderate, 350 deg F or gas 4 (180 deg C).
2. Grease a deep, round 8-inch (20cm) cake tin. Line with greaseproof paper. Grease the paper.
3. Sift flour. Put all the ingredients except the cherries in a bowl.
4. Wash the cherries in warm water. Dry well. Cut up and toss in a little extra flour.
5. Add cherries to bowl. Beat well for 2 minutes with a wooden spoon.
6. Put mixture in prepared tin.
7. Bake in centre of preheated oven for 50 minutes to 1 hour, or until firm.
8. Turn out to cool on a wire cooling rack.

EASY-MIX COFFEE CAKE
Gives 4 portions

4oz (100gm) self-raising flour
4oz (100gm) soft margarine
4oz (100gm) caster sugar
2 large eggs, well beaten
½ level teaspoon baking powder
4 tablespoons very strong liquid black coffee, unsweetened
2 tablespoons chocolate spread

1. Preheat oven to moderate to moderately hot, 375 deg F or gas 5 (190 deg C).
2. Grease two 7½-inch (19cm) sandwich tins. Line bases with greaseproof paper. Grease the paper.
3. Sift flour. Put all the ingredients except chocolate spread in a bowl. Beat for 2 minutes, using a wooden spoon.
4. Divide mixture between the prepared tins and smooth tops.
5. Bake in centre of preheated oven for 25–30 minutes, or until firm.
6. Turn out to cool.
7. Sandwich with chocolate spread.

EASY-MIX ALMOND CAKE
Gives 4 portions

4oz (100gm) soft margarine
4oz (100gm) caster sugar
2 large eggs, beaten
4oz (100gm) self-raising flour, sifted
½ level teaspoon baking powder
4 tablespoons milk
1 small can cream
1oz (25gm) whole almonds, skinned and chopped

1. Preheat oven to moderate to moderately hot, 375 deg F or gas 5 (190 deg C).
2. Grease two 7½-inch (19cm) sandwich tins. Line bases with greaseproof paper and grease the paper.
3. Put all ingredients except cream and nuts in a bowl. Beat for 2 minutes, using a wooden spoon.
4. Divide mixture between the prepared tins and smooth tops.
5. Bake in centre of preheated oven for 25–30 minutes, or until firm.
6. Turn out to cool.
7. Sandwich with cream and nuts mixed.

SPEEDY CITRUS CAKE
Gives 4 portions

4oz (100gm) self-raising flour
4oz (100gm) soft margarine
4oz (100gm) caster sugar
2 large eggs, beaten
2 level teaspoons baking powder
strained juice of a small orange
1 rounded teaspoon grated orange rind
2 tablespoons lemon curd

1. Preheat oven to moderate to moderately hot, 375 deg F or gas 5 (190 deg C).
2. Grease two 7½-inch (19cm) sandwich tins. Line bases with greaseproof paper. Grease the paper.
3. Sift flour. Put all ingredients except lemon curd in a bowl. Beat for 2 minutes with a wooden spoon.
4. Divide between the prepared tins and smooth tops.
5. Bake in centre of preheated oven for 20–25 minutes, or until firm to the touch.
6. Turn out to cool on a wire cooling rack.
7. Sandwich cakes with lemon curd.

SPEEDY CHOCOLATE CAKE
Gives 4 portions

4oz (100gm) soft margarine
4oz (100gm) caster sugar
2 large eggs, beaten
3oz (75gm) plain chocolate
4oz (100gm) self-raising flour
1 can (6oz or 150gm) cream

1. Preheat oven to moderate to moderately hot, 375 deg F or gas 5 (190 deg C).
2. Grease two 7½-inch (19cm) sandwich tins. Line bases with greaseproof paper. Grease the paper.
3. Put margarine and sugar in a bowl.
4. Add eggs and stir well.
5. Put chocolate in a bowl over a pan of gently simmering water and leave until melted.
6. Stir into margarine mixture.
7. Add sifted flour and beat for 2 minutes, using a wooden spoon.
8. Divide between prepared tins and smooth the tops.
9. Bake in centre of preheated oven for 20–25 minutes, or until firm to the touch.
10. Turn out to cool on a wire cooling rack.
11. Sandwich cakes with cream.

QUICK-MIX SULTANA CAKE
Gives 5 portions

12oz (300gm) self-raising flour
1 level teaspoon baking powder
large pinch of salt
8oz (200gm) soft margarine
8oz (200gm) caster sugar
4 large eggs
14oz (350gm) sultanas

1. Preheat oven to moderate, 350 deg F or gas 4 (180 deg C).
2. Grease a deep, round 8-inch (20cm) cake tin. Line with greaseproof paper. Grease the paper.
3. Sift flour, baking powder and salt into a bowl.
4. Add rest of ingredients and mix for 5 minutes using a wooden spoon, not mixer.
5. Put into prepared tin and smooth the top.
6. Bake in centre of preheated oven for 2¼ hours, or until firm to the touch.
7. Leave cake to cool in tin for 10 minutes, then turn out to complete cooling on a wire rack. Store in an airtight tin and eat within a week.

CUP OF TEA CAKE
Gives 8 portions

9oz (225gm) sultanas
9oz (225gm) currants
4oz (100gm) caster sugar
4oz (100gm) soft brown sugar
½ pint (250ml) medium strength strained cold tea
1lb (½ kilo) self-raising flour
4 tablespoons milk
1 level tablespoon golden syrup
2 large eggs

1. Put the fruits, sugars and tea in a bowl – not metal – and leave overnight.
2. Preheat oven to moderate to moderately hot, 375 deg F or gas 5 (190 deg C).
3. Grease a deep, round 8-inch (20cm) cake tin. Line base and sides with greaseproof paper. Grease the paper.
4. Sift the flour and stir it into the fruit mixture. Add milk, syrup and beaten eggs. Mix well.
5. Spoon into prepared tin.
6. Bake in centre of preheated oven for 1¼ hours, or until firm to the touch.
7. Turn out to cool on a wire cooling rack.

MIXER CELEBRATION CAKE
Gives 6 portions

This is a very economical cake for Christmas or a birthday. Leave at least two weeks before icing.

6oz (150gm) self-raising flour
1 level teaspoon mixed spice
½ level teaspoon nutmeg
6oz (150gm) margarine
6oz (150gm) soft brown sugar
4 large eggs
10oz (250gm) sultanas
2oz (50gm) glacé cherries, chopped
1oz (25gm) chopped mixed peel
rum essence, to taste
half a packet bought almond paste
8oz (200gm) icing sugar

1. Preheat oven to moderate, 350 deg F or gas 4 (180 deg C).
2. Grease a round, deep 8-inch (20cm) cake tin. Line with greaseproof paper. Grease the paper.
3. Sift the flour with spice and nutmeg.
4. Put margarine and brown sugar in bowl of mixer. Start it up and leave till mixture is light and creamy.
5. Add 3 lightly beaten eggs, fruit and peel. Run mixer for 2 minutes.
6. Using a metal spoon, fold in the flour.
7. Flavour with rum essence.
8. Put in prepared tin. Make a small hollow in centre.
9. Bake in centre of preheated oven for about 1 hour 40 minutes or until firm to the touch.
10. Turn out to cool.
11. Store in airtight tin.
12. Complete the cake four days before the celebration. Separate the remaining egg.
13. Roll out almond paste into a round to fit top of cake.
14. Brush top of cake with egg yolk, then fit almond paste on.
15. Put sifted icing sugar and egg white in mixer. Beat for 3 minutes or until thick and standing up in peaks.
16. Spoon icing on to top of cake only. Peak with a knife. Leave overnight to set hard.
17. Put a red or gold paper cake frill round sides of cake and pin in place.

EVERYDAY MIXER SPONGE
Gives 4 portions

6oz (150gm) margarine
4oz (100gm) caster sugar
2 large eggs, lightly beaten
4oz (100gm) self-raising flour
2oz (50gm) icing sugar
2 tablespoons lemon juice

1. Preheat oven to moderate to moderately hot, 375 deg F or gas 5 (190 deg C).
2. Grease two 7½-inch (19cm) sandwich tins. Line the bases with greaseproof paper. Grease the paper.
3. Put 4oz (100gm) margarine and the caster sugar in an electric mixer. Start it up to cream mixture.
4. When mixture is very light in colour and creamy, add lightly beaten eggs and run mixer for about 2 minutes.
5. Using a metal spoon, fold in the sifted flour.
6. Spoon into prepared tins.
7. Bake in centre of preheated oven for 25–30 minutes, or until firm to the touch.
8. Turn out cakes to cool on a wire rack.
9. Put rest of margarine in mixer bowl with sifted icing sugar and lemon juice. Run mixer for about 2 minutes, or until mixture is creamy. Put to chill in refrigerator.
10. Sandwich cakes with lemon icing and eat the same day.

MOCHA MIXER GATEAU
Gives 4 portions

6oz (150gm) margarine
4oz (100gm) caster sugar
2 large eggs, lightly beaten
4oz (100gm) self-raising flour
4 level teaspoons instant coffee powder
2oz (50gm) icing sugar
1 tablespoon evaporated milk
1oz (25gm) milk or plain chocolate, grated

1. Preheat oven to moderate to moderately hot, 375 deg F or gas 5 (190 deg C).
2. Grease two 7½-inch (19cm) sandwich tins. Line bases with greaseproof paper. Grease the paper.
3. Put 4oz (100gm) margarine and the caster sugar in a mixer.
4. Start it up and leave till mixture is creamy and light in colour.
5. Add eggs and run mixer for 2 minutes.
6. Sift the flour with half the coffee powder.
7. Using a metal spoon, fold flour into creamed mixture.
8. Spoon into prepared tins and smooth tops.
9. Bake in centre of preheated oven for 25–30 minutes, or until firm to the touch.
10. Turn out cakes to cool on a wire cooling rack.
11. Put rest of margarine in bowl of mixer with rest of coffee, the icing sugar and milk. Run mixer for about 2 minutes.
12. Stir chocolate into icing and put to chill in the refrigerator.
13. Sandwich cakes with the mocha icing.

MANY LAYERED GATEAU
Gives 4 portions

4 standard egg whites
8oz (200gm) caster sugar
1 can (6oz or 150gm) cream
1 can (8oz or 200gm) raspberries, well drained

1. Preheat oven to very cool, 225 deg F or gas ¼ (110 deg C).
2. Line three baking sheets with foil or use a double layer of foil without a baking sheet.
3. Whisk egg whites until very stiff.
4. Whisk in half the sugar, then fold in the rest.
5. Put some of the mixture in a large piping bag fitted with a large plain nozzle.
6. Pipe two fairly large rings on each piece of foil.
7. Spread rest of meringue in centres of rings to make flat rounds.
8. Bake in oven, on three shelf positions, for 2 hours, or until well dried out, but not coloured.
9. Leave to cool.
10. Put cream and fruit in bowl of electric mixer. Run mixer for 1 minute. Use the cream to sandwich the rounds into one cake. Serve within an hour of adding the filling.

ORANGE GADGET CAKE
Gives 4 portions

5 trifle sponges
3oz (75gm) icing sugar
3oz (75gm) margarine
1 can (11oz or 275gm) mandarin oranges
1 tablespoon orange squash

1. Well oil or grease a loose-based, deep, round 6-inch (15cm) cake tin.
2. Put sponges into liquidizer and run it to make crumbs.
3. Meanwhile, put sugar, margarine, half the drained fruit and the orange squash in the bowl of the mixer. Run it for 2 minutes, or until mixture is creamy.
4. Layer the crumbs and orange mixture in prepared tin. Put a saucer on top and place a heavy weight on saucer.
5. Leave cake in refrigerator for 3 hours.
6. Turn out to serve. Decorate with rest of fruit and serve the same day.

COFFEE GADGET CAKE
Gives 4 portions

5 trifle sponges
3oz (75gm) icing sugar
3oz (75gm) margarine
3 tablespoons very strong liquid black coffee, unsweetened

1. Well oil or grease a loose-based, deep, round 6-inch (15cm) cake tin.
2. Put sponges in liquidizer and run it to make crumbs.
3. Meanwhile, put the icing sugar, margarine and coffee into bowl of electric mixer and run it until mixture is creamy (about 2 minutes).
4. Layer cake crumbs and coffee mixture in prepared tin. Put a saucer on top and place a heavy weight on the saucer.
5. Leave in refrigerator for 3 hours.
6. Turn out to serve and eat the same day.

FRUITY MIXER CAKE
Gives 4 portions

4oz (100gm) margarine
4oz (100gm) caster sugar
2 large eggs, lightly beaten
4oz (100gm) sultanas
4oz (100gm) self-raising flour

1. Preheat oven to moderate, 350 deg F or gas 4 (180 deg C).
2. Grease a deep, round 8-inch (20cm) cake tin. Line with greaseproof paper. Grease the paper.
3. Put margarine and caster sugar in an electric mixer. Start it up to cream mixture.
4. When mixture is very creamy and light in colour, add the eggs and fruit and run mixer for about 2 minutes.
5. Using a metal spoon, fold sifted flour into creamed mixture.
6. Spoon mixture into prepared tin.
7. Bake in centre of preheated oven for 1 hour, or until firm to the touch.
8. Leave to cool in tin for 5 minutes, then turn out to complete cooling on a wire rack.
9. Store in an airtight tin and eat within a week.

FEATHER SPONGE
Gives 4 portions

This cake would be difficult to make without a mixer as it would require a lot of strenuous whisking.

3 large eggs
3oz (75gm) caster sugar
3oz (75gm) self-raising flour
1 tablespoon tepid water
1 can (6oz or 150gm) cream or fresh cream
2 heaped tablespoons raspberry jam

1. Preheat oven to moderately hot, 400 deg F or gas 6 (200 deg C).
2. Grease two 7½-inch (19cm) sandwich tins. Line bases with greaseproof paper. Grease the paper.
3. Put eggs and sugar in the mixer and whisk until very thick and mousse-like – mixture should have almost doubled in volume.
4. Using a metal spoon, fold in sifted flour and water.
5. Spoon quickly into the prepared tins.
6. Bake at once in centre of preheated oven for 15–20 minutes or until golden.
7. Turn out very gently on to a wire rack and leave to cool.
8. Sandwich with cream and jam. Eat that day.

NO-COOK GADGET GATEAU
Gives 4 portions

5 trifle sponges
3 heaped tablespoons lemon curd
3oz (75gm) icing sugar
3oz (75gm) margarine
2 tablespoons lemon juice

1. Well oil or grease a loose-based, deep, round 6-inch (15cm) cake tin.
2. Put sponges in liquidizer and run it until cakes are crumbs.
3. Meanwhile, put lemon curd and icing sugar in bowl of electric mixer with margarine and lemon juice. Run it until mixture is creamy.
4. Layer crumbs and lemon mixture in prepared cake tin. Put a saucer on top and place a heavy weight on top of saucer.
5. Leave in refrigerator for 3 hours.
6. Turn out to serve and eat the same day.

CHOCOLATE NO-BAKE CAKE
Gives 4 portions

4oz (100gm) plain chocolate
2oz (50gm) rice krispies
1 cup cold, thick custard
half a 14½oz (362gm) can apricot pie filling

1. Put chocolate in a bowl over a pan of gently simmering water and leave until melted.
2. Stir rice krispies into the melted chocolate.
3. Press into a greased shallow sandwich tin. Leave to set.
4. Mix custard and fruit. Put on top of set mixture. Leave in refrigerator for an hour and eat the same day.

BISCUIT CRUST GATEAU
Gives 4 portions

6oz (150gm) digestive biscuits
3oz (75gm) margarine
1 cup cold, thick custard
8oz (200gm) can peach slices, drained, then chopped
1oz (25gm) plain chocolate, grated

1. Crush biscuits.
2. Melt the margarine and mix with biscuits.
3. Press into a shallow sandwich tin – one with a loose base is best.
4. Leave in refrigerator to set.
5. Mix custard with fruit.
6. Spoon into flan and top with the chocolate. Serve at once.

CHIFFON FLAN
Gives 6 portions

6oz (150gm) digestive biscuits
3oz (75gm) margarine
half a strawberry jelly
hot water to mix
half a 6oz (150gm) can evaporated milk

1. Crush the biscuits.
2. Melt the margarine and mix into the biscuits.
3. Press into a shallow sandwich tin – one with a loose base is best.
4. Leave in refrigerator.
5. Make up jelly as instructed on the packet.
6. When jelly is cool, stir in the milk. Whisk well. Put in refrigerator for about 30 minutes.
7. Pour jelly into flan. Leave to set.

RASPBERRY CRUNCHY CAKE
Gives 4 portions

6oz (150gm) digestive biscuits
3oz (75gm) margarine
1 can (8oz or 200gm) raspberries or fresh raspberries when in season
arrowroot, to thicken
1 large banana
1 cup cold, thick custard, chilled

1. Crush the biscuits.
2. Melt the margarine and mix with the biscuits.
3. Press into a shallow sandwich tin – one with a loose base is best so flan can be removed for serving.
4. Leave in refrigerator to harden.
5. Drain raspberries and thicken the juice with arrowroot, as instructed on the packet.
6. Put fruit in thickened juice.
7. Peel and slice banana and put in base of flan. Pour the custard over.
8. Add the raspberries and serve within an hour of adding filling.

BORDER CAKE
Gives 5 portions

1 oblong bought Madeira cake
1 heaped tablespoon apricot jam
1 standard egg white
2oz (50gm) caster sugar
half a 14½oz (362gm) can apricot pie filling

1. Cut the bought cake into two layers. Stick them together with jam.
2. Preheat oven to very cool, 225 deg F or gas ¼ (110 deg C).
3. Line a baking sheet with foil.
4. Whisk egg white until very stiff.
5. Whisk in half the sugar, then fold in the rest with a metal spoon.
6. Put in a large piping bag fitted with a star nozzle.
7. Measure the cake, then pipe a meringue shape, on the foil, the same size.
8. Bake in centre of preheated oven for 2 hours.
9. Leave to cool.
10. Place meringue on top of cake.
11. Fill the centre with the pie filling and eat within 3 hours.

Small cakes

Small cakes are easy to make and children adore them. Here are the well-loved, traditional ones plus some novel ways of decorating plain sponge buns.

ORANGE SPECIALS
Makes 8

If you have no piping bag make a cone of doubled greaseproof paper and pipe through that.

3oz (75gm) self-raising flour
2oz (50gm) margarine
2oz (50gm) caster sugar
1 standard egg
1 can (11oz or 275gm) mandarin oranges
arrowroot, to thicken
4oz (100gm) plain chocolate

1. Preheat oven to moderate, 350 deg F or gas 4 (180 deg C).
2. Grease eight bun tins.
3. Sift the flour.
4. Cream margarine with caster sugar until light and fluffy.
5. Gradually add the egg, beating well.
6. Using a metal spoon, fold in the flour.
7. Divide mixture between the prepared tins.
8. Bake in centre of preheated oven for 15 minutes, or until golden and firm to the touch.
9. Leave to cool.
10. Drain the fruit and reserve the juice.
11. Thicken the juice with the arrowroot, as directed on the packet.
12. Put fruit back in juice and stir well. Leave to cool.
13. Spoon fruit on top of buns.
14. Put the chocolate in a bowl over a pan of gently simmering water. Leave until melted.
15. Spoon melted chocolate into a piping bag fitted with a very small plain nozzle. Pipe a whirly pattern of chocolate lines on each bun.
16. Leave to set and serve within 3 hours.

SNOWBALLS
Makes 8

6oz (150gm) self-raising flour
4oz (100gm) margarine
4oz (100gm) caster sugar
2 large eggs
small sachet powdered creamy topping
milk to mix
3 tablespoons raspberry jam
5oz (125gm) desiccated coconut

1. Preheat oven to moderate, 350 deg F or gas 4 (180 deg C).
2. Grease 16 bun tins.
3. Sift the flour.
4. Cream the margarine with the caster sugar until light and fluffy.
5. Beat the eggs and gradually add them to creamed mixture, beating well.
6. Using a metal spoon, fold in the flour.
7. Divide mixture between the prepared tins.
8. Bake in centre of preheated oven for 15 minutes, or until golden and firm to the touch.
9. Leave to cool.
10. Trim top of each cake to make it level.
11. Chop or liquidize the cake trimmings to make crumbs.
12. Make up the creamy topping as directed on the packet, using the milk.
13. Mix topping with crumbs and use to sandwich buns in pairs, so you have eight roundish shapes.
14. Put the jam in a small pan with 2 tablespoons water. Heat gently until melted, then brush over the cakes to coat.
15. Roll cakes in coconut and sprinkle more on them to make them look like snowballs.
16. Leave for 30 minutes before serving and eat within 3 hours.

BUTTERFLIES
(Illustrated on page 35)
Makes 12

4oz (100gm) plain flour
1 level teaspoon baking powder
pinch of salt
5oz (125gm) margarine
3oz (75gm) caster sugar
1 large egg, beaten
4oz (100gm) icing sugar, sifted

1. Preheat oven to moderate to moderately hot, 375 deg F or gas 5 (190 deg C).
2. Line 12 bun tins with paper cake cases.
3. Sift the flour with the baking powder and salt.
4. Cream 3oz (75gm) margarine with the caster sugar until light and fluffy.
5. Add beaten egg a little at a time, beating well.
6. Using a metal spoon, fold in the flour.
7. Spoon the mixture into the cake cases.
8. Bake in the centre of the preheated oven for 15 minutes, or until golden and firm to the touch.
9. Leave buns to cool in paper cases.
10. Beat the rest of the margarine with the icing sugar until light and very creamy.
11. Cut top off each bun. Cut each top in half to make two semi-circles.
12. Pipe or spoon the icing on top of each bun.
13. Place two semi-circles on top of each bun, at an angle and with the straight sides outwards, so they look like butterfly wings.

CANDLE CUP CAKES

(Illustrated on page 36)
Makes 12

This is an inexpensive and pretty idea for a children's party if you don't want to go to the expense of a large cake. Serve one to each child.

4oz (100gm) plain flour
1 level teaspoon baking powder
pinch of salt
3oz (75gm) margarine
3oz (75gm) caster sugar
1 large egg, beaten
1 tablespoon orange squash, undiluted
4oz (100gm) icing sugar
edible pink food colouring
12 tiny birthday candles in holders

1. Preheat oven to moderate to moderately hot, 375 deg F or gas 5 (190 deg C).
2. Line 12 bun tins with paper cases.
3. Sift the flour with the baking powder and salt.
4. Cream the margarine with the caster sugar until light and fluffy.
5. Add beaten egg to creamed mixture a little at a time.
6. Stir in the orange squash.
7. Fold in the flour.
8. Spoon mixture into cake cases.
9. Bake in the centre of the preheated oven for 15 minutes. Leave to cool in their paper cases.
10. Mix icing sugar with enough cold water to make an icing which will thickly coat the back of a wooden spoon.
11. Colour the icing a delicate pink, dropping colour from top of skewer or knitting needle.
12. Spoon icing on to cakes.
13. While the icing is still wet, add a tiny candle in its holder to centre of each cake. Leave to set.

EXTRA MOIST CUP CAKES

Makes 12

4oz (100gm) plain flour
1 level teaspoon baking powder
pinch of salt
4oz (100gm) margarine
4oz (100gm) caster sugar
1 large egg
3 heaped tablespoons sultanas
1 tablespoon canned cream

1. Preheat oven to moderate to moderately hot, 375 deg F or gas 5 (190 deg C).
2. Grease 12 bun tins.
3. Sift flour, baking powder and salt.
4. Cream the margarine with the caster sugar until light and fluffy.
5. Gradually beat in the egg.
6. Using a metal spoon, fold in the flour and sultanas, then stir in cream.
7. Spoon mixture into tins and smooth the tops.
8. Bake in centre of preheated oven for 15 minutes, or until golden and firm to the touch.
9. Turn out to cool. Store in an airtight tin and eat within eight days.

COCONUT ICE CAKES

Makes 12

4oz (100gm) plain flour
1 level teaspoon baking powder
pinch of salt
3oz (75gm) margarine
3oz (75gm) caster sugar
1 large egg, beaten
1 tablespoon milk
half a 6oz (150gm) can cream
3oz (75gm) coconut ice

1. Preheat oven to moderate to moderately hot, 375 deg F or gas 5 (190 deg C).
2. Line 12 bun tins with paper cake cases.
3. Sift the flour with the baking powder and salt.
4. Cream margarine with caster sugar until light and fluffy.
5. Gradually add the beaten egg.
6. Using a metal spoon, fold in the flour and milk.
7. Spoon into cake cases.
8. Bake in centre of preheated oven for 15 minutes, or until firm and golden.
9. Leave to cool.
10. Spread some cream on each cake.
11. Crush the coconut ice and sprinkle it over the cakes.

APPLE SQUARES

(Illustrated on page 35)
Makes 9

1 large cooking apple
1oz (25gm) granulated sugar
4oz (100gm) self-raising flour
4oz (100gm) margarine
4oz (100gm) caster sugar
2 standard eggs
milk to mix
1 medium-sized can cream
¼ pint (125ml) cold, thick custard
1 large red eating apple

1. Preheat oven to moderate to moderately hot, 375 deg F or gas 5 (190 deg C).
2. Line an 8-inch (20cm) square, fairly deep cake tin. Line tin with greaseproof paper. Grease the paper.
3. Peel, core and slice the cooking apple and stew with granulated sugar and one tablespoon water. Drain well and leave to cool.
4. Sift the flour.
5. Cream the margarine with the caster sugar until light and fluffy.
6. Add the beaten eggs a little at a time and beating well.
7. Using a metal spoon, carefully fold in the flour.
8. Add enough milk to give a consistency which will drop easily from a spoon when shaken.
9. Spoon mixture into prepared tin and bake in centre of the preheated oven for 30–45 minutes, or until golden brown and firm to the touch.
10. Leave the cake to cool on wire rack.
11. Drain any liquid off the cream and then mix half of it with the cold custard and stewed apple.
12. Cut the cake into nine equal pieces. Cut each piece into two layers and sandwich them with cream mixture.
13. Wash and core the red apple but don't peel it. Cut it into wedges.
14. Spread the rest of the cream on top of the cakes. Decorate with apple wedges and serve immediately. (If you can't serve the cakes at once, dip the apple slices in lemon juice to prevent them from discolouring.)

ORANGE STRIPES
Makes 6

6oz (150gm) self-raising flour
8oz (200gm) margarine
6oz (150gm) caster sugar
3 standard eggs
milk
4oz (100gm) icing sugar, sifted
8oz (200gm) orange jelly marmalade

1. Preheat oven to moderate, 350 deg F or gas 4 (180 deg C).
2. Grease an 8-inch (20cm) fairly deep, square tin. Line with greaseproof paper. Grease the paper.
3. Sift the flour into a bowl.
4. Cream 6oz (150gm) of the margarine with the caster sugar until light and fluffy.
5. Add eggs one at a time to creamed mixture, beating well.
6. Using a metal spoon, fold in the flour.
7. Add enough milk to give a soft consistency which will drop from spoon as soon as it is shaken.
8. Put mixture in prepared tin and bake in centre of preheated oven for 35–40 minutes, or until golden and firm.
9. Leave cake to cool on wire rack.
10. Beat the rest of the margarine with the icing sugar until light and fluffy.
11. Cut the cake into four thin layers, then sandwich them together with most of the marmalade and two-thirds of the icing. Spread the rest of the marmalade on top.
12. Put the rest of the icing in a piping bag fitted with a medium-sized plain nozzle.
13. Pipe straight lines, a little apart, across width of the cake. If you haven't got a piping bag, spread icing all over the marmalade.
14. Cut the cake into six equal-sized oblongs and serve.

PEPPERMINT FONDANT CAKES
Makes 12

4oz (100gm) plain flour
1 level teaspoon baking powder
pinch of salt
3oz (75gm) margarine
3oz (75gm) caster sugar
2 large eggs
1 tablespoon milk
4oz (100gm) icing sugar, sifted
peppermint essence, to taste
edible green food colouring

1. Preheat oven to moderate to moderately hot, 375 deg F or gas 5 (190 deg C).
2. Line 12 bun tins with paper cake cases.
3. Sift the flour with the baking powder and salt.
4. Cream margarine with caster sugar until light and fluffy.
5. Separate one egg. Beat yolk with whole egg. Gradually beat in.
6. Using a metal spoon, fold in the flour.
7. Stir in the milk.
8. Spoon into paper cases.
9. Bake in centre of preheated oven for 15 minutes, or until well risen and golden brown.
10. Leave to cool in cases.
11. Mix the egg white with enough icing sugar to give a soft, pliable mixture. Flavour with peppermint to taste.
12. Knead in a tiny amount of green colouring to give a delicate shade.
13. Roll out thinly. Cut into 12 rounds the same size as the buns and put a round on top of each bun. Eat within 3 hours of adding decoration.

SYRUP WHIRLS
Makes 12

4oz (100gm) self-raising flour
pinch of salt
2oz (50gm) margarine
1oz (25gm) caster sugar
1 large egg, separated
4oz (100gm) golden syrup
2 tablespoons orange squash mixed with 2 tablespoons water
1½oz (37gm) plain or milk chocolate
4oz (100gm) icing sugar, sifted
1 tablespoon warm milk

1. Preheat oven to moderate to moderately hot, 375 deg F or gas 5 (190 deg C).
2. Line a set of 12 bun tins with paper cases.
3. Sift the flour with the salt into a bowl.
4. In another bowl cream the margarine with the caster sugar until light and fluffy.
5. Whisk the egg yolk until pale and thick, then add it to the creamed mixture.
6. Stir in 3oz (75gm) syrup.
7. Stir in the flour and the diluted orange squash in alternate spoonfuls. Do not beat.
8. Whisk the egg white until very stiff, then fold it into the mixture.
9. Divide the mixture between the paper cases and bake at once in centre of preheated oven for about 18 minutes, or until risen and golden.
10. Leave to cool in paper cases.
11. Meanwhile, melt the chocolate in a basin over a small pan of gently simmering water. Stir in rest of syrup.
12. Take the basin off the heat.
13. Stir the icing sugar and warm milk into the chocolate. The consistency should be fudge-like, so add a little more milk if needed.
14. Spoon the icing on top of each cake and make a swirl pattern with a teaspoon.
15. Leave to cool and eat that day.

GOLDEN TOPPERS
Makes 12

4oz (100gm) plain flour
1 level teaspoon baking powder
pinch of salt
3oz (75gm) margarine
3oz (75gm) caster sugar
1 large egg
1 tablespoon milk
12 pink marshmallows
3 heaped tablespoons desiccated coconut

1. Preheat oven to moderate to moderately hot, 375 deg F or gas 5 (190 deg C).
2. Grease 12 bun tins.
3. Sift the flour with baking powder and salt.
4. Cream margarine with caster sugar until light and fluffy.
5. Gradually beat in the egg.
6. Using a metal spoon, fold in the flour.
7. Stir in the milk.
8. Spoon into bun tins.
9. Bake in centre of preheated oven for 15 minutes, or until firm and golden.
10. Leave in bun tins.
11. Turn on the grill.
12. Sprinkle coconut over the buns to cover them.
13. Put a marshmallow on top of each bun.
14. Grill for a few seconds, or until very pale golden.
15. Leave to cool and eat within 3 hours of toasting marshmallows.

TWO-FRUIT BASKETS
Makes 10

4oz (100gm) margarine
4oz (100gm) caster sugar
2 large eggs
3oz (75gm) self-raising flour
1oz (25gm) custard powder
½ level teaspoon baking powder
2 large oranges
6oz (150gm) small, green grapes or fresh raspberries when in season
2 tablespoons canned or fresh double, whipped cream

1. Preheat oven to moderate to moderately hot, 375 deg F or gas 5 (190 deg C).
2. Grease 10 bun tins.
3. Cream the margarine with the caster sugar until light and fluffy.
4. Beat the eggs, then add them to mixture, beating well.
5. Sift the flour with custard powder and baking powder. Do this twice.
6. Using a metal spoon, fold flour mixture into creamed mixture.
7. Divide mixture between the prepared bun tins.
8. Bake in centre of preheated oven for 15 minutes, or until golden and firm to the touch.
9. Turn out and leave to cool.
10. Cut top off each bun to make it flat, then slightly hollow out the centres. Reserve trimmings.
11. Peel off the orange rind in long thin strips and cut into 10 long, thin neat strips about 3 inches long.
12. Cut the oranges into neat chunks by slicing and then cutting up the slices.
13. Mix orange pieces with grapes.
14. Pound up the cake trimmings and mix with the cream.
15. Put this mixture into the cake hollows and put the fruit on top.
16. Push a piece of orange rind into both sides of each cake to make a basket handle. Eat the same day.

TOFFEE APPLE CAKES
Makes 8

3oz (75gm) self-raising flour
2oz (50gm) margarine
2oz (50gm) caster sugar
1 standard egg
milk to mix
1 large cooking apple
1 rounded tablespoon soft brown sugar
4oz (100gm) granulated sugar

1. Preheat oven to moderate, 350 deg F or gas 4 (180 deg C).
2. Put eight paper cake cases in eight bun tins.
3. Sift the flour.
4. Cream the margarine with the caster sugar until light and fluffy.
5. Gradually beat in the egg.
6. Using a metal spoon, fold in the flour.
7. Add enough milk to give a mixture which will drop easily from a spoon when shaken.
8. Divide mixture between cake cases.
9. Bake in centre of preheated oven for 15 minutes, or until golden and firm to the touch.
10. Leave to cool in paper cases.
11. Peel and core the apple. Cut it into neat slices and stew with 2 tablespoons water and the brown sugar until tender but not broken up.
12. Leave apples to cool in their cooking liquid.
13. Lift apple slices with a draining spoon and put on top of cakes.
14. Put granulated sugar and ¼ pint (125ml) cold water in a pan. Heat, without stirring, until golden brown. To test: a little sugar mixture dropped into a cup of cold water should form a soft ball.
15. Spoon toffee over apple on cakes and leave to set. Eat the same day.

LIME CAKES
Makes 12

4oz (100gm) plain flour
1 level teaspoon baking powder
pinch of salt
3oz (75gm) margarine
3oz (75gm) caster sugar
1 large egg
2 tablespoons lime marmalade
4oz (100gm) icing sugar
lime cordial, undiluted, to mix

1. Preheat oven to moderate to moderately hot, 375 deg F or gas 5 (190 deg C).
2. Line 12 bun tins with paper cake cases.
3. Sift flour with baking powder and salt.
4. Cream the margarine with the caster sugar until light and fluffy.
5. Gradually beat in the egg.
6. Stir in the marmalade.
7. Using a metal spoon, fold in the flour.
8. Spoon into cake cases.
9. Bake in centre of preheated oven for 15 minutes, or until firm and golden.
10. Leave to cool in paper cases.
11. Mix the sifted icing sugar with enough cordial to give a mixture which will coat the back of a wooden spoon.
12. Spoon icing on each cake and leave to set. Store in an airtight tin and eat within three days.

CHERRY RIPE CAKES

Makes 12

4oz (100gm) plain flour
1 level teaspoon baking powder
pinch of salt
3oz (75gm) margarine
3oz (75gm) caster sugar
1 large egg
1 can (8oz or 200gm) red cherries
1 tablespoon raspberry milk shake syrup
arrowroot, to thicken

1. Preheat oven to moderate to moderately hot, 375 deg F or gas 5 (190 deg C).
2. Line 12 bun tins with paper cake cases.
3. Sift flour with baking powder and salt.
4. Cream margarine with caster sugar until light and fluffy.
5. Gradually beat in the egg.
6. Using a metal spoon, fold in the flour.
7. Spoon into paper cake cases.
8. Bake in centre of preheated oven for 15 minutes, or until firm and golden.
9. Leave in paper cases to cool.
10. Drain cherries and reserve juice.
11. Mix juice with milk shake syrup, then thicken with arrowroot as directed on packet.
12. Put cherries in thickened liquid.
13. Spoon on top of cakes and eat within three hours of decorating.

CHOCOLATE LOGS

Makes 6

You can make these two days in advance and keep them in an airtight tin, but don't fill until the day you are serving them.

5oz (125gm) margarine
2oz (50gm) caster sugar
1 small egg
3oz (75gm) plain flour
1 oz (25gm) cornflour
½ level teaspoon baking powder
large pinch of salt
almond essence, to taste
3oz (75gm) icing sugar
2oz (50gm) chocolate

1. Preheat oven to hot, 425 deg F gas 7 (220 deg C).
2. Grease a baking sheet.
3. Cream 2oz (50gm) margarine with caster sugar until light and fluffy.
4. Gradually beat in the egg.
5. Sift the flour with cornflour, baking powder and salt. Do this twice.
6. Using a metal spoon, fold flour into creamed mixture.
7. Add almond essence, to taste.
8. Put mixture in a large piping bag fitted with a large star nozzle.
9. Pipe 12 short lines, well spaced, on the prepared baking sheet.
10. Bake in centre of preheated oven for 7–10 minutes, or until golden and firm.
11. Leave to cool.
12. Beat the rest of the margarine with sifted icing sugar until creamy.
13. Put the chocolate in a bowl over a pan of gently simmering water and leave until melted.
14. Beat melted chocolate into icing and leave to cool.
15. Sandwich cakes with icing.

CLOVER LEAF CAKES

Makes 8

2oz (50gm) margarine
2oz (50gm) caster sugar
1 standard egg, beaten
4oz (100gm) self-raising flour
vanilla essence
3 tablespoons apricot jam

1. Preheat oven to moderately hot, 400 deg F or gas 6 (200 deg C).
2. Grease a baking sheet.
3. Cream the margarine with the caster sugar until light and fluffy.
4. Beat in half the egg.
5. Using a metal spoon, fold in the sifted flour.
6. Flavour to taste with vanilla essence.
7. Form the mixture into 24 balls. Put three balls together in a clover leaf shape and use rest of egg to seal edges. Repeat until you have eight clover leaves.
8. Put on prepared baking sheet.
9. Bake in centre of preheated oven for 10–15 minutes or until golden and firm.
10. Leave to cool.
11. Melt the jam with 2 tablespoons cold water in a small pan. Let it thicken slightly, then spoon hot jam on top of each cake. Leave to cool.

ORANGE-ICED FANCIES

Makes 8

3oz (75gm) self-raising flour
2oz (50gm) margarine
2oz (50gm) caster sugar
1 large egg
rum essence, to taste
4oz (100gm) icing sugar
strained juice of 1 large orange
2 teaspoons orange squash
1 heaped teaspoon grated orange rind

1. Preheat oven to moderate, 350 deg F or gas 4 (180 deg C).
2. Grease eight bun tins.
3. Sift the flour.
4. Beat the margarine with the caster sugar until light and fluffy.
5. Gradually add the egg, beating well.
6. Using a metal spoon, fold in the flour.
7. Flavour with rum essence.
8. Divide mixture between the prepared tins.
9. Bake in the centre of the preheated oven for 15 minutes, or until golden and firm to the touch.
10. Leave to cool.
11. Mix the sifted icing sugar with enough of the orange juice and squash to give a mixture which will thickly coat the back of a wooden spoon.
12. Stir orange rind into icing.
13. Spoon icing on centre of each cake and leave to set. Store in an airtight tin and eat within two days.

JEWEL CAKES
Makes 8

1 packet raspberry jelly
3oz (75gm) self-raising flour
2oz (50gm) margarine
2oz (50gm) caster sugar
1 standard egg
4oz (100gm) icing sugar, sifted

1. Make up the jelly, following instructions on packet but using only 10 tablespoons hot water. Put jelly to set in a shallow, wetted tin.
2. Preheat oven to moderate, 350 deg F or gas 4 (180 deg C).
3. Put eight paper cake cases in eight bun tins.
4. Sift the flour into a bowl.
5. Cream margarine with caster sugar until light and fluffy.
6. Gradually beat in the egg.
7. Using a metal spoon, fold in the flour.
8. Spoon mixture into paper cases.
9. Bake in centre of preheated oven for 15 minutes, or until golden and well risen.
10. Leave to cool.
11. Add enough cold water to the icing to give a mixture which will thickly coat the back of a wooden spoon.
12. Spoon icing on top of buns and leave to set.
13. Turn out the set jelly and, using a sharp knife, chop it up very finely.
14. Put jelly into a large piping bag fitted with a very large plain nozzle.
15. Pipe a ring of jelly round top edge of each bun.

RASPBERRY RINGS
Makes 8

3oz (75gm) self-raising flour
3 tablespoons raspberry jam
2oz (50gm) margarine
2oz (50gm) caster sugar
1 standard egg
small sachet powdered creamy topping or ¼ pint (125ml) fresh double cream
milk to mix topping if used

1. Preheat oven to moderate, 350 deg F or gas 4 (180 deg C).
2. Grease eight bun tins.
3. Sift the flour into a bowl.
4. Heat and sieve the jam. Leave to cool.
5. Cream the margarine with the caster sugar until very creamy and light and fluffy.
6. Add egg to creamed mixture, beating well.
7. Gradually fold in the flour.
8. Spoon mixture into the prepared bun tins.
9. Bake buns in centre of the preheated oven for 15 minutes, or until well risen and golden.
10. Leave buns to cool on wire rack.
11. Make up the powdered topping, following instructions on packet, or whip the fresh cream if used.
12. Put the topping in a piping bag fitted with a medium star nozzle. Pipe a small circle of stars round the top of each bun. If you are using fresh cream, spread this round the top of each bun.
13. Fill the centre of each with jam, spooning in very carefully. Eat by next day.

MARBLE BUNS
Makes 12

These are best kept for two days in an airtight tin before serving, to allow them to become more moist.

3oz (75gm) margarine
3oz (75gm) caster sugar
1 large egg
3oz (75gm) self-raising flour
1oz (25gm) cocoa
1 level teaspoon baking powder

1. Preheat oven to moderate to moderately hot, 375 deg F or gas 5 (190 deg C).
2. Line 12 bun tins with paper cake cases.
3. Cream margarine with caster sugar until light and fluffy.
4. Gradually beat in the egg.
5. Put half the mixture into another bowl.
6. To one lot of mixture fold in 2oz (50gm) flour.
7. To the other mixture fold in rest of flour sifted with cocoa and baking powder.
8. Put alternate small teaspoonfuls of mixture into cake cases.
9. Bake in the centre of the preheated oven for 15 minutes.
10. Leave to cool in paper cases.

MARSHMALLOW BUNS
Makes 12

4oz (100gm) plain flour
1 level teaspoon baking powder
pinch of salt
3oz (75gm) margarine
3oz (75gm) caster sugar
1 large egg, beaten
1 tablespoon raspberry milk shake syrup
4oz (100gm) pink marshmallows

1. Preheat oven to moderate to moderately hot, 375 deg F or gas 5 (190 deg C).
2. Line 12 bun tins with paper cake cases.
3. Sift the flour with the baking powder and salt.
4. Cream the margarine with the caster sugar until light and fluffy.
5. Gradually beat in the egg.
6. Stir in the milk shake syrup.
7. Using a metal spoon, fold in the flour.
8. Spoon mixture into cake cases.
9. Bake in the centre of the preheated oven for 15 minutes, or until golden.
10. Leave to cool in paper cases.
11. Put the marshmallows in a wetted bowl. Stand the bowl over a pan of gently simmering water until marshmallows have melted, which will take about 10–15 minutes. Stir occasionally, taking care not to allow it to become dry.
12. Spoon melted marshmallow on to the cakes.
13. Leave to set, then serve at once.

SIMPLE PETIT FOURS
Makes 18

8oz (200gm) margarine
4oz (100gm) caster sugar
2 standard eggs
4oz (100gm) self-raising flour
12oz (300gm) icing sugar
pink and green edible food colouring
a few silver balls
1 heaped teaspoon cocoa
half an 11oz (275gm) can mandarin oranges

1. Preheat oven to moderate to moderately hot, 375 deg F or gas 5 (190 deg C).
2. Line an 8-inch (20cm) square, fairly deep cake tin.
3. Cream half the margarine with caster sugar until light and fluffy.
4. Beat eggs together and add gradually to creamed mixture, beating well.
5. Using a metal spoon, fold in the sifted flour.
6. Spoon mixture into prepared tin. Smooth the top.
7. Bake in centre of preheated oven for 35–45 minutes, or until golden and firm to the touch.
8. Turn out to cool. Cut into nine equal-sized pieces, then cut each piece in half to make 18 triangles.
9. Put half the cakes on a wire rack with a plate underneath.
10. Sift 8oz (200gm) icing sugar with enough cold water to give an icing which will coat the back of a wooden spoon.
11. Put half the icing into another bowl.
12. Colour one lot of icing pale pink and the other pale green.
13. Pour green icing over half the cakes on the racks. Pour pink icing over the rest of the cakes on the rack.
14. Sprinkle silver balls on the iced cakes and leave to set.
15. Beat rest of icing sugar with rest of margarine until creamy.
16. Beat in cocoa until well blended.
17. Spread over remaining cakes and rough up with a knife.
18. Decorate these cakes with mandarin oranges.

GINGER CUP CAKES
Makes 12

4oz (100gm) plain flour
1 level teaspoon baking powder
pinch of salt
1 level teaspoon ground ginger
3oz (75gm) margarine
3oz (75gm) caster sugar
1 large egg, beaten
4oz (100gm) icing sugar
edible yellow food colouring

1. Preheat oven to moderate to moderately hot, 375 deg F or gas 5 (190 deg C).
2. Line 12 bun tins with paper cake cases.
3. Sift the flour with the baking powder, salt and ginger.
4. Cream the margarine with caster sugar until light and fluffy.
5. Gradually beat in egg.
6. Using a metal spoon, fold in the flour.
7. Spoon into paper cases.
8. Bake in centre of preheated oven for 15 minutes, or until golden.
9. Leave in cases to cool.
10. Mix sifted icing sugar with enough cold water to make an icing which will coat the back of a wooden spoon.
11. Colour icing a delicate yellow.
12. Spoon icing on to cakes in paper cases. Leave to set.

CARAMEL TOPPERS
Makes 8

3oz (75gm) self-raising flour
2oz (50gm) margarine
2oz (50gm) caster sugar
1 standard egg
1 can (6oz or 150gm) cream or ¼ pint (125ml) fresh double cream, whipped
4oz (100gm) granulated sugar
3 tablespoons water

1. Preheat oven to moderate, 350 deg F or gas 4 (180 deg C).
2. Grease eight bun tins.
3. Sift the flour.
4. Cream the margarine with the caster sugar until light and fluffy.
5. Gradually add the egg, beating all the time.
6. Using a metal spoon, fold in the flour.
7. Divide mixture between the prepared tins.
8. Bake in the centre of the preheated oven for 15 minutes, or until golden and firm to the touch.
9. Leave to cool.
10. Spread some cream on each cake.
11. Put the sugar and water in a small pan. Heat slowly until the sugar dissolves, then bring to the boil and boil until pale golden.
12. Pour on to an oiled or a greased surface. Leave to set.
13. Break set caramel into splinters, sprinkle them on the cakes. Serve within an hour.

CHOCOLATE TOWERS
Makes 12

5½oz (137gm) self-raising flour
½oz (12gm) cocoa
pinch of salt
½ level teaspoon baking powder
6oz (150gm) margarine
6oz (150gm) caster sugar
3 standard eggs, beaten
1 heaped tablespoon orange jelly marmalade or apricot jam
2oz (50gm) desiccated coconut
6 glacé cherries

1. Preheat oven to moderate, 350 deg F or gas 4 (180 deg C).
2. Grease 12 dariole tins or castle pudding tins.
3. Sift the flour with the cocoa, salt and baking powder. Do this twice.
4. Cream the margarine with the sugar until light and fluffy.
5. Add eggs gradually to creamed mixture, beating all the time.
6. Using a metal spoon, fold in the flour mixture.
7. Divide the mixture between the prepared tins.
8. Bake in the centre of the preheated oven for 15–20 minutes, or until well risen and firm to the touch.
9. Turn out to cool on a wire cooling rack.
10. Gently heat the marmalade or apricot jam in a small pan. Brush the top and sides of cooled cakes with this.
11. Roll the cakes in coconut so they are coated. Top each cake with half a glacé cherry.

PRUNE VELVETS
Makes 8

4oz (100gm) dried prunes
3oz (75gm) self-raising flour
2oz (50gm) margarine
2oz (50gm) caster sugar
1 standard egg
small sachet of powdered creamy topping
milk to mix

1. Leave prunes to soak overnight.
2. Stew the prunes in the soaking water, without adding sugar, for 25 minutes, or until tender. Drain well.
3. Sieve the prunes and discard the stones. Leave to cool.
4. Preheat oven to moderate, 350 deg F or gas 4 (180 deg C).
5. Grease eight bun tins.
6. Sift the flour.
7. Cream the margarine and caster sugar until light and fluffy.
8. Gradually beat in the egg.
9. Using a metal spoon, fold in the flour.
10. Divide mixture between the prepared tins.
11. Bake in the centre of the preheated oven for 15 minutes, or until golden and firm to the touch.
12. Turn out to cool.
13. Make up the topping as directed on the packet.
14. Mix the prune purée into the topping.
15. Top buns with prune cream and serve within an hour.

CUSTARD CAKES
Makes 8

4oz (100gm) margarine
4oz (100gm) caster sugar
1 standard egg yolk
6oz (150gm) plain flour
2oz (50gm) custard powder
milk to mix
1 can (1lb or ½ kilo) pineapple rings
1 dessertspoon pineapple milk shake syrup
arrowroot, to thicken

1. Preheat oven to hot, 425 deg F or gas 7 (220 deg C).
2. Grease a baking sheet.
3. Cream the margarine and caster sugar until light and fluffy.
4. Gradually beat in egg yolk.
5. Sift flour with custard powder. Do this twice.
6. Using a metal spoon, fold flour into creamed mixture.
7. Add just enough milk to give a stiff mixture.
8. Roll out mixture to about ½ inch thick. Cut out eight rounds with a large pastry cutter.
9. Put rounds on prepared baking sheet.
10. Bake in centre of preheated oven for 15–20 minutes, or until golden and firm.
11. Leave to cool.
12. Trim fruit rings, if necessary, to make them same size as cakes.
13. Place a fruit ring on top of each cake.
14. Mix milk shake syrup with pineapple juice.
15. Thicken this liquid with arrowroot, following instructions on the packet. Leave to cool for 2 minutes.
16. Spoon mixture on top of the fruit and leave to cool. Eat the same day.

EASTERN CAKES
Makes 9

4oz (100gm) self-raising flour
6oz (150gm) margarine
4oz (100gm) caster sugar
2 standard eggs
2oz (50gm) icing sugar
2oz (50gm) Turkish delight

1. Preheat oven to moderate to moderately hot, 375 deg F or gas 5 (190 deg C).
2. Grease an 8-inch (20cm) square, fairly deep cake tin. Line tin with greaseproof paper. Grease the paper.
3. Sift the flour.
4. Cream 4oz (100gm) margarine with caster sugar until light and fluffy.
5. Beat the eggs, then add to the creamed mixture, beating well.
6. Using a metal spoon, fold in the flour.
7. Put in prepared tin. Smooth the top.
8. Bake in centre of preheated oven for 30–45 minutes, or until golden and firm to the touch.
9. Turn out to cool on wire cooling rack.
10. Cut into nine squares.
11. Beat the rest of the margarine with the sifted icing sugar until light and fluffy.
12. Cut up the Turkish delight with scissors and stir into icing.
13. Spread the icing on top of the cakes.

COCONUT AND LIME CAKES
Makes 9

4oz (100gm) self-raising flour
4oz (100gm) margarine
4oz (100gm) caster sugar
2 standard eggs
4oz (100gm) desiccated or shredded coconut
5 tablespoons lime marmalade

1. Preheat oven to moderate to moderately hot, 375 deg F or gas 5 (190 deg C).
2. Grease an 8-inch (20cm) square, fairly deep cake tin. Line tin with greaseproof paper. Grease the paper.
3. Sift the flour.
4. Cream margarine with caster sugar until light and fluffy.
5. Gradually beat in eggs.
6. Using a metal spoon, fold in the flour.
7. Put mixture in prepared tin and bake in centre of preheated oven for 30–45 minutes, or until golden and firm to the touch.
8. Turn out to cool on a wire rack.
9. Cut into nine equal pieces.
10. Toast the coconut under a medium hot grill until golden.
11. Heat the marmalade with 2 tablespoons water in a pan.
12. Use a little marmalade to brush the sides of the cakes.
13. Coat sides of cakes with toasted coconut.
14. Spoon rest of marmalade on the top. Leave to cool.

APRICOT CAKES
Makes 9

4oz (100gm) margarine
4oz (100gm) caster sugar
2 standard eggs
4oz (100gm) self-raising flour
1 can (1lb or ½ kilo) apricot halves
4½ glacé cherries
3 heaped tablespoons apricot jam

1. Preheat oven to moderate to moderately hot, 375 deg F or gas 5 (190 deg C).
2. Line an 8-inch (20cm) square, fairly deep cake tin.
3. Line tin with greaseproof paper. Grease the paper.
4. Cream margarine with the caster sugar until light and fluffy.
5. Beat the eggs, then gradually add to creamed mixture, beating well.
6. Sift the flour, then fold it into mixture with a metal spoon.
7. Put mixture into prepared tin and smooth the top.
8. Bake in the centre of preheated oven for 30–45 minutes, or until golden, well risen and firm to the touch.
9. Turn out to cool on wire cooling rack.
10. Cut cake into nine equal-sized pieces.
11. Drain the fruit – juice is not needed.
12. Place an apricot half on top of each cake.
13. Put half a cherry on top of each apricot half.
14. Gently heat jam with 2 tablespoons cold water. When mixture is runny, spoon on top of the cakes.
15. Leave to cool. Serve within 2 hours.

MOCHA WHEELS
Makes 8

3 standard eggs
4oz (100gm) caster sugar
3oz (75gm) self-raising flour
2oz (50gm) margarine
2oz (50gm) icing sugar
3 tablespoons strong liquid black coffee
5oz (125gm) plain chocolate

1. Preheat oven to hot, 450 deg F or gas 8 (230 deg C).
2. Grease a Swiss roll tin about 12 inches (30cm) by 9 inches (23cm). Line with greaseproof paper and grease the paper.
3. Put the eggs and caster sugar in a bowl. Whisk until mixture is very thick and the whisk leaves an impression on mixture for 5 seconds after it is removed from bowl.
4. Using a metal spoon, fold in the flour.
5. Spoon mixture into prepared tin.
6. Bake in centre of preheated oven for 7–10 minutes, or until well risen and golden.
7. Turn out on to greaseproof paper and roll up with the help of the greaseproof.
8. Leave to cool.
9. Unroll the cooled roll.
10. Beat the margarine with icing sugar until creamy. Stir in coffee to taste.
11. Spread the icing on the cake. Roll up tightly. Cut into eight slices. Put on a wire rack.
12. Put the chocolate in a bowl over a pan of gently simmering water. Leave until melted.
13. Spoon melted chocolate over cake slices and leave to set. Eat the same day.

LEMON SPONGE WHEELS
Makes 8

3 standard eggs
4oz (100gm) caster sugar
3oz (75gm) self-raising flour
3 heaped tablespoons lemon curd
orange squash to mix
4oz (100gm) icing sugar, sifted

1. Preheat oven to hot, 450 deg F or gas 8 (230 deg C).
2. Grease a Swiss roll tin about 12 inches (30cm) by 9 inches (23cm). Line tin with greaseproof paper and grease the paper.
3. Whisk the eggs with caster sugar until very thick. Whisk should leave an impression on mixture for 5 seconds after it is removed from bowl.
4. Using a metal spoon, fold in the sifted flour.
5. Put into prepared tin.
6. Bake in centre of preheated oven for 7–10 minutes, or until well risen and golden.
7. Turn out on to greaseproof paper and roll up with the help of the paper.
8. Leave to cool.
9. Unroll and spread the lemon curd on the cake. Then roll up again.
10. Cut the roll into eight slices.
11. Put the slices on a wire rack.
12. Add enough orange squash to the icing sugar to make an icing which will coat the back of a wooden spoon.
13. Spoon icing on to cake slices. Leave to set and eat the same day.

VARIETY MERINGUES
Makes 10

2 standard egg whites
4oz (100gm) caster sugar
3oz (75gm) milk chocolate buttons
2 heaped tablespoons apricot jam
1 tablespoon lemon juice
half an 11oz (275gm) can mandarin oranges

1. Preheat oven to very cool, 225 deg F or gas ¼ (110 deg C).
2. Line two baking sheets with foil.
3. Whisk egg whites until stiff. Whisk in half the sugar, then fold in the rest.
4. Put into a large piping bag with a medium star nozzle.
5. Pipe a Catherine-wheel shape so you have a solid base. Make nine more, using up all the meringue.
6. Cook in centre of preheated oven for 2 hours, or until really dry.
7. Leave to cool.
8. When meringues are cool, put chocolate buttons all round the edges.
9. Heat the jam with 1 tablespoon water and the lemon juice.
10. Mix jam with fruit.
11. Spoon mixture into centre of each meringue and leave to cool. Eat within 3 hours.

TEATIME MERINGUES
Makes 6

2 standard eggs, separated
4oz (100gm) caster sugar
$\frac{1}{3}$ pint (166ml) hot, thick custard, not too sweet
coffee essence to taste
1oz (25gm) plain chocolate, grated

1. Preheat oven to very cool, 225 deg F or gas $\frac{1}{4}$ (110 deg C).
2. Line a large baking sheet with foil.
3. Whisk the egg whites until very stiff.
4. Whisk in half the sugar, then fold in rest with a metal spoon.
5. Put in a large piping bag fitted with a medium-sized star nozzle.
6. Pipe 12 small swirls on to prepared baking sheet. If you have no piping bag, spoon on neat heaps of mixture using two dessertspoons.
7. Cook in centre of preheated oven for 2 hours, or until really dry. (It doesn't matter if they colour slightly.)
8. Beat the egg yolks into the hot custard. Stir over heat for a few seconds. Leave to cool.
9. Flavour with coffee essence.
10. Stir chocolate into the coffee custard and use the mixture to sandwich meringues in pairs. Serve within an hour of adding the filling.

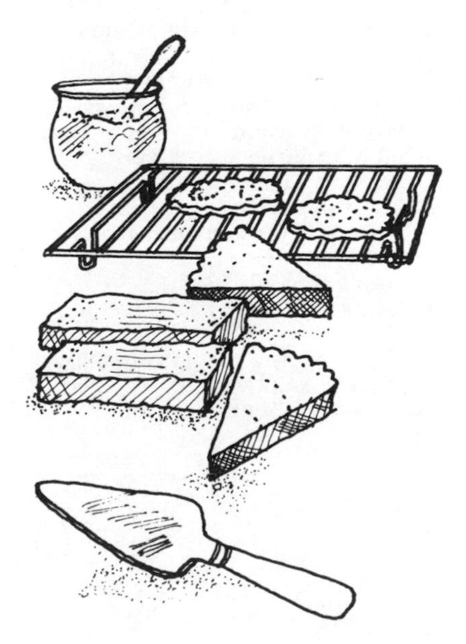

MERINGUE PYRAMIDS
Makes 6

4 standard egg whites
8oz (200gm) caster sugar
1 can (1lb or $\frac{1}{2}$ kilo) peach halves
1 heaped teaspoon arrowroot
small sachet of powdered creamy topping or $\frac{1}{4}$ pint double cream, whipped
milk to mix
3 glacé cherries

1. Preheat oven to very cool, 225 deg F or gas $\frac{1}{4}$ (110 deg C).
2. Line a large baking sheet with foil.
3. Whisk the egg whites until very stiff.
4. Whisk in half the sugar.
5. Using a metal spoon, fold in the other half.
6. Put the meringue in a large piping bag fitted with a medium star nozzle.
7. Pipe six solid rounds, each about 3 inches in diameter on the foil for bases of baskets. If you have no piping bag, just spoon mixture on.
8. Now pipe a ring of stars round edge of each base, then pipe another line of stars on top so making a 'wall'. Or just spoon mixture on and peak up with a knife.
9. Cook in the centre of the preheated oven for $2\frac{1}{2}$–3 hours, or until meringues are really dried out.
10. Leave meringues to cool.
11. Drain peach halves and reserve the juice.
12. Put a peach half, rounded side up, in each meringue.
13. Thicken the peach juice with arrowroot as directed on the packet. Cool slightly, then spoon it on to fruit and leave to cool completely.
14. Make up the powdered topping as directed on the packet. Or use whipped double cream. Pipe or spoon cream on to each fruit half.
15. Top with half a cherry and serve within 2 hours of adding decoration.

BLACK AND WHITE MERINGUES
Makes 6

2 standard egg whites
4oz (100gm) caster sugar
4oz (100gm) plain chocolate
1 can 6oz (150gm) cream or $\frac{1}{4}$ pint (125ml) fresh double cream, whipped

1. Preheat oven to very cool, 225 deg F or gas $\frac{1}{4}$ (110 deg C).
2. Line a large baking sheet with foil.
3. Whisk the egg whites until very stiff.
4. Whisk in half the sugar, then fold in the rest using a metal spoon.
5. Put the mixture in a large piping bag fitted with a large star nozzle.
6. Pipe 12 straight lines about 3 inches long, well spaced, on the baking sheet.
7. Cook in the centre of the preheated oven for 2 hours, or until really dry.
If the meringues show signs of colouring, then take them out of the oven for 15 minutes and, when you put them back, leave the oven door slightly ajar.
8. Leave to cool.
9. Put the chocolate in a bowl over a pan of gently simmering water. Leave until melted.
10. Dip half of each meringue in the melted chocolate.
11. Leave to set.
12. Sandwich meringues in pairs with the cream.

MOCHA BASKETS
Makes 6

4 standard egg whites
8oz (200gm) caster sugar
small sachet of chocolate blancmange powder
milk to mix
granulated sugar to mix
1 level teaspoon instant coffee powder
½oz (12gm) margarine
3 tablespoons evaporated milk
1 tablespoon grated plain chocolate

1. Preheat oven to very cool, 225 deg F or gas ¼ (110 deg C).
2. Line a large baking sheet with foil.
3. Whisk the egg whites until very stiff.
4. Whisk in half the sugar, then, using a metal spoon, fold in rest of sugar.
5. Put mixture in a large piping bag fitted with a medium star nozzle.
6. Pipe six solid rounds on the foil, each about 3 inches in diameter for bases of baskets. If you have no piping bag, just spoon mixture on.
7. Now pipe a line all round edge of base, then another line on top to make a 'wall'. Or just spoon mixture on and peak with knife.
8. Cook in centre of preheated oven for 2½–3 hours, or until really dry.
9. Leave meringues to cool.
10. Make up the blancmange as directed on the packet, using milk and sugar. Add coffee before bringing to the boil.
11. Beat margarine into made-up blancmange. (This makes it look glossy.)
12. Stir in the evaporated milk.
13. Leave mixture to cool.
14. Fill baskets with the cooled blancmange, taking care not to stir it.
15. Sprinkle grated chocolate on top and serve within an hour.

FRUIT BASKETS
Makes 6

Use the left-over egg yolks to make scrambled eggs or mayonnaise.

4 standard egg whites
8½oz (212gm) caster sugar
2oz (50gm) margarine
1½oz (37gm) plain flour
just under ½ pint (250ml) milk
1 egg yolk
vanilla essence, to taste
1 can (1lb or ½ kilo) fruit cocktail

1. Preheat oven to very cool, 225 deg F or gas ¼ (110 deg C).
2. Line a large baking sheet with foil.
3. Whisk the egg whites until very stiff.
4. Whisk in 4oz (100gm) sugar.
5. Fold in another 4oz (100gm) sugar with a metal spoon.
6. Put the mixture in a large piping bag fitted with a medium star nozzle.
7. Pipe six solid rounds on the foil, each 3 inches in diameter, for bases of baskets. If you have no piping bag, just spoon the mixture on.
8. Pipe meringue stars round the sides of bases. Pipe a second row on top to make a 'wall'. Alternatively, spoon mixture on and peak up with a knife.
9. Cook in the centre of the preheated oven for 2½–3 hours, or until really dry.
10. Leave meringues to cool.
11. Now make custard. Melt the margarine and stir in the flour. Cook on a gentle heat for 1 minute.
12. Gradually whisk the milk into flour.
13. Bring to the boil, stirring all the time until thick.
14. Add the remaining ½oz (12gm) sugar, the egg yolk and vanilla essence. Cook gently for two minutes, stirring all the time.
15. Leave custard to cool.
16. Fill the meringue baskets with custard.
17. Drain juice off fruit; juice is not needed. Spoon fruit on top of custard and serve within an hour.

MERINGUE LETTERS
Makes 6

2 standard egg whites
4oz (100gm) caster sugar
1 can (6oz or 150gm) cream or ¼ pint (125ml) fresh double cream, whipped

1. Preheat oven to very cool, 225 deg F or gas ¼ (110 deg C).
2. Line a baking sheet with foil.
3. Whisk egg whites until very stiff.
4. Whisk in half the caster sugar, then, using a metal spoon, fold in the rest.
5. Put mixture in a large piping bag fitted with a large star nozzle.
6. Pipe 'S' shapes on foil.
7. Cook in centre of preheated oven for 2 hours, or until really dry.
8. Leave to cool.
9. Sandwich in pairs with cream and serve within an hour.

MERINGUE RINGS
Makes 6

2 standard egg whites
4oz (100gm) caster sugar
small sachet powdered creamy topping
milk to mix
1 heaped tablespoon rough-cut orange marmalade

1. Preheat oven to very cool, 225 deg F or gas ¼ (110 deg C).
2. Line a baking sheet with foil.
3. Whisk egg whites until very stiff.
4. Whisk in half the sugar, then, using a metal spoon, fold in rest.
5. Put mixture in large piping bag fitted with large star nozzle.
6. Pipe ring shapes on foil.
7. Cook in centre of preheated oven for 2 hours, or until really dry.
8. Leave to cool.
9. Make up topping as directed on the packet.
10. Mix topping and marmalade.
11. Use to sandwich meringues. Eat within 2 hours of filling.

PIXIE TOADSTOOL CAKES
Makes 12

2 standard egg whites
4oz (100gm) caster sugar
3oz (75gm) plain chocolate

1. Preheat oven to very cool, 225 deg F or gas ¼ (110 deg C).
2. Line a baking sheet with foil.
3. Whisk the egg whites until very stiff.
4. Whisk in half the sugar then, using a metal spoon, fold in the rest.
5. Put meringue in a large piping bag with a large plain nozzle.
6. Pipe 12 large blobs on foil.
7. Cook in centre of preheated oven for 2 hours, or until really dry.
8. Leave to cool.
9. Put chocolate in a bowl over a pan of gently simmering water and leave until melted.
10. Put chocolate in piping bag fitted with small plain nozzle. Pipe small chocolate dots on each meringue. Leave to set and eat the same day.

MERINGUE FRUIT BARS
Makes 6

2 standard egg whites
4oz (100gm) caster sugar
2 tablespoons apricot jam
1 can (8oz or 200gm) fruit cocktail

1. Preheat oven to very cool, 225 deg F or gas ¼ (110 deg C).
2. Line a baking sheet with foil.
3. Whisk egg whites until very stiff.
4. Whisk in half the sugar, then, using a metal spoon, fold in the rest.
5. Put in a large piping bag fitted with a medium star nozzle.
6. Pipe four lines, close together so they just touch, on foil, each about 3 inches long.
Now pipe stars all round edges of this oblong.
7. Make five more oblongs in same way.
8. Cook in centre of preheated oven for 2 hours, or until really dry.
9. Leave to cool.
10. Gently heat the jam, then sieve it.
11. Mix jam and drained fruit, spoon on to meringue bars. Eat 2 hours after adding the topping.

GINGER SNAP MERINGUES
Makes 6

2 standard egg whites
4oz (100gm) caster sugar
2 bought ginger snaps, fairly finely crushed
1 can (6oz or 150gm) cream or ¼ pint (125ml) fresh double cream, whipped

1. Preheat oven to very cool, 225 deg F or gas ¼ (110 deg C).
2. Line a baking sheet with foil.
3. Whisk the egg whites until very stiff.
4. Whisk in half the sugar then, using a metal spoon, fold in the rest.
5. Gently but thoroughly, fold in the crushed biscuits.
6. Put mixture in large heaps on the foil.
7. Cook in centre of preheated oven for 2 hours, or until really dry.
8. Leave to cool.
9. Sandwich with the cream and eat the same day.

CUSHION MERINGUES
Makes 5

2 standard egg whites
4oz (100gm) caster sugar
3oz (75gm) marshmallows
a few canned mandarin orange segments, chopped
3oz (75gm) marshmallows
2 tablespoons canned cream

1. Preheat oven to very cool, 225 deg F or gas ¼ (110 deg C).
2. Line a baking sheet with foil.
3. Whisk the egg whites until very stiff.
4. Whisk in half the sugar then, using a metal spoon, fold in the rest.
5. Put the mixture in smooth mounds on the foil.
6. Cook in centre of preheated oven for 2 hours, or until really dry.
7. Leave to cool.
8. Put marshmallows in a bowl over a pan of gently simmering water and leave until melted.
9. Cool for 1 minute then stir in fruit and cream.
10. Sandwich meringues with filling, while still warm. Leave to cool and eat 2 hours after adding filling.

CARDINALS' HATS
Makes 10

2 standard egg whites
4oz (100gm) caster sugar
1 can (8oz or 200gm) strawberries or fresh strawberries when in season
3 heaped tablespoons strawberry jam
1 can (6oz or 150gm) cream or ¼ pint (125ml) fresh double cream, whipped

1. Preheat oven to very cool, 225 deg F or gas ¼ (110 deg C).
2. Line two baking sheets with foil.
3. Whisk egg whites until very stiff.
4. Whisk in half the sugar, then fold in the rest using a metal spoon.
5. Put meringue in a large piping bag fitted with a large plain nozzle.
6. Pipe 10 flat rounds on the foil about 3 inches in diameter. Pipe a ring round the edge to raise it slightly.
7. Bake in centre of preheated oven for 2 hours, or until really dry. Leave to cool.
8. Drain the fruit thoroughly, keeping it whole.
9. Mix the fruit with the jam.
10. Spread some cream in each meringue.
11. Top with fruity mixture.

FIGURE ECLAIRS

Makes 12

These are very good for a children's party.

5oz (125gm) plain flour
pinch of salt
2oz (50gm) margarine
3 standard eggs, beaten
3 heaped tablespoons apricot jam
3oz (75gm) icing sugar, sifted
1 heaped tablespoon hundreds and thousands

1. Preheat oven to hot, 425 deg F or gas 7 (220 deg C).
2. Grease a baking sheet.
3. Sift the flour and salt into a bowl.
4. Put the margarine in a pan with ½ pint (250ml) cold water. Heat gently until margarine melts. Do not boil.
5. Using a wooden spoon, mix flour into melted margarine. Beat well over a gentle heat until mixture leaves sides of pan.
6. Take off heat and allow to cool slightly.
7. Very gradually, add the eggs to the mixture, beating well.
8. When mixture is very smooth, put in a piping bag fitted with a large plain pipe.
9. Pipe figure eights on prepared baking sheet.
10. Bake in centre of preheated oven for 30 minutes, or until golden brown and firm to the touch.
11. Carefully cut each cake in half and remove any soft paste from inside. Leave to cool.
12. Gently heat the jam and spoon into lower half of each cake. Add top of cake.
13. Put the icing sugar in a bowl. Add enough water to give an icing thick enough to coat the back of a wooden spoon.
14. Spoon icing on to cakes.
15. Sprinkle with hundreds and thousands. Leave to set.

CHOCOLATE ECLAIRS

(Illustrated on page 35)
Makes 12

5oz (125gm) plain flour
pinch of salt
2oz (50gm) margarine
3 standard eggs, beaten
small sachet powdered creamy topping or ½ pint (250ml) fresh double cream, whipped
milk to mix topping if used
2oz (50gm) icing sugar
1 level tablespoon cocoa

1. Preheat oven to hot, 425 deg F or gas 7 (220 deg C).
2. Grease a large baking sheet.
3. Sift the flour and salt into a bowl.
4. Put the margarine in a pan with ½ pint (250ml) cold water. Heat gently until the margarine has melted but do not allow to boil.
5. Using a wooden spoon, mix in the flour. Beat well over a gentle heat until mixture leaves sides of pan.
6. Take off heat and allow to cool slightly.
7. Very gradually, add the beaten eggs to the mixture, beating all the time.
8. When the mixture is very smooth, put it in a piping bag fitted with a ¾-inch (2cm) plain nozzle.
9. Pipe 12 lines, each 5 inches long on two baking sheets.
10. Bake in the centre of the preheated oven for 30 minutes, or until golden brown and fairly crisp.
11. Cut each éclair in half and, using a small spoon, carefully scoop out any soft mixture.
12. Make up the creamy topping as instructed on the packet or use the fresh cream.
13. Spoon topping or cream into both the hollowed-out halves and sandwich together again.
14. Sift the icing sugar with the cocoa. Add enough hot water to make an icing which will coat the back of a wooden spoon.
15. Spoon some icing on top of each bun, or quickly dip the top of each bun in icing. Leave to set and eat the same day.

SPICY GINGERBREAD

Makes 6

These cakes taste best if stored for a week in an airtight tin before they are eaten.

12oz (300gm) plain flour
2 level teaspoons ground ginger
1 level teaspoon cinnamon
1 level teaspoon bicarbonate of soda
4oz (100gm) margarine
2oz (50gm) caster sugar
4oz (100gm) golden syrup
4oz (100gm) black treacle
4 tablespoons milk
1 large egg, beaten

1. Preheat oven to very moderate, 325 deg F or gas 3 (170 deg C).
2. Lightly grease a 6-inch (15cm) square, fairly deep cake tin. Line base of tin with greaseproof paper, then grease the paper.
3. Sift the flour with the ginger, cinnamon and bicarbonate of soda into a bowl.
4. Melt the margarine in a small pan with sugar, syrup and treacle. Cool for 2 minutes.
5. Stir milk into treacle mixture and mix into dry ingredients.
6. Beat in the egg.
7. Spoon into prepared tin and bake in centre of preheated oven for 1½–1¾ hours, or until firm to the touch.
8. Leave to cool in tin for 10 minutes, then turn out to complete cooling on a wire rack.
9. Cut into six for serving.

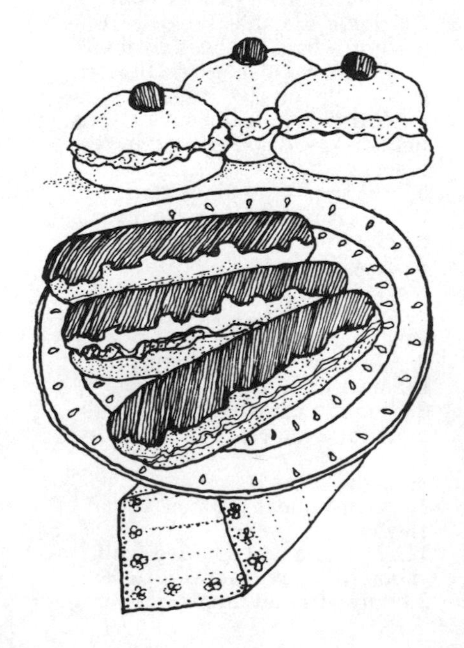

ICED PARKIN
Makes 12

6oz (150gm) wholemeal flour
6oz (150gm) oatmeal (not the instant kind)
2 level teaspoons mixed spice
1½ level teaspoons ground ginger
1 level teaspoon cinnamon
1 level teaspoon bicarbonate of soda
2 level teaspoons cream of tartar
4oz (100gm) margarine
3oz (75gm) soft brown sugar
¾ teacup golden syrup
1 large egg
4oz (100gm) icing sugar
strained juice of 1 small lemon

1. Preheat oven to very moderate, 325 deg F or gas 3 (170 deg C).
2. Well grease a Yorkshire pudding tin or any fairly shallow cake tin of same size.
3. Put the wholemeal flour in a bowl with the oatmeal, spice, ginger, cinnamon, bicarbonate of soda, and cream of tartar. Mix well.
4. Rub in the margarine until mixture resembles fine breadcrumbs.
5. Put the brown sugar in a pan with the syrup. Heat gently until sugar has completely dissolved. Leave to cool for 2 minutes.
6. Stir syrup into dry ingredients.
7. Add the beaten egg and mix well.
8. Pour mixture into prepared tin.
9. Bake in centre of preheated oven for 1–1¼ hours, or until firm and slightly springy to the touch.
10. Leave to cool in tin, then turn out.
11. Mix the sifted icing sugar with enough lemon juice to make a mixture which will thickly coat the back of a wooden spoon. Add a little cold water if necessary.
12. Cut cake into equal-sized pieces.
13. Spoon icing on top of cakes. Don't worry if it dribbles down the sides – this looks very appetizing.
14. Leave to set and serve the same day once it is iced.

BRANDY SNAPS
Makes about 8

These will keep well in an airtight tin, but add the cream only on the day of serving.

3oz (75gm) golden syrup
2oz (50gm) caster sugar
3oz (75 gm) margarine
2oz (50gm) plain flour
1 level teaspoon ginger
1 can (6oz or 150gm) cream or ¼ pint (125ml) fresh double cream, whipped

1. Preheat oven to moderate to moderately hot, 375 deg F or gas 5 (190 deg C).
2. Well grease a baking sheet.
3. Melt the syrup in a small pan with the sugar and margarine.
4. Sift the flour with the ginger.
5. Leave syrup mixture to cool a little, then pour it into flour and mix well.
6. Put teaspoons of the mixture 4 inches apart on prepared baking sheet.
7. Bake in centre of preheated oven for 15–20 minutes, or until well spread and golden brown.
8. Grease the handle of a wooden spoon.
9. Lift each brandy snap off the baking sheet with palette knife and roll it quickly round the handle of the spoon. Then slide it off carefully.
10. Leave to harden and cool.
11. Fill each end with cream and serve at once.

CRUNCHY GOLDEN CAKES
Makes about 10

4oz (100gm) plain flour
6oz (150gm) caster sugar
2oz (50gm) crushed cornflakes
2oz (50gm) desiccated coconut
1 level teaspoon powdered ginger
4oz (100gm) margarine
1 level tablespoon golden syrup
1 level teaspoon bicarbonate of soda

1. Preheat oven to very moderate, 325 deg F or gas 3 (170 deg C).
2. Grease two baking sheets.
3. Sift the flour into a bowl.
4. Stir in sugar, cornflakes, coconut and powdered ginger.
5. Melt the margarine in a small pan with the syrup; do not allow to boil.
6. Stir in bicarbonate of soda.
7. Stir margarine mixture into flour mixture and blend together.
8. Put in heaps, well spaced, on prepared baking sheets.
9. Bake in centre of preheated oven for 15 minutes.
10. Leave to cool, and eat the same day.

CREAM HORNS
(Illustrated on page 35)
Makes 6

7½oz (187gm) packet frozen puff pastry, thawed
1 small egg yolk, beaten
2 heaped tablespoons red jam
1 small can cream or ¼ pint (125ml) fresh double cream, whipped

1. Preheat oven to hot, 450 deg F or gas 8 (230 deg C).
2. Wet a baking sheet but don't grease it. Grease six cream horn tins.
3. Roll out pastry into a thin, neat oblong. Cut six neat strips and wet these lightly.
4. Starting at pointed end of tin, and overlapping pastry as you work, wind pastry strip around each tin. Seal with a little egg yolk and brush rest over pastry.
5. Bake in centre of preheated oven for 15–20 minutes or until pale golden. Remove tins. Allow to cool.
6. Fill first with jam, then cream and eat within 2 hours.

STRAWBERRY TARTLETS
(Illustrated on page 36)
Makes 12

5oz (125gm) plain flour
pinch of salt
$2\frac{1}{2}$oz (62gm) margarine
1 small egg yolk, beaten
2 heaped tablespoons strawberry jam, sieved
1lb ($\frac{1}{2}$ kilo) fresh strawberries (when in season) or 1 large can strawberries
small sachet powdered creamy topping
milk to mix

1. Preheat oven to hot, 425 deg F or gas 7 (220 deg C).
2. Lightly grease 12 patty tins.
3. Sift flour and salt into a bowl.
4. Rub in margarine.
5. Add enough egg yolk to give stiff dough.
6. Use to line prepared tins.
7. Prick bases well or add bits of greaseproof paper and baking beans if you have them. Bake blind for 15–20 minutes. Remove paper and beans if used. Allow to cool.
8. Spoon jam into each tartlet and cover it with prepared or drained fruit.
9. Make up topping with the milk as directed on packet. Decorate with piped stars and eat the same day.

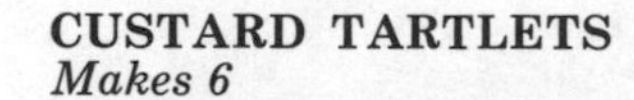

CUSTARD TARTLETS
Makes 6

4oz (100gm) self-raising flour
pinch of salt
2oz (50gm) margarine
1 small egg yolk
1 large egg
1 large egg yolk
1oz (25gm) caster sugar
$\frac{1}{2}$ pint (250ml) milk, less 4 tablespoons
powdered nutmeg

1. Preheat oven to hot, 425 deg F or gas 7 (220 deg C).
2. Lightly grease six fairly deep patty tins.
3. Sift the flour with the salt into a mixing bowl.
4. Rub in the margarine until mixture resembles fine breadcrumbs.
5. Add enough of the small egg yolk to make a stiff dough.
6. Roll out dough thinly and use to line patty tins. (Do not prick pastry.)
7. Bake the pastry for 10 minutes in the centre of the preheated oven.
8. Take tarts out of oven and reduce oven heat to moderate, 350 deg F or gas 4 (180 deg C). Leave for 10 minutes.
9. Meanwhile, mix the large egg and the large egg yolk with the sugar.
10. Heat the milk but do not let it boil. Stir it into the egg mixture.
11. Return mixture to rinsed pan and cook gently until the mixture will lightly coat the back of a wooden spoon – do not boil.
12. Pour the mixture into the pastry tarts.
13. Sprinkle nutmeg over top of custard.
14. Bake tarts in centre of preheated oven for 15–20 minutes, or until custard is set.

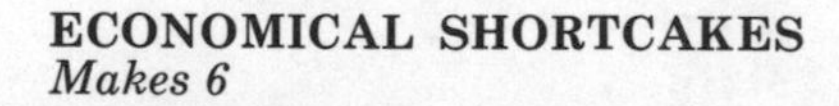

ECONOMICAL SHORTCAKES
Makes 6

8oz (200gm) self-raising flour
4oz (100gm) margarine
4oz (100gm) caster sugar
1 standard egg, beaten
3 heaped tablespoons blackcurrant jam
1 can (6oz or 150gm) cream

1. Preheat oven to moderate to moderately hot, 375 deg F or gas 5 (190 deg C).
2. Grease a baking sheet with lard.
3. Sift the flour into a bowl.
4. Rub in margarine until mixture resembles fine breadcrumbs.
5. Stir in the sugar.
6. Mix to a stiff dough with the beaten egg.
7. Roll out to $\frac{1}{4}$-inch thick.
8. Put on prepared baking sheet.
9. Bake in centre of preheated oven for 20–25 minutes, or until golden.
10. While still hot, cut into. 12 rounds. Leave to cool.
11. Chop up the trimmings and mix them with the jam.
12. Sandwich cooled cakes with jam and cream and eat within 2 hours of adding the filling.

EVERYDAY CAKES
Makes about 12

8oz (200gm) self-raising flour
pinch of salt
4oz (100gm) margarine
4oz (100gm) caster sugar
3oz (75gm) desiccated coconut
2oz (50gm) dates, chopped
1 standard egg
milk to mix

1. Preheat oven to hot, 425 deg F or gas 7 (220 deg C).
2. Grease a large baking sheet.
3. Dredge baking sheet with flour.
4. Sift the flour and salt into a bowl.
5. Rub in the margarine.
6. Stir in sugar, coconut and dates.
7. Mix in the egg and, if needed, a little milk to give a stiff mixture.
8. Put in heaps on prepared baking sheet.
9. Bake in centre of preheated oven for 15–20 minutes.
10. Leave to cool and store no longer than one day.

COFFEE MORNING CAKES
Makes 12

5½oz (137gm) self-raising flour
1 level dessertspoon cocoa
large pinch of salt
1oz (25gm) caster sugar
1 small egg yolk
1 can (8oz or 200gm) raspberries
arrowroot, to thicken
1 tablespoon raspberry jam
1 can (6oz or 150gm) cream
1oz (25gm) grated chocolate

1. Preheat oven to moderately hot, 400 deg F or gas 6 (200 deg C).
2. Grease 12 patty tins.
3. Sift the flour with cocoa and salt into a bowl. Do this three times.
4. Stir in the sugar and enough egg yolk to give a stiff dough.
5. Roll out the dough thinly.
6. Use dough to line patty tins.
7. Bake in centre of preheated oven for 15–20 minutes.
8. Leave to cool.
9. Drain juice off the fruit.
10. Thicken the juice with arrowroot, following instructions on the packet.
11. Put fruit back in thickened juice.
12. Mix jam into fruit and leave to cool.
13. Mix the cream with the chocolate.
14. Fill the pastry cases with cream mixture. Top with fruit and serve within 2 hours of adding the filling.

LEMON TOPPERS
Makes about 12

8oz (200gm) self-raising flour
pinch of salt
4oz (100gm) margarine
4oz (100gm) caster sugar
3oz (75gm) desiccated coconut
1 standard egg
milk to mix
4oz (100gm) icing sugar, sifted
strained juice of large lemon

1. Preheat oven to hot, 425 deg F or gas 7 (220 deg C).
2. Grease two baking sheets.
3. Sift flour and salt into a bowl.
4. Rub in margarine until mixture resembles fine breadcrumbs.
5. Stir in sugar and coconut.
6. Add egg and enough milk to give a stiff mixture.
7. Put in heaps on prepared baking sheets.
8. Bake in centre of preheated oven for 15–20 minutes.
9. Leave to cool.
10. Mix icing sugar with enough lemon juice to give a thick icing. Spoon on completely cooled cakes. Leave to set.

ORANGE PEEL CAKES
Makes about 12

8oz (200gm) self-raising flour
pinch of salt
4oz (100gm) margarine
4oz (100gm) caster sugar
3oz (75gm) desiccated coconut
1 standard egg
milk to mix
6 sugar lumps
2 heaped teaspoons grated orange rind

1. Preheat oven to hot, 425 deg F or gas 7 (220 deg C).
2. Grease two baking sheets.
3. Sift flour and salt into a bowl.
4. Rub in margarine until mixture resembles fine breadcrumbs.
5. Stir in sugar and coconut.
6. Add egg and enough milk to mix to a stiff dough.
7. Put in heaps on prepared baking sheets.
8. Bake in centre of preheated oven for 15–20 minutes, or until golden.
9. While the buns are still warm, crush sugar and mix with orange rind. Sprinkle on the cakes and leave to cool.

APPLE FOOL CAKES
Makes 12

6oz (150gm) plain flour
pinch of salt
4oz (100gm) margarine
1 small egg yolk
1 cup stewed apple, well drained
1 cup cold thick custard, chilled
a little grated chocolate to decorate

1. Preheat oven to moderately hot, 400 deg F or gas 6 (200 deg C).
2. Grease 12 patty tins.
3. Sift the flour and salt into a bowl.
4. Rub in the margarine until mixture resembles fine breadcrumbs.
5. Stir in beaten egg yolk and enough cold water to give a stiff dough.
6. Roll out dough thinly and cut out 12 rounds.
7. Use to line patty tins; prick the pastry.
8. Cook in centre of preheated oven for 15–20 minutes, or until golden.
9. Mix the apple with the custard
10. Use mixture to fill the pastry cases.
11. Decorate with the chocolate and serve within an hour of adding the filling.

BANBURY CAKES
Makes about 6

7½oz (187gm) packet frozen puff pastry, thawed
2oz (50gm) raisins
2oz (50gm) currants
1oz (25gm) chopped mixed peel
2oz (50gm) caster sugar, plus a little extra for sprinkling
1oz (25gm) margarine, melted
large pinch of nutmeg
large pinch of mixed spice
1 small egg, separated

1. Preheat oven to hot, 425 deg F or gas 7 (220 deg C).
2. Wet a baking sheet.
3. Roll out the pastry thinly and cut into six 5-inch rounds.
4. Mix the fruit and peel with the sugar and melted margarine.
5. Mix in the nutmeg and spice.
6. Spoon a little of the fruit mixture into centre of each pastry round.
7. Brush the edges of each round with beaten egg yolk.
8. Draw the edges of each round together and seal with your fingertips.
9. Turn each cake over and roll out or press lightly into an oval shape.
10. Make two or three cuts across each cake to expose the filling.
11. Brush cakes with egg white then sprinkle with a little caster sugar.
12. Bake in the centre of the preheated oven for 25 minutes, or until golden brown.
13. Eat them the same day, hot or cold.

CHERRY EVERYDAY CAKES
Makes about 12

8oz (200gm) self-raising flour
pinch of salt
4oz (100gm) margarine
4oz (100gm) caster sugar
3oz (75gm) desiccated coconut
1oz (25gm) glacé cherries, chopped
1 standard egg
diluted orange squash, to mix

1. Preheat oven to hot, 425 deg F or gas 7 (220 deg C).
2. Grease two large baking sheets.
3. Sift the flour and salt into a bowl.
4. Rub in the margarine.
5. Stir in sugar, coconut and cherries.
6. Add egg and enough orange squash to mix to a stiff dough.
7. Put in heaps on prepared baking sheets.
8. Bake in centre of preheated oven for 15–20 minutes.
9. Leave to cool, then store in an airtight tin. Eat within two days.

COCONUT PYRAMIDS
Makes 8

2 large egg whites
5oz (125gm) caster sugar
5oz (125gm) desiccated coconut
edible pink food colouring

1. Preheat oven to cool, 300 deg F or gas 2 (150 deg C).
2. Grease a baking sheet.
3. Whisk the egg whites until very stiff and snowy.
4. Using a metal spoon, fold in the sugar and coconut.
5. Divide the mixture in half and colour one half pink.
6. Drop piles of the mixture, well spaced, on to prepared baking sheet.
7. Bake in centre of preheated oven for 1 hour, or until white ones are very pale fawn.
8. Leave to cool. Store in an airtight tin for one day only.

APRICOT FLUFF CAKES
Makes 12

6oz (150gm) plain flour
pinch of salt
4oz (100gm) margarine
1 standard egg yolk
1 can (15oz or 375gm) apricot halves
cornflour to thicken
1 standard egg white
2oz (50gm) caster sugar

1. Preheat oven to moderately hot, 400 deg F or gas 6 (200 deg C).
2. Grease 12 patty tins.
3. Sift the flour and salt into a bowl.
4. Rub in margarine until mixture resembles fine breadcrumbs.
5. Add beaten egg yolk and enough cold water to make a stiff dough.
6. Roll out thinly and cut out 12 rounds.
7. Use to line the prepared patty tins. Prick the pastry.
8. Bake in centre of preheated oven for 15 minutes. Remove from oven and leave the oven on, but turn down to very moderate, 325 deg F or gas 3 (170 deg C).
9. Drain juice off the fruit.
10. Thicken the juice with cornflour, as instructed on the packet.
11. Put an apricot half, rounded part up into each pastry case. Spoon juice on top.
12. Whisk the egg white until very stiff. Fold in the caster sugar.
13. Put mixture in a piping bag with medium sized star nozzle.
14. Pipe a ring round edge of each piece of fruit.
15. Cook in centre of preheated oven for 20 minutes, or until golden.
16. Leave to cool and serve within 2 hours.

ROCK CAKES
Makes 8

8oz (200gm) self-raising flour
½ level teaspoon salt
large pinch mixed spice
3oz (75gm) margarine
3oz (75gm) caster sugar
4oz (100gm) currants
1oz (25gm) chopped mixed peel
1 standard egg, beaten
milk to mix

1. Preheat oven to hot, 425 deg F or gas 7 (220 deg C).
2. Grease a large baking sheet.
3. Sift the flour with the salt and spice into a bowl.
4. Rub in the margarine until the mixture looks like fine breadcrumbs.
5. Stir in the sugar, currants and peel.
6. Mix in the beaten egg and enough milk to give a stiff dropping consistency – the spoon should need a really good shake before the mixture will drop off it.
7. Spoon the mixture in eight heaps on the prepared baking sheet.
8. Bake in centre of preheated oven for 25–30 minutes, or until golden brown and firm to the touch.
9. Leave cakes to cool on a wire rack, and eat them the same day.

RASPBERRY BUNS
Makes 6

8oz (200gm) self-raising flour
large pinch of salt
3oz (75gm) margarine
4oz (100gm) caster sugar
milk to mix
half a 1lb (½ kilo) jar raspberry jam

1. Preheat oven to hot, 450 deg F or gas 8 (230 deg C).
2. Lightly grease a baking sheet.
3. Sift the flour and salt into a mixing bowl.
4. Rub in the margarine until mixture resembles fine breadcrumbs.
5. Stir in the sugar.
6. Add enough milk to mix to a stiff dough.
7. Turn on to a lightly floured surface and roll out to ¼-inch thickness.
8. Cut into six large rounds.
9. Place 1 heaped teaspoon of raspberry jam in the centre of each bun.
10. Wet edges of dough and gather them together so that the jam is enclosed.
11. Place balls of dough on the prepared baking sheet.
12. Bake in the centre of the preheated oven for 20 minutes, or until pale golden and firm to the touch. Eat the same day, hot or cold.

CINNAMON KNOTS
Makes 8

4oz (100gm) self-raising flour
pinch of salt
1oz (25gm) margarine
1oz (25gm) caster sugar
half a standard egg, beaten
milk to mix
clean lard or corn oil for deep frying
1oz (25gm) granulated sugar
1½ level teaspoons cinnamon

1. Sift the flour with the salt into a mixing bowl.
2. Rub the margarine into the flour until mixture resembles fine breadcrumbs.
3. Stir in the caster sugar.
4. Beat in the egg and just enough milk to give a fairly soft dough.
5. Wrap the dough in foil and leave to chill in the refrigerator for 3 hours.
6. Unwrap dough and roll out to about ¼-inch thickness.
7. Cut into thin strips each about ½ inch wide and 6 inches long.
8. Tie each strip into a simple knot.
9. Heat the lard or oil and fry each strip for 3–5 minutes, or until golden brown and fairly crisp.
10. Drain on soft paper.
11. Toss the knots in a mixture of sugar and cinnamon. These will keep for a day if stored in an airtight tin.

PINEAPPLE FOAM CAKES
Makes 12

6oz (150gm) plain flour
pinch of salt
4oz (100gm) margarine
1 standard egg yolk
1 can (8oz or 200gm) pineapple pieces
cornflour to thicken
1 standard egg white
2oz (50gm) caster sugar

1. Preheat oven to moderately hot, 400 deg F or gas 6 (200 deg C).
2. Grease 12 patty tins.
3. Sift the flour and salt into a bowl.
4. Rub in margarine until mixture resembles fine breadcrumbs.
5. Add the beaten egg yolk and enough cold water to give a stiff dough. Roll out thinly and cut into 12 rounds.
6. Use the pastry to line the patty tins. Prick the pastry.
7. Bake in centre of preheated oven for 15 minutes, then take out of oven. Leave oven on but reduce heat to very moderate, 325 deg F or gas 3 (170 deg C).
8. Drain fruit and thicken juice with cornflour as instructed on the packet. Stir in the fruit.
9. Spoon fruit into pastry cases.
10. Whisk the egg white until very stiff. Fold in sugar.
11. Spoon meringue on top of fruit.
12. Put back in oven and cook for about 20 minutes, or until golden.
13. Leave to cool. Serve within 2 hours.

RING DOUGHNUTS

(Illustrated on page 36)

Makes 12

The dough can be made the day before and kept in the refrigerator well wrapped, ready to fry.

8oz (200gm) plain flour
pinch of salt
2 level teaspoons baking powder
2oz (50gm) margarine
2½oz (62gm) caster sugar
1 standard egg, beaten
milk to mix
clean lard or corn oil for deep frying

1. Sift the flour with the salt and baking powder into a mixing bowl.
2. Rub margarine into flour until mixture resembles fine breadcrumbs.
3. Mix in 2oz (50gm) sugar.
4. Beat in the egg and enough milk to give a fairly soft, but not sticky, consistency.
5. Turn dough on to lightly floured board and knead gently until smooth.
6. Roll out the dough to ½-inch thickness.
7. Using a plain 2-inch (5cm) cutter, cut out nine rounds. Using a much smaller cutter or a knife, cut out the centre of the rounds to make rings. Re-roll centres and make more rings.
8. Fry the doughnuts in a deep pan of hot fat or oil for 5–7 minutes, or until golden brown and crisp.
9. Drain doughnuts on soft kitchen paper and toss them in rest of sugar. Eat the same day, hot or cold.

OLD-FASHIONED DOUGHNUTS

Makes 12

8oz (200gm) plain flour
2oz (50gm) margarine
½oz (12gm) fresh yeast
4 tablespoons tepid milk
1 standard egg
large pinch of salt
1oz (25gm) caster sugar, plus extra for coating doughnuts
2 heaped tablespoons red jam
clean lard or oil for deep frying

1. Sift flour into a bowl.
2. Rub in the margarine until mixture resembles fine breadcrumbs.
3. Cream the yeast with a little of the milk then mix it with rest of milk, and the egg.
4. Beat well for at least 5 minutes.
5. Grease the inside of a large polythene bag with melted lard or oil.
6. Put the bowl of dough inside the bag and leave in a warm place – not near direct heat or boiler – for about 1 hour, or until dough has doubled in bulk.
7. Knead the salt and 1oz (25gm) caster sugar into the risen dough. Knead lightly.
8. Divide dough into 12 pieces and form each piece into a ball.
9. Put the balls on a lightly floured surface and leave for 5 minutes.
10. Flour your index finger and push it well into the centre of the dough to make a dent. Fill carefully with jam.
11. Moisten the edges of the hole you have made and then seal it with fingertips.
12. Heat the lard or oil.
13. Fry the doughnuts, in batches, in the hot lard or oil for about 8 minutes. Drain them on soft paper.
14. Toss in sugar and serve the same day, hot or cold.

ANGEL BUNS

Makes 8

3oz (75gm) sultanas
8oz (200gm) self-raising flour
pinch of salt
2oz (50gm) margarine
2½oz (62gm) caster sugar
1 standard egg, beaten
1 small egg, beaten
milk to mix
corn oil for deep frying

1. Leave sultanas to soak in hot water for 1 hour. Drain well.
2. Sift the flour with the salt into a bowl.
3. Rub in margarine until mixture resembles fine breadcrumbs.
4. Stir in sugar.
5. Add beaten standard egg and enough milk to mix to a soft dough.
6. Roll out thinly on a lightly floured board.
7. Using a large plain pastry cutter, cut into eight rounds.
8. Put some sultanas in the centre of each round.
9. Brush pastry edges with small beaten egg. Fold over and press edges to seal.
10. Deep fry in hot oil for 3–5 minutes, or until golden.
11. Drain on soft absorbent paper and serve within an hour, hot or cold.

LITTLE MIXER CAKES

Makes 12

4oz (100gm) margarine
4oz (100gm) caster sugar
2 large eggs, lightly beaten
1 heaped teaspoon grated lemon rind
4oz (100gm) self-raising flour

1. Preheat oven to moderate to moderately hot, 375 deg F or gas 5 (190 deg C).
2. Put 12 paper cake cases in 12 patty tins.
3. Put margarine and caster sugar in bowl of mixer. Start it up to cream.
4. When mixture is very creamy and light in colour, add eggs and lemon rind and run mixer for 2 minutes.
5. Using a metal spoon fold in sifted flour.
6. Spoon into cake cases.
7. Bake in centre of preheated oven for 15 minutes, or until firm to the touch.
8. Turn out to cool and eat the same day.

CHOCOLATE MIXER CAKES

Makes 12

4oz (100gm) margarine
4oz (100gm) caster sugar
2 large eggs, lightly beaten
3oz (75gm) plain chocolate, melted
4oz (100gm) self-raising flour

1. Preheat oven to moderate to moderately hot, 375 deg F or gas 5 (190 deg C).
2. Put 12 paper cake cases in 12 patty tins.
3. Put margarine and caster sugar in your electric mixer bowl. Start it up to cream.
4. When mixture is very light and creamy, add eggs and melted chocolate. Run mixer for 2 minutes.
5. Using a metal spoon, fold in sifted flour.
6. Spoon into paper cake cases.
7. Bake in centre of preheated oven for 15 minutes, or until firm to the touch.
8. Leave to cool. Store in an airtight tin for one day before serving.

BANANA MIXER BUNS

Makes 12

7oz (175gm) margarine
4oz (100gm) caster sugar
2 large eggs, lightly beaten
4oz (100gm) self-raising flour,
3oz (75gm) icing sugar
1 large ripe banana

1. Preheat oven to moderate, 375 deg F or gas 5 (190 deg C).
2. Put 12 paper cake cases in 12 patty tins.
3. Put 4oz (100gm) margarine and caster sugar into your electric mixer bowl. Start it up to cream the mixture.
4. When mixture is very light and creamy, add eggs and run mixer for 2 minutes.
5. Using a metal spoon, fold in the sifted flour.
6. Spoon into paper cases.
7. Bake in centre of preheated oven for 15 minutes, or until firm to the touch.
8. Leave to cool.
9. Wipe out mixer bowl. Add rest of margarine, the icing sugar and peeled banana. Run mixer for 2 minutes.
10. Spoon on top of cold buns. Serve within 2 hours.

COFFEE FROSTED MIXER CAKES

Makes 12

7oz (175gm) margarine
4oz (100gm) caster sugar
2 large eggs, lightly beaten
6 tablespoons very strong liquid black coffee, unsweetened
4oz (100gm) self-raising flour
3oz (75gm) icing sugar

1. Preheat oven to moderate, 375 deg F or gas 5 (190 deg C).
2. Put 12 paper cake cases in 12 patty tins.
3. Put 4oz (100gm) margarine and caster sugar in your electric mixer bowl. Start it up to cream.
4. When mixture is very creamy and light in colour, add eggs and half the coffee. Run mixer for 2 minutes.
5. Using a metal spoon fold in the sifted flour.
6. Spoon into paper cake cases.
7. Bake in centre of preheated oven for 15 minutes, or until firm to the touch.
8. Leave to cool.
9. Wipe mixer bowl. Add rest of margarine, rest of coffee and the icing sugar. Run mixer for 2 minutes. Put to chill in refrigerator.
10. Pipe icing on top of buns and eat the same day.

GOOSEBERRY MIXER CAKES

Makes 12

7oz (175gm) margarine
4oz (100gm) caster sugar
2 large eggs, lightly beaten
4oz (100gm) self-raising flour
3oz (75gm) icing sugar
1 can (8oz or 200gm) gooseberries or fresh gooseberries, stewed, when in season

1. Preheat oven to moderate to moderately hot, 375 deg F or gas 5 (190 deg C).
2. Put 12 paper cake cases in 12 patty tins.
3. Put 4oz (100gm) margarine and caster sugar in your electric mixer bowl. Start it up to cream mixture.
4. When very light and creamy, add eggs and run mixer for 2 minutes.
5. Using a metal spoon, fold in the sifted flour.
6. Spoon into cake cases.
7. Bake in centre of preheated oven for 15 minutes, or until firm to the touch.
8. Leave to cool.
9. Wipe out mixer bowl.
10. Add rest of margarine, the icing sugar and drained fruit. Run mixer for 2 minutes, or until well blended. Spoon on top of cold buns.

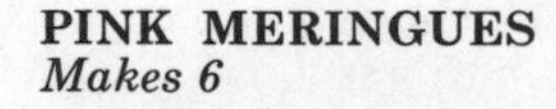

CANDY FLOSS BUNS
Makes 12

4oz (100gm) margarine
4oz (100gm) caster sugar
2 large eggs plus 1 small egg, lightly beaten
4oz (100gm) self-raising flour
1 small egg white
3 tablespoons raspberry jam
5 tablespoons evaporated milk

1. Preheat oven to moderate to moderately hot, 375 deg F or gas 5 (190 deg C).
2. Put 12 paper cake cases in 12 patty tins.
3. Put margarine and caster sugar in your electric mixer bowl. Start it up to cream mixture.
4. When mixture is very light and creamy, add beaten egg mixture and run mixer for 2 minutes.
5. Using a metal spoon, fold in sifted flour.
6. Spoon mixture into paper cake cases.
7. Bake in centre of preheated oven for 15 minutes, or until firm to the touch.
8. Leave to cool.
9. Wipe out mixer bowl. Add egg white, jam and milk. Run it for 2 minutes, or until mixture is very stiff and snowy.
10. Put mixture on top of buns and serve at once.

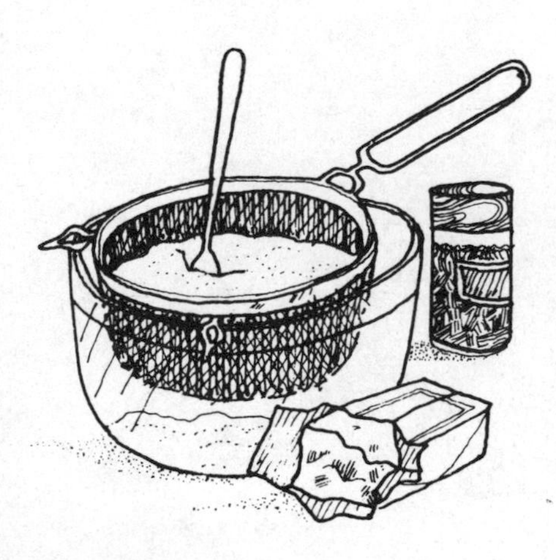

PINK MERINGUES
Makes 6

2 standard egg whites
4oz (100gm) caster sugar
3 drops pink food colouring
3oz (75gm) icing sugar
3oz (75gm) margarine
3 drops vanilla essence

1. Preheat to very cool, 225 deg F or gas ¼ (110 deg C).
2. Line baking sheet with foil.
3. Put egg whites and caster sugar in your electric mixer bowl. Add colouring. Run mixer until mixture is very stiff and snowy.
4. Put into a large piping bag fitted with large star nozzle.
5. Pipe 12 swirls on prepared baking sheet.
6. Bake in centre of preheated oven for 2 hours, or until dry.
7. Leave to cool.
8. Wipe out mixer bowl. Add icing sugar, margarine and vanilla essence. Run mixer for 2 minutes, or until mixture is very creamy.
9. Sandwich meringues with the vanilla icing. Serve within 3 hours of adding the filling.

COFFEE MERINGUES
Makes 6

2 standard egg whites
4oz (100gm) caster sugar
2 teaspoons very strong liquid black coffee, unsweetened
1 can (6oz or 150gm) cream or ¼ pint (125ml) fresh double cream, whipped

1. Preheat oven to very cool, 225 deg F or gas ¼ (110 deg C).
2. Line baking sheet with foil.
3. Put egg whites and caster sugar in your electric mixer bowl. Add coffee. Run mixer until mixture is very stiff and snowy.
4. Put into large piping bag with large star nozzle.
5. Pipe large swirls on the prepared baking sheet.
6. Bake in centre of preheated oven for 2 hours or until dry.
7. Leave to cool.
8. Sandwich meringues with cream and serve within 2 hours of adding the filling.

ALMOND MERINGUES
Makes 6

2 standard egg whites
4oz (100gm) caster sugar
3 drops almond essence
3oz (75gm) margarine
3oz (75gm) icing sugar
2 heaped tablespoons cornflakes

1. Preheat oven to very cool, 225 deg F or gas ¼ (110 deg C).
2. Line a baking sheet with foil.
3. Put egg whites and caster sugar in your electric mixer bowl. Add almond essence and whisk until very stiff and snowy.
4. Put mixture in large piping bag and pipe 12 swirls on prepared baking sheet.
5. Bake in centre of preheated oven for 2 hours, or until dry.
6. Wipe out mixer bowl and add margarine and icing sugar. Run mixer for 2 minutes, or until mixture is creamy.
7. Stir in cornflakes.
8. Sandwich meringues with the cornflake mixture and serve within 2 hours of adding the filling.

LAZY COOK'S CAKES
Makes 6

6oz (150gm) plain chocolate
1 can (6oz or 150gm) cream
2oz (50gm) crystallized ginger, finely chopped

1. Put the chocolate in a basin over a pan of gently simmering water. Leave until melted.
2. Pour melted chocolate into six small, deep foil cases. Swish chocolate about to cover base and sides. Leave to set, then remove the foil.
3. Mix the cream with the ginger and spoon into chocolate cases.

Chocolate fancies (see page 74)

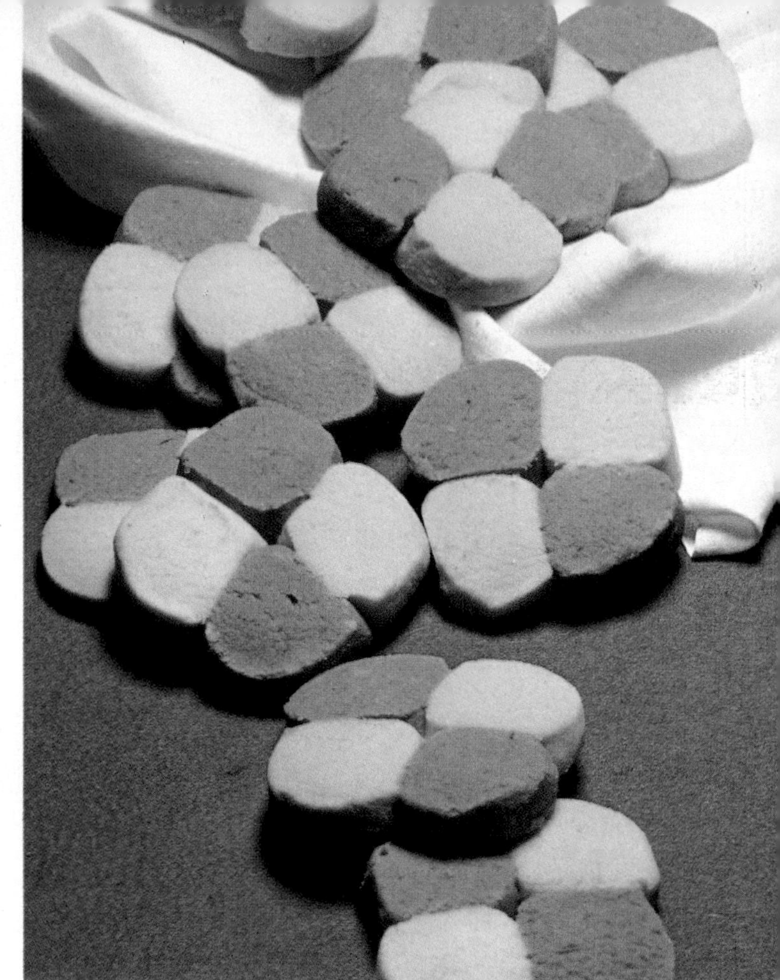

Demerara biscuits (see page 73)

Coconut biscuits (see page 80)

Gingerbread men (see page 76)

Jam circles (see page 78)

Cornish scones (see page 84)

Ginger scones (see page 85)

Lemon scones (see page 89)

LAZY PINEAPPLE CAKES
Makes 6

6oz (150gm) plain chocolate
1 can (8oz or 200gm) pineapple pieces
cornflour to thicken
1 bought sponge trifle cake

1. Put the chocolate in a bowl over a pan of gently simmering water. Leave until melted.
2. Pour melted chocolate into six small deep foil cases. Swish chocolate about to coat base and sides. Leave to set, then remove from foil.
3. Drain juice off fruit.
4. Thicken the fruit juice with cornflour, following the instructions on the packet.
5. Put fruit back in thickened juice and leave to cool.
6. Pound up or liquidize the cake.
7. Mix cake crumbs and fruit.
8. Spoon into chocolate cases and eat the same day.

CHOCOLATE BOXES
Makes 12

1 oblong bought Madeira cake, or bake one in a medium-sized loaf tin, see page 6
8oz (200gm) chocolate-flavoured cake covering
4 heaped tablespoons marmalade

1. Cut the cake into two layers.
2. Cut each layer into small squares.
3. Melt the chocolate covering as directed on the packet and spread it in a fairly thick layer on waxed paper or plastic working top.
4. Measure the size of the sides of each cake square.
5. Using a sharp knife, which has been heated by dipping in hot water, cut out four squares for each cake. (The squares are to go on the four sides of the cake and should protrude about ½ inch above them.)
6. Use some of the marmalade to brush the sides of the cakes
7. Stick chocolate squares on to sides of cakes to make boxes.
8. Spoon a little marmalade into centre of boxes. Eat that day.

NO-BAKE CRACKLES
Makes 6

4oz (100gm) plain chocolate
4 plain chocolate digestive biscuits
half a teacup of cornflakes

1. Put the chocolate in a basin over a pan of gently simmering water. Leave until melted.
2. Crush biscuits – not too finely – or liquidize them.
3. Mix melted chocolate with crushed biscuits and cornflakes.
4. Spoon into six paper cake cases.
5. Leave in cold place to set. Eat the same day.

TEN-MINUTE CAKES
Makes 6

1 chocolate-coated soft toffee bar
2oz (50gm) pink marshmallows
half a cup of rice krispies

1. Put toffee bar and marshmallows in a bowl over a pan of gently simmering water. Leave to melt, stirring now and then.
2. Mix rice krispies into the melted mixture.
3. Spoon into six paper bun cases and leave to set. Eat the same day.

SULTANA SNOWBALLS
Makes 8

2oz (50gm) sultanas
4 bought sponge trifle cakes
1 can (6oz or 150gm) cream
4oz (100gm) desiccated coconut

1. Leave sultanas to soak in warm water for 1 hour. Drain.
2. Pound up or liquidize the trifle cakes.
3. Mix sultanas with the cake.
4. Stir in all but 3 tablespoons of the cream.
5. Form mixture into eight balls.
6. Coat balls with rest of cream.
7. Toss in coconut to cover completely and eat within 4 hours.

QUICKY STICKY CAKES
Makes 6

3oz (75gm) milk chocolate
3oz (75gm) plain chocolate
1 tablespoon golden syrup
1 cup cornflakes
1 can (11oz or 275gm) mandarin oranges
2 large, ripe bananas, mashed

1. Put all the chocolate in a bowl over a pan of gently simmering water. Leave until melted.
2. Stir in syrup and cornflakes.
3. Spoon mixture into six paper cake cases and spread round base and sides of cases. Leave to set.
4. Drain oranges and mix with the bananas. Spoon into chocolate cases and serve.

ORANGE BITES
Makes 8

4 bought trifle sponge cakes
strained juice of 1 small orange
2 tablespoons canned cream
5 tablespoons lemon curd
4oz (100gm) desiccated coconut

1. Pound or liquidize the cakes.
2. Mix the orange juice with the cream and 2 tablespoons lemon curd.
3. Mix in the cake crumbs.
4. Form the mixture into eight balls.
5. Spread rest of lemon curd round balls.
6. Toss in coconut to coat and eat the same day.

Biscuits

Home-baked biscuits are delicious – and quick – to make. They keep very well, too, if they are stored in an airtight tin.

COFFEE OBLONGS

Makes 12

8oz (200gm) plain flour
½ level teaspoon baking powder
4oz (100gm) margarine
2oz (50gm) caster sugar
1 large egg yolk
3 tablespoons extra strong black coffee, made with instant coffee and hot water

1. Preheat oven to moderate to moderately hot, 375 deg F or gas 5 (190 deg C).
2. Grease a shallow baking tin about 10 inches (25cm) by 6 inches (15cm).
3. Sift the flour with the baking powder.
4. Rub in the margarine until mixture resembles fine breadcrumbs.
5. Stir in the sugar.
6. Add enough egg yolk to mix to a stiff dough.
7. Add coffee to taste.
8. Press into prepared tin. Smooth the top and prick with a fork.
9. Bake in centre of the preheated oven for 20 minutes, or until golden and firm.
10. Leave in the tin to cool.
11. Cut into 12 equal-sized fingers.

PINEAPPLE OBLONGS

Makes 12

8oz (200gm) plain flour
½ level teaspoon baking powder
4oz (100gm) margarine
2oz (50gm) caster sugar
1 large egg yolk
pineapple milk shake syrup, to taste

1. Preheat oven to moderate to moderately hot, 375 deg F or gas 5 (190 deg C).
2. Grease a shallow baking tin about 10 inches (25cm) by 6 inches (15cm).
3. Sift the flour and the baking powder.
4. Rub in the margarine until mixture looks like fine breadcrumbs.
5. Stir in the sugar.
6. Add enough of the egg yolk to give a firm dough.
7. Add pineapple syrup, to taste.
8. Press into prepared tin and smooth the top.
9. Prick dough with a fork then bake in centre of preheated oven for 20 minutes, or until golden and firm.
10. Allow to cool in the tin.
11. Cut into 12 equal-sized fingers.

BOURBONS

Makes 6

6oz (150gm) plain flour
1oz (25gm) cocoa
½ level teaspoon baking powder
4oz (100gm) margarine
4oz (100gm) caster sugar
1 standard egg yolk
water, if necessary
vanilla essence
3oz (75gm) plain chocolate
caster sugar, to decorate

1. Preheat oven to hot, 425 deg F or gas 7 (220 deg C).
2. Grease a shallow tin about 10 inches (25cm) by 6 inches (15cm).
3. Sift the flour with the cocoa and baking powder. Do this three times.
4. Rub in the margarine until mixture resembles fine breadcrumbs.
5. Stir in the sugar.
6. Mix to a stiff dough with egg yolk, adding water only if needed.
7. Flavour to taste with vanilla essence.
8. Roll out to an oblong to fit the tin. Place in the tin.
9. Using a knife, mark into 12 equal oblongs.
10. Bake in the centre of the preheated oven for 10–15 minutes or until firm.
11. Leave to cool in the tin.
12. Cut into oblongs.
13. Put the chocolate in a bowl over a pan of gently simmering water until melted.
14. Spread chocolate on six of the oblongs. Put the plain oblongs on top. Leave to set.
15. Sift caster sugar over the tops of the biscuits and store in an airtight tin in the refrigerator.

CHOCOLATE FINGERS
Makes 12

8oz (200gm) plain flour
½ level teaspoon baking powder
4oz (100gm) margarine
2oz (50gm) caster sugar
1 large egg yolk
4oz (100gm) plain chocolate

1. Preheat oven to moderate to moderately hot, 375 deg F or gas 5 (190 deg C).
2. Grease a shallow baking tin about 10 inches (25cm) by 6 inches (15cm).
3. Sift the flour and baking powder.
4. Rub in the margarine until mixture resembles fine breadcrumbs.
5. Stir in sugar and enough egg yolk to give a firm dough.
6. Press mixture into tin and smooth the top. Prick with a fork.
7. Bake in the centre of the preheated oven for 20 minutes, or until pale golden and firm.
8. Leave in tin to cool.
9. Cut into 12 equal-sized fingers.
10. Put the chocolate in a bowl over a pan of gently simmering water until it melts.
11. Dip half of each finger biscuit in chocolate.
12. Leave to set and store for no longer than one day.

DIGESTIVE BISCUITS
Makes 10

6oz (150gm) plain flour
1 level teaspoon salt
1½oz (37gm) coarse oatmeal
1oz (25gm) caster sugar
½ level teaspoon baking powder
3oz (75gm) lard
milk to mix

1. Preheat oven to hot, 425 deg F or gas 7 (220 deg C).
2. Grease a baking sheet.
3. Thoroughly mix the flour, salt, oatmeal, sugar and baking powder.
4. Rub in the lard.
5. Add enough milk to mix to a firm dough.
6. Roll out quite thinly and cut into rounds with a large pastry cutter.
7. Put on prepared baking sheet.
8. Bake in centre of preheated oven for 12–15 minutes, or until pale golden.
9. Leave to cool. Store in an airtight tin and eat within a week.

CHOCOLATE DIGESTIVE BISCUITS
Makes 10

6oz (150gm) plain flour
1 level teaspoon salt
1½oz (37gm) coarse oatmeal
1oz (25gm) caster sugar
½ level teaspoon baking powder
3oz (75gm) lard
milk to mix
6oz (150gm) milk or plain chocolate

1. Preheat oven to hot, 425 deg F or gas 7 (220 deg C).
2. Grease a baking sheet.
3. Thoroughly mix the flour, salt, oatmeal, sugar and baking powder.
4. Using your fingertips, rub in the lard.
5. Mix in enough milk to make a firm dough.
6. Roll out quite thinly and cut into rounds using a large pastry cutter.
7. Put on prepared baking sheet.
8. Bake in centre of preheated oven for 12–15 minutes, or until pale golden.
9. Leave biscuits to cool on wire rack.
10. Put the chocolate in a bowl and put the bowl over a pan of gently simmering water until chocolate has melted.
11. Carefully spoon the melted chocolate on the tops of the biscuits, then, using the prongs of a fork, make a pattern. Leave to set.

DEMERARA BISCUITS
(Illustrated on page 69)
Makes 14

6oz (150gm) margarine
5oz (125gm) demerara sugar
1 tablespoon golden syrup
8oz (200gm) oatmeal (not the instant kind)
large pinch of salt
3oz (75gm) milk or plain chocolate

1. Preheat oven to moderate to moderately hot, 375 deg F or gas 5 (190 deg C).
2. Grease an oblong baking tin about 11 inches (28cm) by 7 inches (18cm).
3. Put the margarine in a pan and melt it over a gentle heat.
4. Stir the sugar into the margarine with the syrup, oatmeal and salt. Stir well.
5. Put mixture in prepared tin; smooth the top and bake in centre of preheated oven for 30 minutes, or until golden.
6. Bring out of oven, mark 14 neat oblongs with a knife and leave to cool in the tin.
7. Melt the chocolate in a basin over a pan of gently simmering water.
8. Cut the cooled mixture into 14 oblongs.
9. Dip half of each oblong into the liquid chocolate. Leave to become hard and set. Eat the same day.

CREAM OAT CRISPS
(Illustrated on page 36)
Makes 6

4oz (100gm) granulated sugar
1oz (25gm) margarine
1 large egg
3oz (75gm) oatmeal (not the instant kind)
½ level teaspoon baking powder
pinch of salt
vanilla essence to taste
1 small can of cream or ¼ pint (125ml) double cream

1. Preheat oven to moderate to moderately hot, 375 deg F or gas 5 (190 deg C).
2. Grease two large baking sheets.
3. Cream the sugar with the margarine until light and fluffy.
4. Add the egg, beating well.
5. Mix the oatmeal with the baking powder and salt. Stir into mixture.
6. Add vanilla essence to taste.
7. Drop mixture in heaped teaspoonfuls on to prepared baking sheets. Space very well apart.
8. Bake in centre of preheated oven for 10 minutes, or until firm to the touch.
9. Leave to cool on baking sheets for 2 minutes then turn out to complete cooling on a wire rack.
10. Drain any liquid off the cream. Whip it slightly and use to sandwich the biscuits together. Serve immediately.

LEMON FINGERS
Makes 12

8oz (200gm) plain flour
½ level teaspoon baking powder
4oz (100gm) margarine
2oz (50gm) caster sugar
1 large egg yolk
3oz (75gm) icing sugar
strained juice of a medium-sized lemon
edible yellow food colouring

1. Preheat oven to moderate to moderately hot, 375 deg F or gas 5 (190 deg C).
2. Grease a shallow tin about 10 inches (25cm) by 6 inches (15cm).
3. Sift the flour with the baking powder.
4. Rub in the margarine until mixture resembles fine breadcrumbs.
5. Stir in the sugar.
6. Mix in enough egg yolk to make a stiff dough.
7. Press into prepared tin. Smooth the top and prick with a fork.
8. Bake in the centre of the preheated oven for 20 minutes, or until pale golden and firm.
9. Leave in the tin to cool.
10. Cut into 12 equal-sized fingers.
11. Mix the icing sugar with enough lemon juice to give a mixture which will coat the back of a wooden spoon.
12. Colour icing a delicate yellow.
13. Dip half of each finger biscuit into the icing. Leave to set. Store in an airtight tin and eat within three days.

ORANGE COCONUT CREAMS
Makes 8

half a small can condensed milk
2 teaspoons orange squash
4oz (100gm) desiccated coconut

1. Preheat oven to moderately hot, 400 deg F or gas 6 (200 deg C).
2. Grease a baking sheet.
3. Mix all the ingredients until well blended.
4. Drop teaspoonfuls of the mixture on to the baking sheet.
5. Bake in centre of preheated oven for 10 minutes, or until firm and very lightly browned.
6. Leave to cool. Eat the same day.

PINK GRASS BISCUITS
Makes about 20

7oz (175gm) plain flour
5oz (125 gm) margarine
4oz (100gm) caster sugar
1 standard egg
4oz (100gm) plain chocolate
4oz (100gm) desiccated coconut
edible pink food colouring

1. Preheat oven to moderate to moderately hot, 375 deg F or gas 5 (190 deg C).
2. Grease two baking sheets.
3. Sift the flour into a bowl.
4. Rub in margarine until mixture resembles fine breadcrumbs.
5. Stir in caster sugar.
6. Add egg and work lightly to a firm dough.
7. Roll out, not too thinly.
8. Using a large plain pastry cutter, cut out 20 rounds.
9. Put on prepared baking sheets.
10. Bake in centre of preheated oven for 15 minutes, or until firm.
11. Leave to cool.
12. Put the chocolate in a bowl over a pan of gently simmering water and leave until chocolate has melted.
13. Coat one side of each biscuit with chocolate.
14. Mix the coconut with a tiny amount of pink colouring. Add a little to top of biscuits before the chocolate sets.

ORANGE SNACKS
Makes 8

6oz (150gm) self-raising flour
1oz (25gm) cocoa
7oz (175gm) margarine
4oz (100gm) caster sugar
1 small egg yolk, beaten
3oz (75gm) icing sugar, sifted
strained juice of 1 small orange
1 heaped teaspoon grated orange rind
1 teaspoon orange squash

1. Preheat oven to hot, 425 deg F or gas 7 (220 deg C).
2. Grease two baking sheets.
3. Sift the flour and cocoa twice.
4. Cream 4oz (100gm) margarine with caster sugar until light and fluffy.
5. Beat in the egg yolk.
6. Fold in flour mixture to give a firm dough and add a little water to bind if necessary.
7. Roll out dough fairly thinly.
8. Cut out 16 rounds using a large pastry cutter.
9. Put on prepared baking sheets.
10. Bake in centre of preheated over for 10–15 minutes, or until firm.
11. Leave to cool.
12. Beat icing sugar with rest of margarine until creamy.
13. Stir in the orange juice, rind and orange squash. Use mixture to sandwich biscuits in pairs. Store in an airtight tin and eat within four days.

CHOCOLATE FANCIES
(Illustrated on page 69)
Makes 26

10oz (250gm) plain flour
large pinch of salt
3oz (75gm) caster sugar
6oz (150gm) margarine
vanilla essence, to taste
½oz (12gm) cocoa

1. Preheat oven to moderate, 350 deg F or gas 4 (180 deg C).
2. Lightly grease two baking sheets.
3. Sift the flour and salt into a mixing bowl.
4. Stir in the sugar.
5. Cut the margarine into small pieces then rub into flour. Knead lightly until you have a smooth dough.
6. Divide the dough into two equal parts.
7. Knead a few drops of vanilla essence into half of the dough.
8. Knead the cocoa into the other half of the dough, making sure it is well blended.
9. Divide each piece of dough into half. Form each piece into an 8-inch roll.
10. Place a vanilla roll next to a chocolate roll, so they are side by side. Place a vanilla roll on top of the chocolate roll. Place the remaining chocolate roll on top of the vanilla roll.
11. Press all the dough lightly together so it is joined.
12. Cut the roll into 26 slices and put on prepared baking sheets.
13. Bake in centre of preheated oven for 25–30 minutes, or until firm. Leave to cool. Store in an airtight tin and eat within 10 days.

GARIBALDI BISCUITS
Makes 10

4oz (100gm) self-raising flour
large pinch of salt
1oz (25gm) margarine
1oz (25gm) caster sugar
milk to mix
3oz (75gm) currants

1. Preheat oven to moderately hot, 400 deg F or gas 6 (200 deg C).
2. Grease a baking sheet.
3. Sift the flour and salt into a bowl.
4. Rub in the margarine.
5. Stir in the sugar.
6. Add just enough milk to mix to a stiff dough.
7. Roll out dough on a floured surface to about ⅛-inch thickness. Roll to an oblong then cut into two equal squares.
8. Put one square on the baking sheet.
9. Chop currants finely and sprinkle on this square.
10. Put the other square on top.
11. Mark out into 10 biscuits.
12. Bake in the centre of the preheated oven for 15 minutes, or until golden.
13. Leave to cool, then cut into squares.

SHORTBREAD FANS
Makes 12

8oz (200gm) self-raising flour
4oz (100gm) margarine
4oz (100gm) caster sugar, plus a little extra for dusting
1 standard egg yolk, beaten

1. Preheat oven to moderate, 350 deg F or gas 4 (180 deg C).
2. Grease two small sandwich tins.
3. Sift the flour into a bowl.
4. Rub in the margarine until mixture resembles fine breadcrumbs.
5. Stir in 4oz (100gm) caster sugar.
6. Mix to a stiff dough with the egg yolk.
7. Divide the dough between the prepared tins and press them in well.
8. Smooth the tops and prick them with a fork.
9. Bake in centre of preheated oven for 20–25 minutes.
10. Cut into triangles while still in the tin. Cool on a wire rack.
11. Sprinkle with sugar and leave to cool. Store in an airtight tin.

CREAMY SHORTBREADS
Makes about 12

8oz (200gm) self-raising flour
4oz (100gm) margarine
4oz (100gm) caster sugar
1 small egg yolk, beaten
1 heaped tablespoon canned cream

1. Preheat oven to moderate, 350 deg F or gas 4 (180 deg C).
2. Grease two small sandwich tins.
3. Sift the flour into a bowl.
4. Rub in the margarine until mixture resembles breadcrumbs.
5. Stir in the sugar and enough egg to give a stiff dough.
6. Stir in the cream.
7. Press mixture into prepared tins. Smooth the tops and prick them with a fork.
8. Bake in centre of preheated oven for 20–25 minutes, or until golden and cooked.
9. Leave in tin and cut into triangles while still warm.
10. Leave to cool on a wire rack. Store in an airtight tin and eat within a week.

LEMONY SNAPS
Makes 20

4oz (100gm) margarine
4oz (100gm) caster sugar
1 large egg
8oz (200gm) plain flour
½ level teaspoon baking powder
large pinch of salt
1 heaped teaspoon grated lemon rind
1 tablespoon lemon juice

1. Cream margarine with caster sugar until light and fluffy.
2. Gradually beat in egg.
3. Sift the flour with baking powder and salt then stir in rind.
4. Using a metal spoon fold flour mixture into creamed mixture.
5. Stir in the lemon juice.
6. Put the mixture in a polythene bag and seal. Keep in the refrigerator for two hours.
7. Preheat oven to moderately hot, 400 deg F or gas 6 (200 deg C).
8. Grease two baking sheets.
9. Take dough out of bag and form into 20 balls.
10. Put on prepared baking sheets and flatten slightly.
11. Bake in centre of preheated oven for 10–15 minutes, or until golden and firm.
12. Leave to cool on cooling rack. Store in an airtight tin.

ICED FANS
Makes about 12

8oz (200gm) self-raising flour
4oz (100gm) margarine
4oz (100gm) caster sugar
1 small egg yolk, beaten
4oz (100gm) icing sugar, sifted
strained lemon juice, to mix
1 teaspoon grated lemon rind

1. Preheat oven to moderate, 350 deg F or gas 4 (180 deg C).
2. Grease two small sandwich tins.
3. Sift the flour into a bowl.
4. Rub in the margarine until mixture resembles fine breadcrumbs.
5. Stir in the sugar.
6. Add enough egg yolk to mix to a stiff dough.
7. Press into prepared tins.
8. Bake in centre of preheated oven for 20–25 minutes, or until golden.
9. Leave in the tin and cut into triangles while still warm.
10. Leave to cool on a wire rack.
11. Mix the sifted icing sugar with enough lemon juice to give an icing which will coat the back of a wooden spoon.
12. Stir lemon rind into icing.
13. Spoon icing on triangles and leave to set. Eat the same day.

APRICOT COOKIES
Makes about 20

7oz (175gm) plain flour
5oz (125gm) margarine
4oz (100gm) caster sugar
1 standard egg
3 heaped tablespoons apricot jam, sieved
3oz (75gm) desiccated coconut

1. Preheat oven to moderate to moderately hot, 375 deg F or gas 5 (190 deg C).
2. Grease two baking sheets.
3. Sift flour into a bowl.
4. Rub in margarine until mixture resembles fine breadcrumbs.
5. Stir in caster sugar.
6. Add beaten egg and work lightly to a firm dough.
7. Roll out, not too thinly.
8. Using a large plain pastry cutter, cut out 20 rounds.
9. Put on prepared baking sheets.
10. Bake in centre of preheated oven for 15 minutes, or until firm.
11. Leave to cool.
12. Spread jam on biscuits and then sprinkle with coconut.

JAMMY SNACKS
Makes about 20

7oz (175gm) plain flour
5oz (125gm) margarine
4oz (100gm) caster sugar
1 standard egg
3 heaped tablespoons raspberry jam
3 heaped tablespoons apricot jam

1. Preheat oven to moderate to moderately hot, 375 deg F or gas 5 (190 deg C).
2. Grease two baking sheets.
3. Sift flour into a bowl.
4. Rub in margarine until mixture resembles fine breadcrumbs.
5. Stir in sugar.
6. Add egg and mix lightly to make a firm dough.
7. Roll out, not too thinly.
8. Using a large plain pastry cutter, cut out 20 rounds. Put on prepared baking sheets.
9. Bake in centre of preheated oven for 15 minutes.
10. Heat jams, in separate pans, until runny and spoon into two greaseproof paper cones or small piping bags. (No nozzles are needed.)
11. Pipe a line of red jam down the middle of each biscuit. Fill in one half of the biscuit with red jam. Pipe a half circle of apricot jam. Leave to cool.

DATE DREAMS
Makes 8

4oz (100gm) margarine
2oz (50gm) caster sugar
1 standard egg
5oz (125gm) plain flour
2oz (50gm) desiccated coconut
2oz (50gm) dates, finely chopped

1. Preheat oven to moderate to moderately hot, 375 deg F or gas 5 (190 deg C).
2. Grease a baking sheet.
3. Cream the margarine with caster sugar until light and fluffy.
4. Gradually beat in the egg.
5. Sift the flour.
6. Using a metal spoon, fold flour, coconut and dates into creamed mixture.
7. Lightly knead then roll out thinly.
8. Using a large, plain pastry cutter, cut out eight rounds.
9. Put rounds on baking sheet.
10. Bake in centre of preheated oven for 15 minutes, or until firm.
11. Leave to cool on wire rack.

GINGER NUTS
Makes 8

4oz (100gm) margarine
4 tablespoons golden syrup
4oz (100gm) caster sugar
10oz (250gm) plain flour
2 level teaspoons ginger
$\frac{1}{4}$ level teaspoon bicarbonate of soda

1. Preheat oven to moderate to moderately hot, 375 deg F or gas 5 (190 deg C).
2. Grease a baking sheet.
3. Put the margarine in a small pan with syrup and sugar. Warm just a little then beat until creamy.
4. Sift the flour with the ginger and bicarbonate of soda.
5. Stir mixture into pan and mix to a stiff dough.
6. Form mixture into eight balls.
7. Place well apart on the baking sheet and flatten with the heel of hand.
8. Bake in centre of preheated oven for 15–20 minutes, or until firm. Leave to cool and store in an airtight tin.

CRISPY GINGERS
Makes 8

3oz (75gm) margarine
3oz (75gm) caster sugar
1 standard egg yolk
1oz (25gm) crystallized ginger, finely chopped
4oz (100gm) plain flour
$1\frac{1}{2}$ level teaspoons powdered ginger
a little milk
half a cup of cornflakes, lightly crushed

1. Preheat oven to moderately hot, 400 deg F or gas 6 (200 deg C).
2. Grease a baking sheet.
3. Cream margarine with caster sugar until light and fluffy.
4. Gradually beat in the egg yolk.
5. Stir in the chopped ginger.
6. Sift flour and powdered ginger and then fold it into creamed mixture.
7. Add a little milk to make a stiff consistency.
8. Form mixture into eight balls and roll them in cornflakes.
9. Put on prepared baking sheet.
10. Bake in centre of preheated oven for 15–20 minutes, or until firm.
11. Leave to cool then store them in an airtight tin.

GINGERBREAD MEN
(Illustrated on page 69)
Makes 12

If you have no gingerbread man cutter make a thin shape out of cardboard and cut round this with a knife.

5oz (125gm) plain flour
pinch of salt
$\frac{1}{2}$ level teaspoon ground ginger
$\frac{1}{4}$ level teaspoon bicarbonate of soda
$1\frac{1}{4}$ tablespoons golden syrup
$\frac{1}{2}$oz (12gm) caster sugar
1oz (25gm) margarine
half a medium egg, beaten
currants, angelica, glacé cherries and silver balls to decorate

1. Preheat oven to moderate, 350 deg F or gas 4 (180 deg C).
2. Lightly grease two large baking sheets.
3. Sift the flour with the salt, ginger and bicarbonate of soda.
4. Put the syrup, caster sugar and margarine in a pan and melt them over a gentle heat.
5. Cool slightly then stir into flour mixture.
6. Add enough of the egg to mix to a stiff dough.
7. Roll out dough thinly.
8. Cut into gingerbread men shapes with cutter or cut round cardboard shape with a knife.
9. Put the men on the prepared baking sheets. Give each a pair of currant eyes, an angelica smiling, upturned mouth and silver balls or chopped glacé cherries for buttons.
10. Bake in centre of preheated oven for 7–10 minutes, or until golden and firm to touch. Leave to cool. (These keep well if stored in an airtight tin.)

CRUNCHY GINGER NUTS
Makes 12

6oz (150gm) plain flour
large pinch of salt
2 level teaspoons ginger
1 level teaspoon mixed spice
½ level teaspoon cinnamon
2oz (50gm) margarine
4oz (100gm) soft brown sugar
1 tablespoon golden syrup

1. Preheat oven to moderate to moderately hot, 375 deg F or gas 5 (190 deg C).
2. Grease a baking sheet.
3. Sift the flour with the salt, ginger, spice and cinnamon.
4. Cream margarine with brown sugar until light and fluffy.
5. Put syrup over a gentle heat to warm it slightly.
6. Stir dry ingredients and creamed margarine into syrup to make a fairly stiff mixture, adding more syrup if needed.
7. Form into 12 balls and put on baking sheet. Flatten them with the heel of your hand.
8. Bake in centre of preheated oven for 15–20 minutes, or until brown and crisp.
9. Leave to cool.

CHOCOLATE GINGERS
Makes 12

5oz (125gm) plain flour
pinch of salt
½ level teaspoon ground ginger
¼ level teaspoon bicarbonate of soda
1¼ tablespoons golden syrup
½oz (12gm) caster sugar
1oz (25gm) margarine
half a medium egg, beaten
4oz (100gm) plain chocolate

1. Preheat oven to moderate, 350 deg F or gas 4 (180 deg C).
2. Lightly grease two baking sheets.
3. Sift the flour with the salt, ginger and bicarbonate of soda.
4. Put the syrup in a small pan with caster sugar and margarine. Heat gently until melted.
5. Cool slightly then stir into the flour mixture.
6. Add enough egg to mix to a stiff dough.
7. Roll out fairly thinly.
8. Using a large plain pastry cutter, cut out 12 rounds.
9. Put on prepared baking sheets.
10. Bake in centre of preheated oven for 7–10 minutes or until pale golden and firm.
11. Leave to cool.
12. Put the chocolate in a basin over a pan of gently simmering water and leave until melted.
13. Dip each biscuit in melted chocolate to coat it on one side only. Leave to set and eat them the same day.

GERMAN GINGERBREAD
Makes 8

These make lovely Christmas or Easter presents. Pipe a greeting on them in icing.

5oz (125gm) plain flour
pinch of salt
½ level teaspoon ground ginger
½ level teaspoon bicarbonate of soda
1¼ level tablespoons golden syrup
½oz (12gm) caster sugar
1oz (25gm) margarine
half a medium egg, beaten

1. Preheat oven to moderate, 350 deg F or gas 4 (180 deg C).
2. Lightly grease two baking sheets.
3. Sift flour with salt, ginger and bicarbonate of soda.
4. Put syrup in a pan with sugar and margarine. Heat gently until melted.
5. Leave mixture to cool slightly then stir it into the flour.
6. Add enough egg to mix to a stiff dough.
7. Roll out dough thinly.
8. Cut out eight heart shapes – make a pattern out of foil to cut around – and place them on baking sheets.
9. Bake in centre of preheated oven for 10 minutes, or until firm.
10. Leave to cool.
11. Pipe a greeting, in icing, on each, if wished.

DATE REFRIGERATOR COOKIES
Makes 10

5oz (125gm) margarine
6oz (150gm) caster sugar
1 standard egg
12oz (300gm) plain flour
1½oz (37gm) custard powder
½ level teaspoon baking powder
large pinch of salt
2oz (50gm) dates
milk, if needed

1. Cream margarine with sugar until light and fluffy.
2. Add the egg a little at a time, beating well.
3. Sift flour with custard, baking powder and salt; do this twice.
4. Chop up dates very finely.
5. Fold flour and dates into creamed mixture. Add a little milk if the mixture does not bind together firmly.
6. Form the dough into a neat, fat roll and wrap in foil.
7. Keep in refrigerator overnight.
8. Preheat oven to hot, 425 deg F or gas 7 (220 deg C).
9. Grease a baking sheet.
10. Unwrap the dough. Cut into 10 neat slices and lay them flat on a baking sheet.
11. Bake in centre of preheated oven for 5–7 minutes.
12. Leave cookies to cool and store them in an airtight tin.

RAISIN SNAPS
Makes 8

4oz (100gm) margarine
2oz (50gm) caster sugar
1 standard egg
5oz (125gm) plain flour
2oz (50gm) desiccated coconut
2oz (50gm) raisins, chopped

1. Preheat oven to moderate to moderately hot, 375 deg F or gas 5 (190 deg C).
2. Grease a baking sheet.
3. Cream margarine with caster sugar until light and fluffy.
4. Gradually beat in the egg.
5. Sift the flour.
6. Using a metal spoon, fold in flour and coconut.
7. Stir in raisins.
8. Knead lightly then roll out thinly.
9. Using a large, plain pastry cutter, cut out eight rounds.
10. Put on prepared baking sheet.
11. Bake in centre of preheated oven for 15 minutes.
12. Leave to cool on wire rack.

RUM BISCUITS
Makes 8

4oz (100gm) margarine
2oz (50gm) caster sugar
1 standard egg
5oz (125gm) plain flour
2 oz (50gm) desiccated coconut
rum essence, to taste

1. Preheat oven to moderate to moderately hot, 375 deg F or gas 5 (190 deg C).
2. Grease a baking sheet.
3. Cream the margarine with caster sugar until light and fluffy.
4. Gradually beat in the egg.
5. Sift the flour.
6. Using a metal spoon, fold flour and desiccated coconut into creamed mixture.
7. Flavour to taste with a tiny amount of rum essence.
8. Lightly knead, then roll out thinly.
9. Using a large, plain pastry cutter, cut out eight rounds.
10. Put on prepared baking sheet.
11. Bake in centre of preheated oven for 15 minutes or until golden.
12. Leave to cool.

JELLY SANDWICHES
Makes 6

4oz (100gm) caster sugar
1oz (25gm) margarine
1 large egg
3oz (75gm) oatmeal (not instant kind)
1 level teaspoon baking powder
pinch of salt
3 heaped tablespoons redcurrant jelly

1. Preheat oven to moderate to moderately hot, 375 deg F or gas 5 (190 deg C).
2. Grease a baking sheet.
3. Cream the sugar and margarine until light and fluffy.
4. Gradually beat in the egg.
5. Fold in oats, baking powder and salt.
6. Drop mixture in teaspoonfuls on prepared baking sheet, spacing them well apart.
7. Bake in centre of preheated oven for 10 minutes. Cool on baking sheet for 2 minutes.
8. Leave to cool completely on wire rack.
9. Sandwich with recurrant jelly and eat the same day.

SPICY BISCUITS
Makes 24

3oz (75gm) plain flour
1oz (25gm) cornflour
½ level teaspoon baking powder
2 level teaspoons ground ginger
1 level teaspoon ground cinnamon
1 level teaspoon ground cloves
2oz (50gm) margarine
2oz (50gm) soft brown sugar
1 tablespoon golden syrup

1. Grease two large baking sheets.
2. Sift the flour with the cornflour, baking powder, ginger, cinnamon and cloves.
3. Cream the margarine with the sugar until very light and fluffy.
4. Beat in the syrup.
5. Fold flour into creamed mixture.
6. Cover the bowl tightly and leave in the refrigerator for 30 minutes.
7. Preheat oven to moderate, 350 deg F or gas 4 (180 deg C).
8. Form the mixture into 24 balls each the size of a large walnut. Flatten them slightly and put on prepared baking sheets.
9. Cook in the centre of the preheated oven for 20 minutes.
10. Leave on baking sheet for 5 minutes then finish cooling on a wire rack. Store in an airtight tin and eat within 10 days.

CHERRY CUSHIONS
Makes 24

4oz (100gm) margarine
4oz (100gm) caster sugar
1 large egg
8oz (200gm) plain flour
½ level teaspoon baking powder
large pinch of salt
1½oz (37gm) chopped glacé cherries, plus 12 whole ones

1. Cream margarine and caster sugar until light and fluffy.
2. Gradually beat in the egg.
3. Sift the flour with the baking powder and salt.
4. Using a metal spoon, fold flour into creamed mixture.
5. Stir in chopped cherries.
6. Wrap the dough in foil and leave in refrigerator to chill for two hours.
7. Preheat oven to moderately hot, 400 deg F or gas 6 (200 deg C).
8. Grease two baking sheets.
9. Unwrap the dough and form it into 24 balls. Flatten a little.
10. Cut each cherry in half and put a cherry, rounded part up, on each biscuit.
11. Bake in centre of preheated oven for 10–15 minutes, or until firm.
12. Leave to cool on wire rack. Store in an airtight tin and eat within two days.

JAM CIRCLES
(Illustrated on page 70)
Makes 15

7oz (175gm) plain flour
large pinch of salt
5oz (125gm) margarine
4oz (100gm) caster sugar
1 standard egg, beaten
1½oz (37gm) icing sugar
3 heaped tablespoons raspberry jam

1. Preheat oven to moderate to moderately hot, 375 deg F or gas 5 (190 deg C).
2. Grease two baking sheets.
3. Sift flour and salt into a bowl.
4. Rub in margarine until the mixture resembles fine breadcrumbs.
5. Stir in the caster sugar.
6. Add the beaten egg and work lightly to a firm dough.
7. Roll out thinly.
8. Using a 2½-inch (6cm) fluted cutter, cut out 15 rounds.
9. Remove centre of each round with a smaller cutter. Re-roll centres and cut out 15 rounds – do not remove the centres from these.
10. Put all the biscuits on the prepared baking sheets and bake in centre of preheated oven for 15 minutes or until golden.
11. Cool the biscuits.
12. Sift the icing sugar and sprinkle it on the biscuit rings.
13. Sandwich biscuits in pairs with the rings on top using a little of the jam. Carefully spoon or pipe the rest of the jam into the centre of each biscuit sandwich.
14. Store in an airtight tin and eat within three days.

JAM FAVOURITES
Makes 6

4oz (100gm) margarine
4oz (100gm) caster sugar
1 standard egg
8oz (200gm) plain flour
1oz (25gm) custard powder
3 heaped tablespoons raspberry jam

1. Preheat oven to very moderate, 325 deg F or gas 3 (170 deg C).
2. Grease two baking sheets.
3. Cream margarine with caster sugar until light and fluffy.
4. Beat in the egg.
5. Sift flour and custard powder.
6. Using a metal spoon, fold flour mixture into creamed mixture.
7. Put mixture in a large piping bag fitted with a large plain nozzle.
8. Pipe 12 large blobs on the prepared baking sheets. Flatten them slightly with a knife blade.
9. Bake in centre of preheated oven for 15 minutes, or until firm,
10. Leave to cool.
11. Sandwich with jam, in pairs.

ALMOND BALLS
Makes 8

3oz (75gm) margarine
1½oz (37gm) caster sugar
2 tablespoons golden syrup
3oz (75gm) oatmeal (not the instant kind)
3oz (75gm) plain flour
good pinch of salt
¼ level teaspoon baking powder
almond essence, to taste

1. Preheat oven to moderately hot, 400 deg F or gas 6 (200 deg C).
2. Grease a baking sheet.
3. Cream the margarine with the caster sugar until light and fluffy.
4. Stir syrup into creamed mixture, mixing well.
5. Mix oatmeal with flour, salt and baking powder and gradually work into creamed mixture.
6. Flavour, to taste, with almond.
7. Form into eight balls and put on prepared baking sheet.
8. Bake in centre of preheated oven for 10–15 minutes, or until golden and firm.
9. Leave to cool and store in an airtight tin.

SPICY BARS
Makes 12

6oz (150gm) inexpensive stoned dates
8oz (200gm) plain flour
large pinch of salt
½ level teaspoon mixed spice
½ level teaspoon grated nutmeg
¼ level teaspoon bicarbonate of soda
6oz (150gm) margarine
4oz (100gm) soft brown sugar
2 tablespoons treacle
2 large eggs, beaten
6oz (150gm) icing sugar, sifted
3 tablespoons orange squash mixed with 3 tablespoons water

1. Preheat oven to moderate, 350 deg F or gas 4 (180 deg C).
2. Grease a 10-inch (25cm) square, shallow cake tin. Line base of tin with greaseproof paper.
3. Finely chop the dates.
4. Sift the flour with the salt, mixed spice, nutmeg and the bicarbonate of soda.
5. Rub in 3oz (75gm) margarine.
6. Stir in the brown sugar and the dates.
7. Warm the treacle in a small pan. Do not let it boil.
8. Cool treacle slightly then add to flour mixture with the eggs and mix well.
9. Turn mixture into prepared tin and smooth the top.
10. Bake in the centre of the preheated oven for 35 minutes, or until firm.
11. Cool in the tin for 5 minutes then turn out and cut into equal-sized oblongs and leave to complete cooling on a wire rack.
12. Beat the rest of the margarine with the icing sugar and the orange squash.
13. Spread some of the icing over each bar and mark a pattern with the prongs of a fork. Store in an airtight tin and eat within a week.

PLAIN BISCUITS
Makes 18

4oz (100gm) margarine
4oz (100gm) caster sugar
1 large egg
8oz (200gm) plain flour, sifted
½ level teaspoon baking powder
vanilla essence
milk to mix
caster sugar, to decorate

1. Preheat oven to moderately hot, 400 deg F or gas 6 (200 deg C).
2. Grease two baking sheets.
3. Cream margarine with caster sugar until light and fluffy.
4. Gradually beat in the egg.
5. Sift the flour with the baking powder.
6. Using a metal spoon, fold flour into creamed mixture.
7. Add vanilla, to taste, and enough milk to give a firm dough.
8. Roll out fairly thinly and cut out 18 rounds with a large, fluted pastry cutter.
9. Put on prepared baking sheets.
10. Bake in centre of preheated oven for 10–15 minutes, or until golden and firm.
11. Leave to cool then sprinkle sugar on the top.

CINNAMON BISCUITS
Makes 18

4oz (100gm) margarine
4oz (100gm) caster sugar
1 large egg
8oz (200gm) plain flour
½ level teaspoon baking powder
1 level teaspoon cinnamon

1. Preheat oven to moderately hot, 400 deg F or gas 6 (200 deg C).
2. Grease two baking sheets.
3. Cream margarine with caster sugar until light and fluffy.
4. Gradually beat in egg.
5. Sift flour with baking powder and cinnamon.
6. Using a metal spoon, fold into creamed mixture.
7. Roll out fairly thinly and cut out plain rounds using a large pastry cutter.
8. Put on prepared baking sheets.
9. Bake in centre of preheated oven for 10–15 minutes, or until firm to the touch.
10. Leave to cool and store in an airtight tin.

COCONUT BISCUITS
(Illustrated on page 69)
Makes 10

4oz (100gm) margarine
2oz (50gm) caster sugar
1 standard egg
5oz (125gm) plain flour, sifted
5oz (125gm) desiccated coconut
2 tablespoons apricot jam
edible pink food colouring
5 glacé cherries

1. Preheat oven to moderate to moderately hot, 375 deg F or gas 5 (190 deg C).
2. Grease a baking sheet.
3. Beat the margarine with the sugar until mixture is light and fluffy.
4. Add the egg and beat well.
5. Using a metal spoon, fold in the flour and 2oz (50gm) of the desiccated coconut.
6. Lightly knead the mixture then roll out very thinly.
7. Cut mixture into 10 rounds and put on prepared baking sheet.
8. Bake in centre of preheated oven for 15 minutes, or until golden.
9. Leave biscuits to cool.
10. Warm jam with 1 tablespoon water then sieve it and brush on tops of biscuits.
11. Mix a tiny amount of colouring with 1 tablespoon water. Stir this into the remaining coconut to colour it a delicate pink.
12. Put the coloured coconut on the top of the biscuits.
13. Decorate each biscuit with half a glacé cherry.

CANDIED PEEL COOKIES
Makes 20

4oz (100gm) margarine
4oz (100gm) caster sugar
1 large egg
8oz (200gm) plain flour
½ level teaspoon baking powder
large pinch of salt
2oz (50gm) chopped candied peel

1. Cream margarine and sugar until light and fluffy.
2. Gradually beat in the egg.
3. Sift the flour with baking powder and salt.
4. Using a metal spoon, fold into creamed mixture.
5. Fold in peel, lightly but thoroughly.
6. Wrap dough in foil and leave in refrigerator for two hours.
7. Preheat oven to moderately hot, 400 deg F or gas 6 (200 deg F).
8. Grease two baking sheets.
9. Unwrap dough and form into 20 balls.
10. Put on prepared baking sheets and flatten slightly.
11. Bake in centre of preheated oven for 10–15 minutes, or until firm and golden.
12. Leave to cool and store in an airtight tin.

TEXAS COOKIES
Makes 10

5oz (125gm) soft margarine
6oz (150gm) caster sugar
1 standard egg
few drops vanilla essence
12oz (300gm) plain flour
½ level teaspoon baking powder
large pinch of salt
1½oz (37gm) cocoa
1oz (25gm) plain chocolate
milk, if needed

1. Cream margarine with sugar until light and fluffy.
2. Gradually beat in the egg.
3. Mix in the vanilla essence.
4. Sift the flour with the baking powder, salt and cocoa. Do this twice.
5. Put the chocolate in a bowl over a pan of gently simmering water until melted.
6. Stir melted chocolate into creamed mixture.
7. Using a metal spoon fold in sifted flour mixture.
8. Mixture should bind firmly together; if not, add a little milk.
9. Form the dough into a neat fat roll. Wrap it in foil and leave overnight in the refrigerator.
10. Preheat oven to hot, 425 deg F or gas 7 (220 deg C).
11. Grease a baking sheet.
12. Unwrap the dough and cut into 10 neat slices.
13. Lay slices flat on the baking sheet.
14. Bake in centre of preheated oven for 5–7 minutes, or until firm.
15. Leave to cool and store in an airtight tin.

TANGY ORANGE ROUNDS
Makes 12

4oz (100gm) margarine
4oz (100gm) caster sugar
1 standard egg
9oz (225gm) plain flour
pinch of salt
1 level teaspoon grated orange rind
1 dessertspoon orange juice

1. Preheat oven to very moderate, 325 deg F or gas 3 (170 deg C).
2. Grease two baking sheets.
3. Cream the margarine with the caster sugar until light and fluffy.
4. Beat in the egg.
5. Sift the flour and salt, then stir in the rind.
6. Using a metal spoon, fold flour mixture into creamed mixture.
7. Stir in orange juice.
8. Knead lightly then roll out thinly.
9. Using a large plain pastry cutter, cut out 12 rounds.
10. Bake in centre of preheated oven for 15 minutes, or until firm.
11. Leave to cool.

GRANTHAMS
Makes 14

8oz (200gm) margarine
8oz (200gm) caster sugar
1 small egg
8oz (200gm) plain flour
¼ level teaspoon bicarbonate of soda
2oz (50gm) desiccated coconut
2 level tablespoons cocoa

1. Preheat oven to cool, 300 deg F or gas 2 (150 deg C).
2. Grease a large baking sheet.
3. Cream the margarine with the caster sugar until light and fluffy.
4. Beat egg and add gradually to the creamed mixture.
5. Sift flour and bicarbonate of soda.
6. Thoroughly mix coconut and cocoa.
7. Stir flour into creamed mixture.
8. Add coconut mixture and blend well.
9. Knead mixture lightly; form into 14 balls and put on baking sheet.
10. Bake in centre of preheated oven for 35–45 minutes, or until firm. Leave to cool.

ORANGE CREAMS
Makes 20

7oz (175gm) plain flour
large pinch of salt
8oz (200gm) margarine
4oz (100gm) caster sugar
1 standard egg
3oz (75gm) icing sugar
orange squash, to taste
1 tablespoon canned cream

1. Preheat oven to moderate to moderately hot, 375 deg F or gas 5 (190 deg C).
2. Grease two baking sheets.
3. Sift the flour and salt into a bowl.
4. Rub in 5oz (125gm) margarine until the mixture resembles fine breadcrumbs.
5. Stir in the caster sugar.
6. Add beaten egg and work lightly to a firm dough.
7. Roll out dough to a thin round and, using a plain, medium-sized pastry cutter, cut out 40 rounds.
8. Put biscuits on prepared baking sheets.
9. Bake in centre of preheated oven for 15 minutes, or until golden.
10. Leave to cool.
11. Beat the rest of the margarine with the sifted icing sugar until light and fluffy.
12. Flavour to taste with orange squash, then stir in the cream.
13. Use the icing to sandwich the biscuits together. Eat that day.

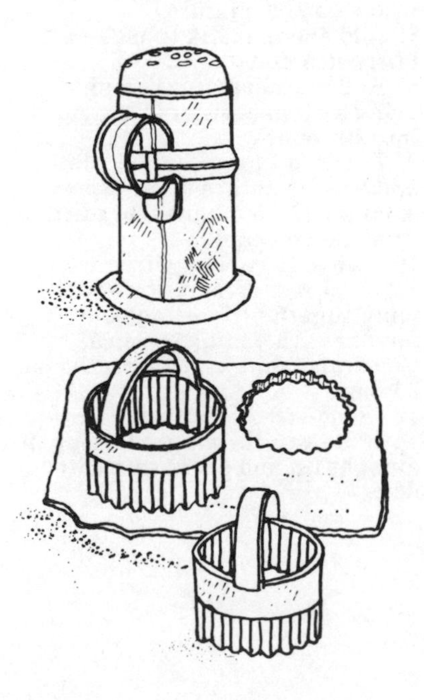

GRANNY'S BISCUITS
Makes 12

8oz (200gm) plain flour
large pinch of salt
½ level teaspoon mixed spice
½ level teaspoon grated nutmeg
¼ level teaspoon bicarbonate of soda
3oz (75gm) margarine
4oz (100gm) soft brown sugar
6oz (150gm) sultanas
2 tablespoons treacle
2 large eggs, beaten

1. Preheat oven to moderate, 350 deg F or gas 4 (180 deg C).
2. Grease a 10-inch (25cm) shallow, square cake tin. Line base and sides of tin with greaseproof paper.
3. Sift the flour with the salt, spice, nutmeg and bicarbonate of soda.
4. Rub in margarine until mixture resembles fine breadcrumbs.
5. Stir in brown sugar and the sultanas.
6. Warm the treacle in a small pan taking care not to let it boil.
7. Let the treacle cool slightly then add it to the flour mixture with the eggs. Mix well.
8. Turn mixture into prepared tin and smooth the top.
9. Bake in centre of preheated oven for 35 minutes, or until firm and golden.
10. Allow to cool in tin for 5 minutes then turn out and cut into 12 equal-sized oblongs.
11. Leave to cool on a wire rack.

MOCHA DELIGHTS
Makes 12

4oz (100gm) margarine
4oz (100gm) caster sugar
1 standard egg
8oz (200gm) plain flour
1oz (25gm) cocoa
1 level dessertspoon instant coffee powder
pinch of salt
1 dessertspoon milk

1. Preheat oven to very moderate, 325 deg F or gas 3 (170 deg C).
2. Grease two baking sheets.
3. Cream margarine with caster sugar until light and fluffy.
4. Gradually beat in the egg.
5. Sift the flour with cocoa, coffee powder and salt. Do this twice.
6. Using a metal spoon, fold flour mixture into creamed mixture.
7. Stir in the milk.
8. Put the mixture in a large piping bag fitted with a large star nozzle.
9. Pipe stars on prepared baking sheets.
10. Bake in centre of the preheated oven for 15 minutes or until firm.
11. Leave biscuits to cool.

FRUITY SNACKS
Makes 12

4oz (100gm) margarine
4oz (100gm) caster sugar
1 standard egg
8oz (200gm) plain flour
1oz (25gm) cocoa
pinch of salt
3oz (75gm) currants and sultanas mixed together
2 dessertspoons milk

1. Preheat oven to very moderate 325 deg F or gas 3 (170 deg C).
2. Grease two baking sheets.
3. Cream the margarine with the caster sugar until light and fluffy.
4. Gradually beat in the egg.
5. Sift the flour, cocoa and salt; do this twice.
6. Fold flour mixture into the creamed mixture with a metal spoon.
7. Mix in fruit and milk.
8. Knead lightly then roll out thinly.
9. Using a large pastry cutter, cut out 12 rounds.
10. Place rounds on the baking sheets.
11. Bake in the centre of the preheated oven for 15 minutes, or until firm.
12. Leave to cool.

FEATHER FANCIES
Makes 12

4oz (100gm) margarine
4oz (100gm) caster sugar
1 standard egg
9oz (225gm) plain flour
1 dessertspoon milk
8oz (200gm) icing sugar
1½ level teaspoons cocoa

1. Preheat oven to very moderate, 325 deg F or gas 3 (170 deg C).
2. Grease two baking sheets.
3. Cream the margarine with the caster sugar until light and fluffy.
4. Beat in the egg.
5. Using a metal spoon, fold flour into creamed mixture.
6. Stir in the milk to mix to a stiff dough.
7. Knead mixture lightly then roll out to a large round.
8. Using a large, plain pastry cutter, cut into 12 rounds.
9. Put on prepared baking sheets.
10. Bake in centre of preheated oven for 15 minutes, or until golden and firm to the touch.
11. Leave biscuits to cool.
12. Mix 6oz (150gm) sifted icing sugar with enough water to give a mixture which will coat the back of a wooden spoon.
13. Spoon icing on to biscuits.
14. Before this icing is set, mix rest of icing sugar with cocoa and enough water to make a soft piping consistency. Put in a piping bag fitted with a writing nozzle.
15. Pipe lines across each biscuit, spacing them well apart. Draw a skewer or knitting needle across the lines to give a feathered effect.

RASPBERRY PEPPERMINT STARS
Makes 12

These are ideal to serve at a children's party.

4oz (100gm) margarine
4oz (100gm) caster sugar
1 standard egg
8oz (200gm) plain flour
1oz (25gm) custard powder
1 tablespoon raspberry milk shake syrup
12 small whole round soft peppermint sweets

1. Preheat oven to very moderate, 325 deg F or gas 3 (170 deg C).
2. Grease two baking sheets.
3. Cream margarine with caster sugar until light and fluffy.
4. Beat in the egg.
5. Sift flour and custard powder. Using a metal spoon, fold it into the creamed mixture.
6. Stir in the raspberry syrup.
7. Put mixture in a large piping bag fitted with a large star nozzle.
8. Pipe 12 stars on to prepared baking sheets.
9. Bake in centre of preheated oven for 15 minutes, or until firm.
10. Leave to cool.
11. Put a sweet on each biscuit.

VANILLA RINGS
Makes 10

2oz (50gm) margarine
2oz (50gm) caster sugar
1 small egg
3oz (75gm) plain flour
1oz (25gm) cornflour
½ level teaspoon baking powder
large pinch of salt
vanilla essence, to taste
3oz (75gm) icing sugar
1 heaped tablespoon hundreds and thousands

1. Preheat oven to hot, (425 deg F or gas 7 (220 deg F).
2. Grease a large baking sheet.
3. Cream the margarine with caster sugar until light and fluffy.
4. Gradually beat in the egg.
5. Sift flour with cornflour, baking powder and salt. Do this twice.
6. Using a metal spoon, fold flour mixture into creamed mixture.
7. Add vanilla essence, to taste.
8. Put the mixture in a large piping bag fitted with a large star nozzle.
9. Pipe 10 rings on the prepared baking sheet.
10. Bake in centre of preheated oven for 7–10 minutes, or until golden and firm.
11. Leave to cool.
12. Mix the sifted icing sugar with enough cold water to give a mixture which will coat the back of a wooden spoon.
13. Spoon icing on top of the rings then sprinkle the hundreds and thousands on top. Leave to set and store in an airtight tin.

CUSTARD CREAMS
Makes 8

6oz (150gm) margarine
4oz (100gm) caster sugar
1 standard egg yolk
4oz (100gm) self-raising flour, sifted
4oz (100gm) custard powder
milk to mix
2oz (50gm) icing sugar
vanilla essence, to taste

1. Preheat oven to hot, 425 deg F or gas 7 (220 deg C).
2. Grease two baking sheets.
3. Cream 4oz (100gm) margarine with caster sugar until light and fluffy.
4. Gradually beat in egg yolk.
5. Sift the flour and custard powder; do this twice.
6. Using a metal spoon, fold it into creamed mixture.
7. Add enough milk to make a fairly stiff dough.
8. Roll out fairly thinly and, using a plain pastry cutter, cut into 16 rounds.
9. Put on prepared baking sheets and bake in centre of preheated oven for 10–15 minutes, or until firm and golden.
10. Leave to cool on wire rack.
11. Beat rest of margarine with icing sugar until creamy and flavour with vanilla essence. Cover and chill in refrigerator for 2 hours.
12. Sandwich biscuits in pairs with the vanilla icing. Store in an airtight tin and eat within three days.

CHOCOLATE PROMISES
Makes 16

8oz (200gm) margarine
8oz (200gm) caster sugar
2 large eggs
15oz (375 gm) self-raising flour
large pinch of salt
4 level tablespoons cocoa
vanilla essence
milk, if needed

1. Preheat oven to moderately hot, 400 deg F or gas 6 (200 deg C).
2. Grease two baking sheets.
3. Cream the margarine with the caster sugar until light and fluffy.
4. Beat the eggs and gradually add to creamed mixture, beating well.
5. Sift the flour with salt and cocoa; do this twice.
6. Using a metal spoon, fold flour into creamed mixture.
7. Add the vanilla and, if needed, a little milk to give a firm piping consistency.
8. Put mixture in a large piping bag fitted with a fairly small plain pipe and pipe a line about 3 inches long on a baking sheet. Then pipe five more lines, close together so they join up when cooked.
9. Use up rest of mixture in same way.
10. Bake in the centre of the preheated oven for 10–15 minutes, or until firm.
11. Leave to cool.

CHOCOLATE STARS
Makes 24

4oz (100gm) margarine
4oz (100gm) caster sugar
1 standard egg
8oz (200gm) plain flour
1oz (25gm) cocoa
pinch of salt
vanilla or rum essence, to taste
1 dessertspoon milk

1. Preheat oven to very moderate 325 deg F or gas 3 (170 deg C).
2. Grease two baking sheets.
3. Cream the margarine with the caster sugar until very light and fluffy.
4. Beat in the egg.
5. Sift flour, cocoa and salt twice then fold into creamed mixture using a metal spoon.
6. Add vanilla or rum essence, to taste.
7. Stir in the milk.
8. Put the mixture into a large piping bag fitted with a large star nozzle.
9. Pipe stars on prepared baking sheets.
10. Bake in centre of preheated oven for 15 minutes, or until firm.
11. Leave biscuits to cool, then store in an airtight tin.

MINIATURE STAR BISCUITS
Makes 12

4oz (100gm) margarine
4oz (100gm) caster sugar
1 standard egg
8oz (200gm) plain flour
1oz (25gm) custard powder
3oz (75gm) icing sugar
edible orange food colouring
tiny pieces of crystallized orange

1. Preheat oven to very moderate, 325 deg F or gas 3 (170 deg C).
2. Grease two baking sheets.
3. Cream margarine with caster sugar until light and fluffy.
4. Beat in the egg.
5. Sift flour and custard powder.
6. Using a metal spoon, fold flour mixture into creamed mixture.
7. Put mixture in a large piping bag fitted with a large star nozzle.
8. Pipe stars on prepared baking sheets.
9. Bake in centre of preheated oven for 15 minutes, or until firm.
10. Leave to cool.
11. Mix icing sugar with enough water to give a mixture which will coat the back of a wooden spoon.
12. Colour icing pale orange and spoon it on to biscuits.
13. Decorate with crystallized orange pieces and leave to set.

CHOCOLATE CAPERS
Makes 10

4oz (100gm) margarine
4oz (100gm) caster sugar
1 large egg
7oz (175gm) plain flour
1oz (25gm) cocoa
½ level teaspoon baking powder
large pinch of salt
small sachet powdered creamy topping
milk to mix
1oz (25gm) plain chocolate, chopped

1. Preheat oven to moderately hot, 400 deg F or gas 6 (200 deg C).
2. Grease two baking sheets.
3. Cream the margarine with the caster sugar until light and fluffy.
4. Gradually beat in egg.
5. Sift flour with cocoa, baking powder and salt. Do this twice.
6. Using a metal spoon, fold into creamed mixture.
7. Put into a piping bag fitted with a large star nozzle.
8. Pipe 20 flat swirls on the prepared baking sheets.
9. Bake in the centre of the preheated oven for 10–15 minutes, or until firm.
10. Leave to cool.
11. Make up the creamy topping as directed on the packet, but using a little less milk to make it as stiff as possible.
12. Stir chocolate into the creamy topping and use to sandwich biscuits together in pairs. Serve immediately, once the filling has been added.

Scones

Scones with jam and cream bring back memories of old-fashioned English teas. Try all these delicious variations – they're simple enough for children to make.

CORNISH SCONES

(Illustrated on page 70)

Makes 7

8oz (200gm) self-raising flour
large pinch of salt
2oz (50gm) margarine
1oz (25gm) caster sugar
1 large egg, beaten
milk to mix
1 carton Cornish clotted cream or ¼ pint (125ml) fresh double cream, whipped
strawberry jam

1. Preheat oven to hot, 450 deg F or gas 8 (230 deg C).
2. Lightly grease a baking sheet.
3. Sift the flour with the salt into a bowl.
4. Rub in the margarine.
5. Stir in sugar.
6. Add egg and enough milk to give soft, light dough.
7. Roll out to at least ½-inch thickness.
8. Using a large plain pastry cutter, cut out seven rounds.
9. Bake in centre of preheated oven for 10–15 minutes, or until golden and firm.
10. Leave to cool.
11. Sandwich with cream and jam.

MANDARIN SCONES

Makes 8

8oz (200gm) self-raising flour
large pinch of salt
4oz (100gm) margarine
1oz (25gm) caster sugar
1 large egg, beaten
milk to mix
half an 11oz (275gm) can mandarin oranges
3oz (75gm) icing sugar, sifted
2 teaspoons orange squash
4 teaspoons apricot jam

1. Preheat oven to hot, 450 deg F or gas 8 (230 deg C).
2. Lightly grease a baking sheet.
3. Sift the flour with the salt into a mixing bowl.
4. Rub in half the margarine.
5. Stir in the caster sugar.
6. Add the beaten egg and enough milk to give a soft, light dough.
7. Roll out the dough to at least ½-inch thickness. Trim dough to a neat square.
8. Cut the dough into four squares then cut each square in half to make two triangles.
9. Put on the prepared baking sheet and bake in centre of preheated oven for 10–15 minutes.
10. Leave scones to cool on a wire rack.
11. Drain the canned fruit and then beat the rest of the margarine with 1 tablespoon of the canned fruit juice. (The rest of the juice will not be needed.)
12. Add the icing sugar and orange squash and beat well.
13. Mix in the fruit.
14. Use the fruit mixture to sandwich the split scones together.
15. Put the jam in a small pan with 2 teaspoons water. Heat gently then sieve and brush over the top of the scones. Eat the same day.

ICED SCONES

Makes 7

8 glacé cherries
8oz (200gm) self-raising flour
large pinch of salt
2oz (50gm) margarine
1oz (25gm) caster sugar
1 large egg, beaten
milk to mix
3oz (75gm) icing sugar, sifted

1. Preheat oven to hot, 450 deg F or gas 8 (230 deg C).
2. Lightly grease a baking sheet.
3. Reserve three and a half cherries. Finely chop the rest.
4. Sift the flour with the salt into a mixing bowl.
5. Rub the margarine into the flour.
6. Stir in the chopped cherries and caster sugar.
7. Add the beaten egg and enough milk to mix to a soft, light dough.
8. Roll out the dough to at least ½-inch thickness.
9. Using a plain 2-inch (5cm) cutter, cut out seven rounds.
10. Put the rounds on a baking sheet and bake in centre of oven for 10–15 minutes or until golden.
11. Leave scones to cool on wire rack.
12. Mix the icing sugar with enough water to make a mixture which will thickly coat the back of a wooden spoon.
13. Carefully spoon some icing on the top of each scone.
14. Decorate with half a cherry. Leave to set and eat that day.

GINGER SCONES
(Illustrated on page 70)
Makes 7

8oz (200gm) self-raising flour
large pinch of salt
1 level teaspoon powdered ginger
2oz (50gm) margarine
1oz (25gm) caster sugar
1 large egg, beaten
milk to mix
1 small can cream or ¼ pint (125ml) fresh double cream, whipped
2 or 3 lumps crystallized ginger or stem ginger

1. Preheat oven to hot, 450 deg F or gas 8 (230 deg C).
2. Lightly grease a baking sheet.
3. Sift the flour with salt and powdered ginger into a bowl. Do this twice.
4. Rub in the margarine.
5. Stir in the sugar.
6. Add the beaten egg and just enough milk to mix to a soft, light dough.
7. Roll out the dough to at least ½-inch thickness.
8. Using a 2-inch (5cm) plain cutter, cut out seven rounds.
9. Put the rounds on the baking sheet and bake in centre of preheated oven for 10–15 minutes, or until golden.
10. Leave scones to cool on wire rack.
11. Split the scones in half.
12. Drain any liquid off the can of cream. Whip slightly.
13. Chop the ginger and stir it into the cream.
14. Sandwich scones with the ginger cream and eat that day.

SCONES IN A RING
Gives 7 portions

8oz (200gm) self-raising flour
large pinch of salt
2oz (50gm) margarine
1oz (25gm) caster sugar
2oz (50gm) dates, chopped
1 large egg, beaten
milk to mix

1. Preheat oven to hot, 450 deg F or gas 8 (230 deg C).
2. Lightly grease a baking sheet.
3. Sift the flour with the salt into a bowl.
4. Rub in the margarine.
5. Stir in the sugar and dates.
6. Add the beaten egg and just enough milk to mix to a soft, light dough.
7. Roll out the dough to at least ½-inch thickness.
8. Using a plain 2-inch (5cm) pastry cutter, cut out seven rounds.
9. Arrange the scones in a ring, overlapping slightly, on the baking sheet. The scones will join together as they cook.
10. Bake in the centre of the preheated oven for 10–15 minutes or until golden.
11. Leave the scone ring to cool on a wire rack and eat the same day.

BUTTERMILK SCONES
Makes 7

8oz (200gm) self-raising flour
large pinch of salt
2oz (50gm) margarine
1oz (25gm) caster sugar
1 large egg, beaten
buttermilk to mix

1. Preheat oven to hot, 450 deg F or gas 8 (230 deg C).
2. Lightly grease a baking sheet.
3. Sift the flour with the salt into a bowl.
4. Rub in the margarine.
5. Stir in the sugar.
6. Add the egg and enough buttermilk to give a soft, light dough.
7. Roll out to at least ½-inch thickness.
8. Using a large plain pastry cutter, cut out seven rounds.
9. Bake in centre of preheated oven for 10–15 minutes, or until golden and firm.
10. Leave to cool.

CHOCOLATE TOPS
(Illustrated on page 87)
Makes 14

1lb (½ kilo) self-raising flour
1 level teaspoon salt
4oz (100gm) margarine
2oz (50gm) caster sugar
2 large eggs, beaten
milk to mix
6oz (150gm) plain chocolate
strawberry jam (optional)

1. Preheat oven to hot, 450 deg F or gas 8 (230 deg C).
2. Lightly grease two baking sheets.
3. Sift the flour with the salt into a bowl.
4. Rub in the margarine
5. Stir in the sugar.
6. Add the beaten eggs and just enough milk to mix to a soft, light dough.
7. Roll out the dough to at least ½-inch thickness.
8. Using a plain 2-inch (5cm) pastry cutter, cut out 14 rounds.
9. Put the rounds on the prepared baking sheets and bake in centre of preheated oven for 10–15 minutes or until golden.
10. Leave the scones to cool on a wire rack.
11. Melt the chocolate in a basin over a pan of gently simmering water.
12. Dip the top of each scone in melted chocolate to coat. Leave to become hard and set.
13. Split the scones in half and sandwich with strawberry jam, if wished. Serve within 3 hours of adding the chocolate.

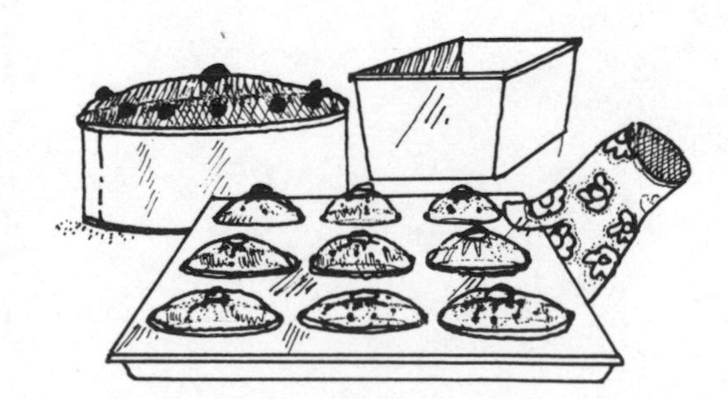

CHOCOLATE RAISIN SCONES

Makes 14

8oz (200gm) raisins
3oz (75gm) plain chocolate
1lb (½ kilo) self-raising flour
1 level teaspoon salt
4oz (100gm) margarine
2oz (50gm) caster sugar
2 large eggs, beaten
milk to mix
2 tablespoons chocolate spread

1. Put the raisins in a small basin. Soak in a little water for 1 hour then drain well.
2. Put the chocolate in a bowl over a pan of gently simmering water. Leave until the chocolate has melted.
3. Stir raisins into melted chocolate.
4. Spread the chocolate mixture on a flat piece of greaseproof paper and leave to get cold.
5. Preheat oven to hot, 450 deg F or gas 8 (230 deg C).
6. Grease two baking sheets.
7. Sift the flour with the salt into a bowl.
8. Rub in margarine until the mixture resembles fine breadcrumbs.
9. Stir in the sugar.
10. Add the eggs and enough of the milk to give a soft, light dough.
11. Roll out dough to at least ½-inch thickness.
12. Using a large, plain pastry cutter, cut out 14 rounds.
13. Put the rounds on the baking sheets.
14. Bake in centre of preheated oven for 10–15 minutes, or until well risen and golden.
15. Leave to cool.
16. Smooth some of the chocolate spread on the scones.
17. Break up the chocolate raisin mixture and sprinkle over scones.

APRICOT SCONES

Makes 7

8oz (200gm) self-raising flour
large pinch of salt
2oz (50gm) margarine
1 large banana
2oz (50gm) dried apricots, stewed and minced
1 large egg, beaten
milk to mix

1. Preheat oven to hot 450 deg F or gas 8 (230 deg C).
2. Grease a large baking sheet.
3. Sift the flour and salt into a bowl.
4. Rub in the margarine until the mixture resembles fine breadcrumbs.
5. Stir in the mashed banana and well-drained apricots.
6. Add the egg and enough milk to give a soft, light dough.
7. Roll out to at least ½-inch thickness.
8. Using a plain pastry cutter, cut into seven rounds.
9. Put on prepared baking sheet.
10. Bake in centre of preheated oven for 10–15 minutes, or until well risen and golden.
11. Leave to cool.

BANANA SCONES

Makes about 7

8oz (200gm) self-raising flour
large pinch of salt
2oz (50gm) margarine
3 large bananas
1 large egg, beaten
milk to mix

1. Preheat oven to hot, 450 deg F or gas 8 (230 deg C).
2. Grease a large baking sheet.
3. Sift flour and salt into a bowl.
4. Rub in margarine until the mixture resembles fine breadcrumbs.
5. Stir in the mashed bananas.
6. Add the egg and enough milk to give a soft, light dough.
7. Roll out dough to at least ½-inch thickness.
8. Using a plain pastry cutter, cut dough into seven rounds.
9. Put on prepared baking sheet.
10. Bake in centre of preheated oven for 10–15 minutes, or until well risen and golden.
11. Leave to cool, then serve immediately.

THREE-LAYER SCONES

Makes 7

8oz (200gm) self-raising flour
large pinch of salt
2oz (50gm) margarine
3 large bananas
1 large egg, beaten
milk to mix
1 can (6oz or 150gm) cream
3 heaped tablespoons raspberry jam

1. Preheat oven to hot, 450 deg F or gas 8 (230 deg C).
2. Grease a large baking sheet.
3. Sift the flour and salt into a bowl.
4. Rub in the margarine until the mixture resembles fine breadcrumbs.
5. Stir in the mashed bananas.
6. Add the egg and enough milk to mix to a soft, light dough.
7. Roll out to at least ½-inch thickness.
8 Using a plain pastry cutter, cut dough into seven rounds.
9. Put on prepared baking sheet.
10. Bake in the centre of the preheated oven for 10–15 minutes, or until well risen and golden.
11. Leave scones to cool.
12. Cut each scone into three layers.
13. Sandwich layers together with cream and jam. Serve within an hour of adding the filling.

Chocolate tops (see page 85)

Marmalade scones (see page 91)

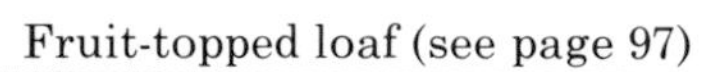

Fruit-topped loaf (see page 97)

Cherry plait (see page 96)

Marmalade loaf (see page 97)

Luxury bun round (see page 98)

Iced bun twists (see page 99)

Chelsea buns (see page 99)

LEMON SCONES

(Illustrated on page 70)
Makes 7

8oz (200gm) self-raising flour
large pinch of salt
3oz (75gm) margarine
1oz (25gm) caster sugar
1 large egg, beaten
milk to mix
3 heaped tablespoons lemon curd
2oz (50gm) icing sugar, sifted
crystallized lemon slices

1. Preheat oven to hot, 450 deg F or gas 8 (230 deg C).
2. Lightly grease a baking sheet.
3. Sift the flour with the salt into a bowl.
4. Rub in 2oz (50gm) of the margarine.
5. Stir in the caster sugar with the beaten egg and enough milk to give a soft, light dough.
6. Roll out the dough to about ½-inch thickness.
7. Using a plain 2 inch (5cm) cutter, cut out seven rounds.
8. Put the scones on the prepared baking sheet and cook in oven for 10–15 minutes, or until golden.
9. Leave scones to cool on wire rack.
10. Split the scones then sandwich with 2 tablespoons of the lemon curd.
11. Beat the rest of the lemon curd with the remaining margarine and the icing sugar until fluffy.
12. Spread this mixture on top of each scone.
13. Cut crystallized lemon slices into small pieces and use to decorate the top of each scone. Serve the same day.

GOOSEBERRY SCONES

Makes 14

1lb (½ kilo) self-raising flour
1 level teaspoon salt
4oz (100gm) margarine
2oz (50gm) caster sugar
2 large eggs, beaten
milk to mix
3 heaped tablespoons gooseberry jam
1 can (8oz or 200gm) gooseberries

1. Preheat oven to hot, 450 deg F or gas 8 (230 deg C).
2. Grease two baking sheets.
3. Sift flour and salt into a bowl.
4. Rub in margarine.
5. Stir in the sugar.
6. Add the eggs and enough milk to mix to a soft, light dough.
7. Roll out to at least ½-inch thickness.
8. Using a large plain pastry cutter, cut out 14 rounds.
9. Put on prepared baking sheets.
10. Bake in centre of preheated oven for 10–15 minutes, or until well risen and golden.
11. Leave to cool.
12. Cut each scone into two layers.
13. Heat 1 tablespoon jam with 1 tablespoon cold water. Sieve.
14. Stir rest of jam into the well-drained fruit.
15. Sandwich the scones with the fruit.
16. Glaze the top of each scone with the warmed jam.

PEAR AND PLUM SCONES

Makes 7

8oz (200gm) self-raising flour
large pinch of salt
2oz (50gm) margarine
1oz (25gm) caster sugar
1 large egg, beaten
1 large can plums
1 large ripe eating pear
2 heaped tablespoons plum jam, sieved

1. Preheat oven to hot, 450 deg F or gas 8 (230 deg C).
2. Grease a large baking sheet.
3. Sift the flour and salt into a bowl.
4. Rub in the margarine until the mixture resembles fine breadcrumbs.
5. Stir in the caster sugar.
6. Add the egg and enough milk to give a soft, light dough.
7. Roll out to at least ½-inch thickness.
8. Using a plain pastry cutter, cut into seven rounds.
9. Put on prepared baking sheet.
10. Bake in centre of preheated oven for 10–15 minutes, or until well risen and golden.
11. Allow to cool.
12. Sandwich split scones with stoned, chopped plums, peeled and chopped pear and jam. Serve within an hour of adding the filling.

PORT AND RASPBERRY SCONES

Makes 7

8oz (200gm) self-raising flour
large pinch of salt
2oz (50gm) margarine
1oz (25gm) caster sugar
1 large egg, beaten
milk to mix
1 small can raspberries
4 tablespoons inexpensive port
1 heaped teaspoon arrowroot

1. Preheat oven to hot, 450 deg F or gas 8 (230 deg C).
2. Grease a large baking sheet.
3. Sift the flour and salt into a bowl.
4. Rub in the margarine until the mixture resembles fine breadcrumbs.
5. Stir in the sugar.
6. Add egg and enough milk to give a soft, light dough.
7. Roll out to at least ½-inch thickness.
8. Using a plain pastry cutter, cut into seven rounds.
9. Put on prepared baking sheet.
10. Bake in centre of preheated oven for 10–15 minutes, or until well risen and golden.
11. Leave to cool.
12. Mix fruit with port. Thicken with arrowroot as directed on packet. Allow to cool, then use to sandwich the split scones. Serve with 3 hours.

RASPBERRY MINT SCONES
Makes 7

8oz (200gm) self-raising flour
large pinch of salt
2oz (50gm) margarine
1oz (25gm) caster sugar, plus a little extra
1 large egg, beaten
milk to mix, plus extra for topping
small sachet powdered creamy topping
1 small can raspberries
1 heaped teaspoon chopped mint, plus a few small leaves
1 small egg white

1. Preheat oven to hot, 450 deg F or gas 8 (230 deg C).
2. Grease a large baking sheet.
3. Sift the flour and salt into a bowl.
4. Rub in the margarine until the mixture resembles fine breadcrumbs.
5. Stir in the 1oz (25gm) caster sugar.
6. Add the egg and enough milk to give a soft, light dough.
7. Roll out to at least ½-inch thickness. Cut into seven rounds.
8. Put on prepared baking sheet.
9. Bake in centre of preheated oven for 10–15 minutes, or until well risen and golden.
10. Allow to cool.
11. Make up topping as directed on packet. Stir in drained fruit and chopped mint.
12. Dry mint leaves well after washing. Dip in egg white then caster sugar.
13. Allow to dry for 20 minutes, then use them to decorate tops of scones. Serve within 3 hours.

EGG NOG SCONES
Makes 7

8oz (200gm) self-raising flour
large pinch of salt
2oz (50gm) margarine
1oz (25gm) caster sugar, plus a little extra
1 large egg, beaten
milk to mix, plus just under ½ pint (250ml)
3 large egg yolks
3 tablespoons inexpensive sweet sherry

1. Preheat oven to hot, 450 deg F or gas 8 (230 deg C).
2. Grease a large baking sheet.
3. Sift the flour and salt into a bowl.
4. Rub in the margarine until the mixture resembles fine breadcrumbs.
5. Stir in sugar.
6. Add the egg and enough milk to give soft, light dough.
7. Roll out to at least ½-inch thickness.
8. Using a plain pastry cutter, cut into seven rounds.
9. Put on prepared baking sheet.
10. Bake in centre of preheated oven for 10–15 minutes, or until well risen and golden.
11. Allow to cool.
12. Put egg yolks and a little caster sugar into a basin. Whisk lightly. Heat milk but do not boil. Stir into eggs.
13. Place basin over small pan of gently boiling water, whisking all the time until mixture thickens. Stir in sherry.
14. Cover basin and leave to cool. Chill for 3 hours. Use to sandwich the split scones. Serve within an hour of adding the filling.

CARAWAY SCONES
Makes 7

8oz (200gm) self-raising flour
large pinch of salt
2oz (50gm) margarine
1oz (25gm) caster sugar
2 level teaspoons caraway seeds
1 large egg, beaten
milk to mix

1. Preheat oven to hot, 450 deg F or gas 8 (230 deg C).
2. Grease a large baking sheet.
3. Sift the flour and salt into a bowl.
4. Rub in the margarine until the mixture resembles fine breadcrumbs. Add the sugar and seeds.
5. Add the egg and enough milk to give a soft, light dough.
6. Roll out to at least ½-inch thickness.
7. Using a plain pastry cutter, cut into seven rounds.
8. Put on prepared baking sheet.
9. Bake in centre of preheated oven for 10–15 minutes, or until well risen and golden.
10. Leave to cool and eat the same day.

GOLDEN APPLE SCONES
Makes 7

8oz (200gm) self-raising flour
large pinch of salt
4oz (100gm) margarine
2oz (50gm) caster sugar
1 large egg, beaten
milk to mix
2 large cooking apples
1 small can cream
1 teacup fresh white breadcrumbs
pinch of cinnamon

1. Preheat oven to hot, 450 deg F or gas 8 (230 deg C).
2. Grease a large baking sheet.
3. Sift the flour and salt into a bowl.
4. Rub in 2oz (50gm) margarine until the mixture resembles fine breadcrumbs.
5. Stir in 1oz (25gm) caster sugar.
6. Add the egg and enough milk to give a soft, light dough.
7. Roll out to at least ½-inch thickness.
8. Using a plain pastry cutter, cut into seven rounds.
9. Put on prepared baking sheet.
10. Bake in centre of preheated oven for 10–15 minutes, or until well risen and golden.
11. Allow to cool.
12. Peel and core apples. Chop them up and stew them with 2 tablespoons water and rest of sugar. Drain, then allow them to cool. Sieve and mix with cream.
13. Fry breadcrumbs and cinnamon in rest of margarine in a shallow pan and toss crumbs while cooking. Drain and allow to cool. Mix with apple.
14. Sandwich the split scones with apple mixture and serve immediately.

MARMALADE SCONES

(Illustrated on page 87)
Makes 7

8oz (200gm) self-raising flour
large pinch of salt
2oz (50gm) margarine
1oz (25gm) caster sugar
1 large egg, beaten
milk to mix
4 heaped tablespoons rough-cut marmalade
rind of 1 small orange

1. Preheat oven to hot, 450 deg F or gas 8 (230 deg C).
2. Lightly grease a baking sheet.
3. Sift the flour with the salt into a large bowl.
4. Rub in the margarine.
5. Stir in the sugar.
6. Add the beaten egg and enough milk to mix to a soft, light dough.
7. Roll out dough to at least ½-inch thickness.
8. Using a plain 2-inch (5cm) cutter, cut out seven rounds.
9. Put the rounds on a baking sheet and bake in centre of preheated oven for 10–15 minutes, or until golden.
10. Leave to cool on a wire rack.
11. Split the scones, and sandwich them with a little of the marmalade.
12. Remove the soft white pith from the orange rind. Using a sharp knife, cut the rind into fine shreds.
13. Put the rind in a pan. And water and boil for 3 minutes. Drain and rinse in cold water then drain again. Leave to cool
14. Spread the rest of the marmalade on the top of the scones.
15. Sprinkle orange rind on top of marmalade and serve that day.

LEMON FLUFF SCONES

Makes 7

8oz (200gm) self-raising flour
large pinch of salt
2oz (50gm) margarine
1oz (25gm) caster sugar
1 large egg, beaten
milk to mix
1 small egg yolk
3 heaped tablespoons lemon curd
half a small can cream
1 small egg white

1. Preheat oven to hot, 450 deg F or gas 8 (230 deg C).
2. Grease a large baking sheet.
3. Sift the flour and salt into a bowl.
4. Rub in the margarine until the mixture resembles fine breadcrumbs.
5. Stir in caster sugar.
6. Add the egg and enough milk to give a soft, light dough.
7. Roll out to at least ½-inch thickness.
8. Using a plain pastry cutter, cut out seven rounds.
9. Put on prepared baking sheet. Brush with beaten small egg yolk.
10. Bake in centre of preheated oven for 10–15 minutes, or until well risen and golden.
11. Allow to cool.
12. Mix lemon curd with cream, then add very stiffly whisked egg white, using metal spoon. Use to sandwich the split scones. Serve immediately.

DAMSON SCONES

Makes 7

8oz (200gm) self-raising flour
large pinch of salt
2oz (50gm) margarine
1oz (25gm) caster sugar
1 large egg, beaten
milk to mix
1 small can damsons or 4 heaped tablespoons damson jam
1 small carton cottage cheese

1. Preheat oven to hot, 450 deg F or gas 8 (230 deg C).
2. Grease a large baking sheet.
3. Sift the flour and salt into a bowl.
4. Rub in the margarine until the mixture resembles fine breadcrumbs. Stir in sugar.
5. Stir in the egg and enough milk to give a soft, light dough.
6. Roll out to at least ½-inch thickness.
7. Using a plain pastry cutter, cut into seven rounds.
8. Put on prepared baking sheet.
9. Bake in centre of preheated oven for 10–15 minutes, or until well risen and golden.
10. Allow to cool.
11. Sandwich the split scones with the drained, sieved damsons or damson jam, and cheese. Serve 2 hours after adding the filling.

HONEY WHIP SCONES

Makes 7

8oz (200gm) self-raising flour
large pinch of salt
2oz (50gm) margarine
1 large egg, beaten
milk to mix and extra for topping
small sachet powdered creamy topping
2 tablespoons clear honey

1. Preheat oven to hot, 450 deg F or gas 8 (230 deg C).
2. Grease a large baking sheet.
3. Sift the flour and salt into a bowl.
4. Rub in the margarine until the mixture resembles fine breadcrumbs.
5. Add the egg and enough milk to give a soft, light dough.
6. Roll out to at least ½-inch thickness.
7. Using a plain pastry cutter, cut into seven rounds.
8. Put on prepared baking sheet.
9. Bake in centre of preheated oven for 10–15 minutes, or until well risen and golden.
10. Allow to cool.
11. Make up topping as directed on packet using milk. Mix with honey and use to sandwich the split scones. Eat within 4 hours.

SWEET AND SOUR SCONES
Makes 7

8oz (200gm) self-raising flour
large pinch of salt
2oz (50gm) margarine
1oz (25gm) caster sugar
1 large egg, beaten
milk to mix
4oz (100gm) cream cheese
3 heaped tablespoons strawberry jam

1. Preheat oven to hot, 450 deg F or gas 8 (230 deg C).
2. Grease a large baking sheet.
3. Sift the flour and salt into a bowl.
4. Rub in the margarine until the mixture resembles fine breadcrumbs. Stir in sugar.
5. Stir in the egg and milk to give a soft, light dough.
6. Roll out to at least ½-inch thickness.
7. Using a plain pastry cutter, cut into seven rounds.
8. Put on prepared baking sheet.
9. Bake in centre of preheated oven for 10–15 minutes.
10. Leave to cool.
11. Split and sandwich with cream cheese and jam. Serve within 2 hours.

MINCEMEAT SCONES
Makes 7

8oz (200gm) self-raising flour
large pinch of salt
2oz (50gm) margarine
2 heaped tablespoons mincemeat
1 large egg, beaten
milk to mix

1. Preheat oven to hot, 450 deg F or gas 8 (230 deg C).
2. Grease a large baking sheet.
3. Sift the flour and salt into a bowl.
4. Rub in the margarine until the mixture resembles fine breadcrumbs.
5. Stir in mincemeat, egg and enough milk to give soft, light dough.
6. Roll out to at least ½-inch thickness.
7. Using a plain pastry cutter, cut into seven rounds.
8. Put on prepared baking sheet.
9. Bake in centre of preheated oven for 10–15 minutes, or until well risen and golden.
10. Leave to cool and eat the same day.

EXTRA CREAMY APRICOT SCONES
Makes 7

1 small can evaporated milk
8oz (200gm) self-raising flour
large pinch of salt
2oz (50gm) margarine
1 large egg, beaten
milk to mix
1 small can apricots

1. Leave can of milk in refrigerator overnight. Next day whisk by hand – or in your electric mixer – until very smooth and thickened. Leave to chill while you are making the scones.
2. Preheat oven to hot, 450 deg F or gas 8 (230 deg C).
3. Grease a large baking sheet.
4. Sift the flour and salt into a bowl.
5. Rub in the margarine until the mixture resembles fine breadcrumbs.
6. Add egg and enough milk to give a soft, light dough.
7. Roll out to at least ½-inch thickness.
8. Using a plain pastry cutter, cut into seven rounds.
9. Put on prepared baking sheet.
10. Bake in centre of preheated oven for 10–15 minutes, or until well risen and golden.
11. Allow to cool.
12. Mix thickened milk with drained fruit. Sandwich the split scones with fruit mixture and serve at once.

CRANBERRY SCONES
Makes 7

8oz (200gm) self-raising flour
large pinch of salt
2oz (50gm) margarine
1 large egg, beaten
milk to mix
1 small can cranberry sauce (not jelly)

1. Preheat oven to hot, 450 deg F or gas 8 (230 deg C).
2. Grease a large baking sheet.
3. Sift the flour and salt into a bowl.
4. Rub in the margarine until the mixture resembles fine breadcrumbs.
5. Stir in the egg and enough milk to give a soft, light dough.
6. Roll out to at least ½-inch thickness.
7. Using a plain pastry cutter, cut into seven rounds.
8. Put on prepared baking sheet.
9. Bake in centre of preheated oven for 10–15 minutes, or until well risen and golden.
10. Leave to cool.
11. Split each scone into two. Sandwich with cranberry sauce and eat within 3 hours.

MARASCHINO SCONES
Makes 7

8oz (200gm) self-raising flour
large pinch of salt
2oz (50gm) margarine
half a small jar of cocktail (maraschino) cherries
1 large egg, beaten
milk to mix

1. Preheat oven to hot, 450 deg F or gas 8 (230 deg C).
2. Grease a large baking sheet.
3. Sift the flour and salt into a bowl.
4. Rub in the margarine until the mixture resembles fine breadcrumbs.
5. Stir in drained, chopped cherries.
6. Add the egg and enough milk to give a soft, light dough.
7. Roll out to at least ½-inch thickness.
8. Using a plain pastry cutter, cut into seven rounds.
9. Put on prepared baking sheet.
10. Bake in centre of preheated oven for 10–15 minutes, or until well risen and golden.
11. Leave to cool and eat the same day.

SEVEN-SCONE CAKE
Gives 7 portions

8oz (200gm) self-raising flour
large pinch of salt
2oz (50gm) margarine
1oz (25gm) caster sugar
1 large egg, beaten
milk to mix
3oz (75gm) icing sugar, sifted
3½ glacé cherries

1. Preheat oven to hot, 450 deg F or gas 8 (230 deg C).
2. Grease a baking sheet.
3. Sift flour and salt into a bowl.
4. Rub in the margarine until mixture resembles fine breadcrumbs.
5. Stir in sugar.
6. Add the egg and enough milk to give a soft, light dough.
7. Roll out to at least ½-inch thickness.
8. Using a large pastry cutter cut out seven rounds.
9. Put the shapes, almost touching, on the baking sheet (they should join up when they are cooked).
10. Bake in centre of preheated oven for 10–15 minutes, or until well risen and golden.
11. Leave to cool.
12. Mix the icing sugar with enough cold water to give a mixture which will coat the back of a wooden spoon.
13. Spoon the icing on centre top of each scone. Add half a cherry and leave to set.

SHERRY-FILLED SCONES
Makes 7

8oz (200gm) self-raising flour
large pinch of salt
5oz (125gm) margarine
1 large egg, beaten
milk to mix
3oz (75gm) icing sugar, sifted
2 tablespoons inexpensive sweet sherry

1. Preheat oven to hot, 450 deg F or gas 8 (230 deg C).
2. Grease a large baking sheet.
3. Sift the flour and salt into a bowl.
4. Rub in 2oz (50gm) of the margarine until the mixture resembles fine breadcrumbs.
5. Add the egg and enough milk to give a soft, light dough.
6. Roll out to at least ½-inch thickness.
7. Using a plain pastry cutter, cut out seven rounds.
8. Put on prepared baking sheet.
9. Bake in centre of preheated oven for 10–15 minutes, or until well risen and golden.
10. Leave to cool.
11. Beat icing sugar with rest of margarine until light and creamy. Mix in sherry and use to sandwich the split scones. Eat within 4 hours of adding the filling.

ICE CREAM SCONES
Makes 7

8oz (200gm) self-raising flour
large pinch of salt
2oz (50gm) margarine
1 large egg, beaten
milk to mix
family size block of strawberry ice cream
3 heaped tablespoons raspberry jam, heated

1. Preheat oven to hot, 450 deg F or gas 8 (230 deg C).
2. Grease a large baking sheet.
3. Sift the flour and salt into a bowl.
4. Rub in the margarine until the mixture resembles fine breadcrumbs.
5. Add egg and enough milk to give a soft, light dough.
6. Roll out to at least ½-inch thickness.
7. Using a plain pastry cutter, cut into seven rounds.
8. Put on baking sheet.
9. Put on baking sheet.
10. Bake in centre of preheated oven for 10–15 minutes, or until well risen and golden.
11. Leave to cool.
12. Using a potato scoop which has been dipped in very hot water, put scoops of ice cream on scones. Top with jam and serve at once.

COUNTRY SCONES
Makes 7

8oz (200gm) self-raising flour
large pinch of salt
2oz (50gm) margarine
1 large egg, beaten
milk to mix
1 medium-sized can blackberries or fresh fruit, when in season
1 small can cream

1. Preheat oven to hot, 450 deg F or gas 8 (230 deg C).
2. Grease a baking sheet.
3. Sift flour and salt into a bowl.
4. Rub in the margarine until the mixture resembles fine breadcrumbs.
5. Stir in egg and enough milk to give a soft, light dough.
6. Roll out to at least ½-inch thickness.
7. Using a plain pastry cutter, cut into seven rounds.
8. Put on prepared baking sheet.
9. Bake in centre of preheated oven for 10–15 minutes, or until well risen and golden.
10. Leave to cool.
11. Split and sandwich with drained fruit and cream. Serve within 2 hours of filling.

SUMMER SCONES
Makes 7

8oz (200gm) self-raising flour
large pinch of salt
2oz (50gm) margarine
1 large egg, beaten
milk to mix
7 tablespoons cherry syrup (made for babies), undiluted
1 heaped teaspoon arrowroot
8oz (200gm) ripe red cherries

1. Preheat oven to hot, 450 deg F or gas 8 (230 deg C).
2. Grease a large baking sheet.
3. Sift the flour and salt into a bowl.
4. Rub in margarine until the mixture resembles fine breadcrumbs.
5. Stir in egg and enough milk to give soft, light dough.
6. Roll out to at least ½-inch thickness.
7. Using a plain pastry cutter, cut into seven rounds.
8. Put on prepared baking sheet.
9. Bake in centre of preheated oven for 10–15 minutes, or until well risen and golden.
10. Leave to cool.
11. Thicken syrup with the arrowroot as directed on packet. Stir in fresh, stoned cherries. Spoon on top of scones when cool. Serve within 2 hours.

APRICOT WINE SCONES
Makes 7

8oz (200gm) self-raising flour
large pinch of salt
2oz (50gm) margarine
1 large egg, beaten
milk to mix
8 tablespoons apricot wine
1 heaped teaspoon arrowroot
1 small can cream

1. Preheat oven to hot, 450 deg F or gas 8 (230 deg C).
2. Grease a large baking sheet.
3. Sift the flour and salt into a bowl.
4. Rub in the margarine until the mixture resembles fine breadcrumbs.
5. Add the egg and enough milk to give a soft, light dough.
6. Roll out to at least ½-inch thickness.
7. Using a plain pastry cutter, cut into seven rounds.
8. Put on prepared baking sheet.
9. Bake in centre of preheated oven for 10–15 minutes, or until well risen and golden.
10. Allow to cool.
11. Thicken wine with arrowroot as directed on packet. Leave to cool then mix with cream. Use to sandwich the split scones and eat within 4 hours.

FUDGE SPECIALS
Makes 7

8oz (200gm) self-raising flour
large pinch of salt
5oz (125gm) margarine
1 large egg, beaten
milk to mix
3oz (75gm) icing sugar, sifted
2oz (50gm) inexpensive bought fudge, finely chopped

1. Preheat oven to hot, 450 deg F or gas 8 (230 deg C).
2. Grease a large baking sheet.
3. Sift the flour and salt into a bowl.
4. Rub in 2oz (50gm) of the margarine until the mixture resembles fine breadcrumbs.
5. Add the egg and enough milk to give a soft, light dough.
6. Roll out to at least ½-inch thickness.
7. Using a plain pastry cutter, cut into seven rounds.
8. Put on prepared baking sheet.
9. Bake in centre of preheated oven for 10–15 minutes, or until well risen and golden.
10. Leave to cool.
11. Cream rest of margarine with icing sugar until light and creamy. Stir in fudge. Use this to sandwich the split scones and eat within 3 hours.

SULTANA SCONES
Makes 24

1lb (½ kilo) plain flour
2oz (50gm) margarine
¾oz (18gm) fresh yeast
½ pint (250ml) tepid milk
1 level teaspoon salt
2oz (50gm) sultanas
a little lard or corn oil for frying

1. Sift the flour into a bowl.
2. Rub in the margarine until the mixture looks like fine breadcrumbs.
3. Cream the yeast with a little of the milk then add rest.
4. Make a well in flour. Add yeast liquid and mix well.
5. Grease or oil the inside of a large polythene bag.
6. Place the bowl of dough inside the large polythene bag.
7. Leave in a warm place for 45 minutes, or until dough has doubled in size.
8. Turn out risen dough. Knead well then knead in salt and sultanas.
9. Roll out the dough to ½-inch thickness.
10. Using a plain cutter, cut out 24 rounds.
11. Grease a girdle or a heavy frying pan with lard or oil. Heat.
12. Cook the scones for about 5 minutes on each side, or until golden and cooked.
13. Serve scones that day, hot or cold, with butter.

DROP SCONES
Makes about 12

These are delicious hot or cold, but they must be eaten within four hours of making. If you are serving them hot, wrap each one in a clean cloth as it is cooked.

8oz (200gm) self-raising flour
pinch of salt
2oz (50gm) margarine
2oz (50gm) caster sugar
1 standard egg
¼ pint (125ml) milk
¼ pint (125ml) water
a little lard or corn oil
butter and jam, for serving

1. Sift the flour with salt into a mixing bowl.
2. Using your fingertips, rub in the margarine until mixture looks like fine breadcrumbs.
3. Stir in the caster sugar.
4. Make a well in the centre and drop in the egg.
5. Mix the milk with the water. Add about a quarter of this liquid to the flour mixture and beat well.
6. When the mixture is smooth, stir in the rest of the liquid.
7. Grease or oil a large, heavy frying pan, or use a girdle if you have one. Heat the pan or girdle until hot.
8. Drop 2 tablespoonfuls of the batter on to the girdle to form a flat round. Cook until bubbles appear on the surface then turn it with a palette knife and cook on the other side until golden. Repeat this until all the mixture is used up.
9. Serve with butter and jam.

Bread and buns

If you've never baked or tasted home-made bread and buns, here's your chance to try some super recipes, old and new.

WHOLEMEAL COB
Gives 4 to 5 portions

1lb (½ kilo) wholemeal flour
½oz (12gm) fresh yeast
½ pint (250ml) tepid water
large pinch of salt
a little raw oatmeal for decoration

1. Sift the flour into a mixing bowl.
2. Cream the fresh yeast with a little of the tepid water then stir in rest of tepid water.
3. Make a well in centre of flour. Add yeast liquid and beat well.
4. Knead the dough for at least 5 minutes, or until smooth and elastic. The dough should leave fingers and sides of bowl clean.
5. Lightly oil or grease the inside of a large polythene bag.
6. Slip the bowl of dough inside the bag.
7. Leave in a warm place – not near direct heat or boiler – until dough has risen to twice its size.
8. Knead salt into risen dough.
9. Form the mixture into a large round and put on a lightly greased baking sheet.
10. Leave in a warm place for 15 minutes, or until swollen.
11. Preheat oven to hot, 450 deg F or gas 8 (230 deg C).
12. Bake bread in centre of preheated oven for 10 minutes, then reduce oven to moderately hot, 400 deg F or gas 6 (200 deg C) and cook for a further 30 minutes, or until loaf sounds hollow when tapped on the base.
13. Leave to cool.
14. Sprinkle oatmeal on top and eat the same day.

MILK LOAF
Gives 8 to 10 portions

2lb (1 kilo) plain flour
1oz (25gm) fresh yeast
1 pint (½ litre) tepid milk
1 level teaspoon salt
1 standard egg, beaten

1. Sift the flour into a mixing bowl.
2. Cream the yeast with a little of the milk then stir in rest of milk.
3. Make a well in centre of flour, then add yeast liquid and mix to a soft dough.
4. Knead the dough until very smooth and elastic.
5. Lightly oil or grease the inside of a large polythene bag.
6. Slip the bowl of dough into the bag.
7. Leave in a warm place – not near direct heat or boiler – for 1–2 hours, or until dough has doubled in size.
8. Knead salt into risen dough.
9. Grease two baking sheets.
10. Knead dough and shape into two neat rounds. Put on baking sheets.
11. Leave in a warm place for 20 minutes.
12. Preheat oven to hot, 425 deg F or gas 7 (220 deg C).
13. Brush tops of loaves with beaten egg.
14. Bake in centre of preheated oven for 10 minutes, then turn oven down to moderate to moderately hot, 375 deg F or gas 5 (190 deg C) and bake for another 35 minutes.
15. Leave to cool. Serve, that day, with butter and strawberry jam.

IRISH TEA BREAD
Gives 5 to 6 portions

1lb (½ kilo) plain flour
¼ level teaspoon grated nutmeg
½ level teaspoon cinnamon
2oz (50gm) margarine
¾oz (18gm) fresh yeast
½ pint (250ml) tepid milk
2 standard eggs, beaten
3oz (75gm) caster sugar
6oz (150gm) sultanas
6oz (150gm) currants
2oz (50gm) mixed chopped peel
pinch of salt

1. Grease an 8-inch (20cm) round, deep cake tin with a little melted lard.
2. Sift the flour with the nutmeg and cinnamon into a large bowl.
3. Rub in the margarine.
4. Cream the yeast with a little of the tepid milk then mix with the rest of the tepid milk.
5. Make a well in the centre of the flour mixture and add yeast liquid and most of the egg.
6. Mix well then knead for 5 minutes or until dough is smooth and elastic.
7. Knead in the sugar, fruit, mixed chopped peel and salt.
8. Press the dough into the prepared cake tin and cover lightly with greased polythene.
9. Leave the dough in a warm place, not near direct heat, for 2 hours, or until the dough has reached the top of the tin.
10. Preheat oven to moderately hot, 400 deg F or gas 6 (200 deg C). Remove polythene.
11. Brush the top of the bread with the rest of the beaten egg.
12. Bake in the centre of the preheated oven for 1 hour, or until golden.
13. Leave in tin for 5 minutes then turn out to finish cooling.

COTTAGE LOAF
Gives 4 to 5 portions

1lb (½ kilo) plain flour
2oz (50gm) margarine
½oz (12gm) fresh yeast
¼ pint (125ml) tepid milk
¼ pint (125ml) tepid water
large pinch of salt

1. Sift the flour into a mixing bowl.
2. Rub in margarine until mixture resembles fine breadcrumbs.
3. Cream yeast with a little of the tepid milk then mix with rest of tepid liquids.
4. Make a well in centre of flour and add the yeast liquid. Beat well.
5. Knead the dough for at least 5 minutes, or until smooth and elastic. The dough should leave fingers and sides of bowl clean.
6. Lightly oil or grease the inside of a large polythene bag.
7. Slip bowl of dough inside the bag.
8. Leave in a warm place – not near direct heat or boiler – until dough has risen to twice its size.
9. Knead salt into risen dough.
10. Form the dough into one large round and one small round.
11. Put the large round on a lightly greased and floured baking sheet. Wet the centre of round and put smaller piece on the top.
12. Flour two fingers and push through centre of small round and halfway through large one, to make deep hole.
13. Leave for 15 minutes in a warm place, or until swollen.
14. Preheat oven to hot, 450 deg F or gas 8 (230 deg C).
15. Bake in centre of preheated oven for 10 minutes then reduce heat to moderately hot, 400 deg F or gas 6 (200 deg C) and bake for a further 30 minutes, or until loaf sounds hollow when tapped on the base.

CHERRY PLAIT
(Illustrated on page 87)
Gives 4 to 5 portions

1oz (25gm) margarine
8oz (200gm) plain flour
½oz (12gm) fresh yeast
4 tablespoons tepid milk
4 tablespoons tepid water
1 small egg, beaten
1½oz (37gm) caster sugar
pinch of salt
2oz (50gm) icing sugar, sifted
3 glacé cherries

1. Sift the flour into a bowl.
2. Rub in the margarine.
3. Cream the yeast with a little of the tepid milk then mix with the rest of the milk and water.
4. Make a well in the centre of the flour and add the yeast liquid and the egg. Mix well.
5. Knead for 5 minutes, or until the dough is smooth and elastic and leaves your fingers and the sides of the bowl clean.
6. Lightly grease or oil the inside of a large polythene bag.
7. Slip the bowl of dough into the bag and leave in the ordinary warmth of the kitchen – not near direct heat or boiler – for 30 minutes to 1 hour, for the dough to rise. (The dough should double in size, so watch it during this time and don't leave it any longer than necessary.)
8. Knead the caster sugar and salt into the risen dough.
9. Divide the dough into three equal parts. Roll each part into a fat sausage shape.
10. Seal the three sausage shapes together at one end. Plait them together then seal the other end.
11. Put the plait on a lightly greased baking sheet. Leave to prove (rise again) for about 15 minutes – the plait should look plump and swollen.
12. Preheat oven to hot, 425 deg F or gas 7 (220 deg C).
13. Bake the plait in the centre of the preheated oven for 30–35 minutes, or until bread is golden and sounds slightly hollow when tapped on the base.
14. Leave the plait to cool.
15. Mix the icing sugar with enough cold water to give a mixture which will thickly coat the back of a wooden spoon.
16. Spoon the icing on to the top of the plait. Decorate with halved glacé cherries.
17. Allow the icing to set before you serve the plait.

MALT BREAD
Gives 4 to 6 portions

12oz (300gm) wholemeal flour
8oz (200gm) plain flour
1oz (25gm) fresh yeast
¾ pint (375ml) plus 2 teaspoons tepid water
1½ level tablespoons caster sugar
1 tablespoon golden syrup
1oz (25gm) malt extract
large pinch of salt
1oz (25gm) sultanas
2 tablespoons milk

1. Sift both lots of flour into a bowl.
2. Cream yeast with ¼ pint (125 ml) tepid water.
3. Make a well in flour mixture. Add yeast liquid and stir well.
4. Dissolve 1 tablespoon of sugar with the syrup and malt in rest of tepid water and add to the flour when cool.
5. Lightly grease or oil the inside of a large polythene bag.
6. Put the bowl of dough inside the polythene bag.
7. Leave in a warm place – not near direct heat or boiler – for 45 minutes, or until dough has risen to twice its size.
8. Knead the risen dough, then knead in the salt and sultanas.
9. Put the dough into two greased 1-lb (½ kilo) loaf tins.
10. Leave in a warm place for 15 minutes, or until dough almost reaches top of tins.
11. Preheat oven to hot, 450 deg F or gas 8 (230 deg C).
12. Mix the remaining sugar with the milk and brush this over the loaves.
13. Bake in the centre of the preheated oven for 5 minutes, then reduce oven heat to moderate, 350 deg F or gas 4 (180 deg C). Bake for 35 minutes.
14. Leave to cool. Store in an airtight tin and serve sliced and buttered within three days.

MARMALADE LOAF

(Illustrated on page 88)
Gives 4 to 6 portions

4oz (100gm) margarine
1lb (½ kilo) plain flour
¾oz (18gm) fresh yeast
¼ pint (125ml) tepid milk
¼ pint (125ml) tepid water
1 standard egg, beaten
pinch of salt
4oz (100gm) caster sugar
3oz (75gm) currants
5oz (125gm) rough-cut marmalade

1. Sift the flour into a mixing bowl.
2. Rub the margarine into the flour.
3. Cream the yeast with a little of the tepid milk, then mix with rest of tepid liquids and the egg.
4. Make a well in the centre of the flour and add the yeast liquid.
5. Mix well then knead for at least 5 minutes until the dough is smooth and elastic and leaves your fingers and the sides of the bowl clean.
6. Lightly grease or oil the inside of a large polythene bag.
7. Slip the bowl of dough inside the polythene bag and leave for 1½ hours in a warm place – not near direct heat, or boiler – or until dough has risen to twice its size.
8. Knead the salt, sugar and currants into the risen dough.
9. Separate about half the peel from the marmalade. Chop this and knead it into the dough.
10. Put the dough into two greased loaf tins, each 6 inches (15cm) by 4 inches (10cm) by 3 inches (7·5cm) and leave to prove (rise again) for 15 minutes, or until the dough has risen to the top of the tins.
11. Preheat oven to hot, 425 deg F or gas 7 (220 deg C).
12. Bake the loaves in the centre of the preheated oven for 30 minutes or until well risen; the loaves should sound hollow when tapped on the base.
13. Leave to cool completely.
14. Top loaves with rest of marmalade and serve sliced and buttered, with more marmalade.

FRUIT-TOPPED LOAF

(Illustrated on page 87)
Gives 4 to 6 portions

1lb (½ kilo) plain flour
4oz (100gm) margarine
¾oz (18gm) fresh yeast
¼ pint (125ml) tepid milk
¼ pint (125ml) tepid water
1 standard egg, beaten
pinch of salt
4oz (100gm) caster sugar
3oz (75gm) currants
2oz (50gm) glacé cherries
1oz (25gm) angelica
2 teaspoons golden syrup or clear honey

1. Sift the flour into a mixing bowl.
2. Rub the margarine into the flour until mixture resembles fine breadcrumbs.
3. Cream the yeast with a little of the tepid milk. Stir in rest of milk, tepid water and egg.
4. Add yeast liquid to flour.
5. Mix well then knead for at least 5 minutes, or until the dough is smooth and elastic and leaves your fingers and the sides of the bowl clean.
6. Lightly grease or oil the inside of a large polythene bag.
7. Slip the bowl of dough into the bag.
8. Leave the dough in a warm place – not near direct heat or boiler – for 1½ hours, or until dough has doubled in size.
9. Knead the salt, sugar and currants into the risen dough.
10. Put the dough in two greased loaf tins each 6 inches (15cm) by 4 inches (10cm) by 3 inches (7·5 cm).
11. Leave the dough in a warm place to prove (rise again) for 15 minutes.
12. Preheat oven to hot, 425 deg F gas 7 (200 deg C).
13. Bake the loaves in the centre of the preheated oven for 30 minutes or until well risen and firm. When the bread is tapped on the base it should sound hollow.
14. Leave to cool completely.
15. Chop up the cherries and angelica fairly finely. Mix them with the syrup. Spoon on top of the loaves.

BRIDGE ROLLS

Makes 10

8oz (200gm) plain flour
½oz (12gm) fresh yeast
4 tablespoons tepid milk
1 standard egg plus 1 small egg, beaten
2oz (50gm) margarine
large pinch of salt

1. Sift the flour into a mixing bowl.
2. Cream the yeast with the tepid milk.
3. Make a well in centre of flour and add the yeast liquid and standard egg.
4. Gently melt margarine and stir into flour mixture.
5. Mix to a dough then knead until smooth.
6. Lightly grease or oil the inside of a large polythene bag.
7. Slip the bowl of dough inside the bag.
8. Leave in a warm place – not near direct heat or boiler – for 1 hour, or until dough has doubled in size.
9. Knead salt into risen dough.
10. Form the dough into 10 narrow rolls, about 3 inches long.
11. Put the rolls on a greased baking sheet.
12. Leave in a warm place for 15 minutes, or until swollen.
13. Preheat oven to hot, 450 deg F or gas 8 (230 deg C).
14. Brush rolls with beaten egg and bake in centre of preheated oven for 15 minutes, or until golden.
15. Leave to cool. Serve the same day, with a sweet or savoury filling.

COTTAGE ROLLS

Makes 12

1lb (½ kilo) plain flour
2oz (50gm) margarine
½oz (12gm) fresh yeast
¼ pint (125ml) tepid milk
¼ pint (125ml) tepid water
large pinch of salt
1 small egg, beaten

1. Sift the flour into a mixing bowl.
2. Rub in margarine until mixture resembles fine breadcrumbs.
3. Cream the yeast with a little tepid milk then mix with rest of tepid liquids.
4. Make a well in centre of flour. Add the yeast liquid and beat well.
5. Knead the dough for at least 5 minutes, or until smooth and elastic. The dough should leave the fingers and sides of the bowl clean.
6. Lightly grease or oil the inside of a large polythene bag.
7. Slip bowl of dough inside the bag.
8. Leave in a warm place – not near direct heat or boiler – until dough has risen to twice its size.
9. Knead salt into risen dough.
10. Shape exactly as for cottage loaf (see page 96) but make 12 tiny ones, and use just one floured finger to make the holes.
11. Put on lightly greased and floured baking sheet.
12. Leave in a warm place for 15 minutes, or until swollen.
13. Brush with beaten egg.
14. Preheat oven to hot, 425 deg F or gas 7 (220 deg C).
15. Bake rolls in centre of preheated oven for 20 minutes, or until cooked and golden.
16. Leave to cool.

BAPS

Makes 8

These delicious, soft Scottish rolls are quite unlike the English version.

1lb (½ kilo) plain flour
2oz (50gm) lard
1oz (25gm) fresh yeast
½ pint (250ml) plus 2 tablespoons tepid milk
1 level teaspoon salt

1. Sift the flour into a mixing bowl.
2. Rub in the lard.
3. Cream the yeast with a little of the milk then stir in enough milk to give ½ pint (250ml) exactly.
4. Make a well in the flour. Add the yeast liquid and stir well. Knead mixture until very smooth.
5. Lightly grease or oil the inside of a large polythene bag.
6. Slip the bowl of dough into the bag.
7. Leave in a warm place – not near direct heat or boiler – for 30 minutes, or until dough has doubled in size.
8. Knead the salt into the risen dough. Knead the dough well.
9. Grease two baking sheets.
10. Shape dough into eight large, flattish rounds. Put on the baking sheets.
11. Leave in a warm place for 20 minutes.
12. Preheat oven to hot, 425 deg F or gas 7 (220 deg C).
13. Brush the tops of the baps with the rest of the milk.
14. Bake in centre of the preheated oven for 15–20 minutes.
15. Leave to cool and eat that day.

LUXURY BUN ROUND

(Illustrated on page 88)
Gives 4 portions

8oz (200gm) plain flour
1oz (25gm) margarine
½oz (12gm) fresh yeast
4 tablespoons tepid milk
4 tablespoons tepid water
1 small egg, beaten
large pinch of salt
1½oz (37gm) caster sugar
1oz (25gm) currants
1 small can cream or ¼ pint fresh double cream, whipped
2 heaped tablespoons strawberry jam
a little sifted icing sugar to decorate

1. Sift the flour into a bowl.
2. Rub in the margarine.
3. Cream the yeast with a little of the tepid milk then add rest of tepid liquids and egg.
4. Make a well in the flour, then add yeast liquid and mix to a soft dough.
5. Knead dough until smooth and elastic.
6. Lightly grease or oil the inside of a large polythene bag.
7. Slip the bowl of dough into the bag.
8. Leave in a warm place – not near direct heat or boiler – for about 1½ hours, or until dough has risen to twice its size.
9. Knead salt into risen dough with sugar and currants.
10. Form mixture into two flat, large rounds and put on to greased baking sheet.
11. Leave in a warm place for 20 minutes.
12. Preheat oven to moderately hot, 400 deg F or gas 6 (200 deg C).
13. Bake in centre of preheated oven for 25–35 minutes or until golden brown and cooked. Leave to cool.
14. Sandwich rounds with cream and jam; decorate top with icing sugar, and serve the same day.

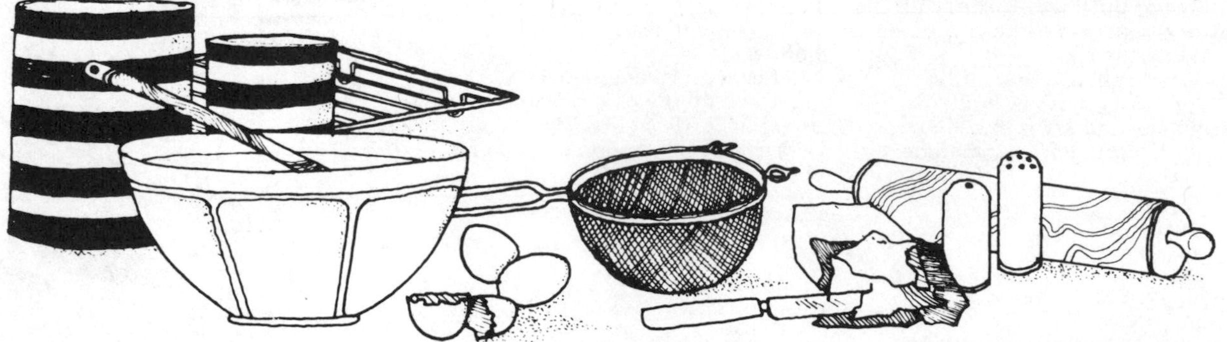

CHELSEA BUNS

(Illustrated on page 88)
Makes 12

8oz (200gm) plain flour
2½oz (62gm) margarine
½oz (12gm) fresh yeast
6 tablespoons tepid milk
1 small egg, beaten
pinch of salt
3½oz (87gm) caster sugar
1oz (25gm) sultanas
1oz (25gm) currants
1oz (25gm) chopped mixed peel

1. Sift the flour into a mixing bowl.
2. Rub in 1½oz (37gm) margarine until mixture resembles fine breadcrumbs.
3. Cream the fresh yeast with a little of the tepid milk then stir in the rest of the milk and the beaten egg.
4. Make a well in the centre of the flour. Add the yeast liquid and beat well.
5. Knead for at least 5 minutes until the dough is smooth and elastic and leaves your fingers and the sides of the bowl clean.
6. Lightly grease or oil the inside of a large polythene bag.
7. Slip the bowl of dough inside the bag and leave in a warm place – not near direct heat or boiler – for 45 minutes, or until dough has doubled in size.
8. Turn dough on to lightly floured board and knead in the salt and ½oz (12gm) sugar.
9. Roll out the dough to an oblong 12 inches by 9 inches.
10. Melt the rest of the margarine in a small pan and stir in the sultanas, currants and peel.
11. Spread the fruit evenly over the dough, leaving a 1-inch space all round the edge.
12. Brush one long edge with water. Starting at the other long edge, roll up dough tightly and press all the edges to seal.
13. Cut the dough roll into 12 slices.
14. Grease a meat tin.
15. Arrange the dough slices in the tin, leaving about ½-inch space between each slice. (They will join up as they cook.)
16. Flatten the buns slightly and leave to prove (rise again) for 15 minutes.
17. Preheat oven to hot, 425 deg F or gas 7 (220 deg C).
18. Bake the buns in the centre of the preheated oven for 20 minutes, or until golden.
19. Take buns out of oven and pull them apart.
20. Sprinkle rest of sugar over the buns and leave to cool. Eat them the same day.

ICED BUN TWISTS

(Illustrated on page 88)
Makes 8

8oz (200gm) plain flour
1oz (25gm) margarine
½oz (12gm) fresh yeast
4 tablespoons tepid milk
4 tablespoons tepid water
1 small egg, beaten
large pinch salt
1½oz (37gm) caster sugar
1oz (25gm) currants
3oz (75gm) icing sugar

1. Sift the flour into a bowl.
2. Rub in the margarine.
3. Cream the fresh yeast with a little of the tepid milk then add rest of tepid liquids and egg.
4. Make a well in the flour, then add yeast liquid and mix to a soft dough.
5. Knead dough until smooth and elastic.
6. Lightly grease or oil the inside of a large polythene bag.
7. Slip bowl of dough into the bag.
8. Leave in a warm place – not near direct heat or boiler – for about 1½ hours, or until dough has risen to twice its size.
9. Knead in salt, sugar and currants.
10. Form mixture into eight, then divide each piece into three. Make into three short fat sausage shapes. Twist lightly together then form into a round shape. Repeat with rest of dough.
11. Leave, on a greased baking sheet, in warm place for 20 minutes.
12. Preheat oven to moderately hot 400 deg F or gas 6 (200 deg C).
13. Bake in centre of preheated oven for 20–25 minutes, or until golden and cooked.
14. Leave to cool.
15. Sift icing sugar and add enough cold water to give thick mixture which will coat back of wooden spoon. Spoon on to top of each bun. Leave to set, and eat the same day.

HOT CROSS BUNS

Makes about 20

1¾lb (700gm) plain flour
1 level teaspoon cinnamon
½ level teaspoon grated nutmeg
1oz (25gm) fresh yeast
¾ pint (375ml) tepid milk
2 large eggs, beaten
4oz (100gm) margarine
4oz (100gm) caster sugar
8oz (200gm) currants
1oz (25gm) finely chopped mixed peel
large pinch of salt
extra caster sugar and milk for glazing

1. Sift flour and spices into a bowl.
2. Cream the yeast with a little of the milk, then stir in rest of milk.
3. Make a well in centre of flour and add yeast liquid and beaten eggs.
4. Melt margarine and stir into dough, then knead until smooth.
5. Lightly grease or oil the inside of a large polythene bag.
6. Slip bowl of dough into the polythene bag.
7. Leave in a warm place – not near direct heat or boiler – for 1 hour or until dough has doubled in size.
8. Knead well then knead in sugar, currants, peel and salt.
9. Form mixture into round buns and place on greased baking sheets. Mark a cross on each bun.
10. Leave in a warm place for 15 minutes, or until swollen.
11. Preheat oven to hot, 450 deg F or gas 8 (230 deg C).
12. Bake on three shelves of the preheated oven for 20–30 minutes or until golden.
13. Mix a little sugar with milk and, when buns are almost cooked, brush this on top of each. Return them to the oven to continue cooking until done. Leave to cool.

CURRANT BUNS
Makes 12

1lb (½ kilo) plain flour
3oz (75gm) margarine
½oz (12gm) fresh yeast
½ pint (250ml) tepid water
5oz (125gm) currants
pinch of salt
2oz (50gm) caster sugar
1 small egg, beaten

1. Sift the flour into a mixing bowl.
2. Rub in the margarine until the mixture resembles fine breadcrumbs.
3. Cream the yeast with a little of the tepid water then mix with rest of water.
4. Make a well in the centre of the flour and add yeast. Beat well.
5. Knead the dough for at least 5 minutes, or until smooth and elastic. The dough should leave your fingers and the sides of the bowl clean.
6. Lightly grease or oil the inside of a large polythene bag.
7. Slip the bowl of dough inside the bag.
8. Leave dough in a warm place – not near direct heat or boiler – for 45 minutes, or until dough has risen to twice its size.
9. Knead the currants, salt and sugar into risen dough.
10. Shape the mixture into 12 rounds.
11. Place the rounds on two greased baking sheets.
12. Leave in a warm place for 15 minutes, or until buns are swollen.
13. Preheat oven to hot, 425 deg F or gas 7 (220 deg C).
14. Brush the buns with beaten egg.
15. Bake the buns in the centre of the preheated oven for 20 minutes, or until golden.
16. Leave to cool and eat that day.

CURRANT CASTLES
Makes 18

1lb (½ kilo) plain flour
3oz (75gm) margarine
½oz (12gm) fresh yeast
½ pint (250ml) tepid water
5oz (125gm) currants
pinch of salt
1 small egg, beaten

1. Sift the flour into a mixing bowl.
2. Rub in the margarine until the mixture resembles fine breadcrumbs.
3. Cream the yeast with a little of the tepid water then mix with rest of water.
4. Make a well in the centre of flour and add yeast. Beat well.
5. Knead for at least 5 minutes, or until the dough is smooth and elastic and leaves your fingers and the sides of the bowl clean.
6. Lightly grease or oil the inside of a large polythene bag.
7. Slip the bowl of dough inside the polythene bag.
8. Leave the bowl in a warm place – not near direct heat or boiler – for 45 minutes, or until dough has risen to twice its size.
9. Knead the currants and salt into the risen dough.
10. Put the mixture into 18 greased dariole moulds (metal castle pudding tins) and leave in a warm place for 15 minutes, or until dough reaches tops of tins.
11. Preheat oven to hot, 425 deg F or gas 7 (220 deg C).
12. Brush the tops with beaten egg.
13. Bake the castles in the centre of the preheated oven for 20 minutes, or until golden.
14. Turn out and leave to cool; eat the same day.

BATH BUNS
Makes 8

8oz (200gm) plain flour
1oz (25gm) margarine
½oz (12gm) fresh yeast
4 tablespoons tepid milk
4 tablespoons tepid water
1 small egg, beaten
large pinch of salt
1½oz (37gm) caster sugar
1oz (25gm) currants
grated rind of 1 small lemon
1oz (25gm) chopped mixed peel
2 teaspoons cold milk
6 sugar lumps, lightly crushed

1. Sift the flour into a bowl.
2. Rub in the margarine.
3. Cream the yeast with a little of the tepid milk then add rest of tepid liquids and egg.
4. Make a well in the flour and add yeast liquid and mix to a soft dough.
5. Knead dough until smooth and elastic.
6. Lightly grease or oil the inside of a large polythene bag.
7. Slip the bowl of dough into the bag.
8. Leave in a warm place – not near direct heat or boiler – for about 1½ hours, or until dough has risen to twice its size.
9. Knead salt into risen dough with sugar, currants, lemon rind, and mixed peel.
10. Form the mixture into eight rounds and put on a greased baking sheet.
11. Leave in a warm place for 20 minutes.
12. Preheat oven to moderately hot, 400 deg F or gas 6 (200 deg C).
13. Brush the buns with milk and sprinkle with crushed sugar.
14. Bake in centre of preheated oven for 20–25 minutes, or until cooked.
15. Leave to cool and eat the same day.

FRUITY TEACAKES
Makes 10

12oz (300gm) plain flour
½oz (12gm) fresh yeast
⅓ pint (166ml) tepid milk and water mixed
1 standard egg
1oz (25gm) lard
large pinch of salt
3oz (75gm) currants and sultanas mixed together

1. Sift the flour into a mixing bowl.
2. Cream the yeast with a little of the tepid liquid then mix in the rest.
3. Make a well in the centre of the flour and stir in the yeast liquid.
4. Add beaten egg to dough.
5. Melt the lard and mix into the dough.
6. Knead mixture until very smooth.
7. Lightly grease or oil the inside of a large polythene bag.
8. Slip the bowl of dough into the bag and leave in a warm place – not near direct heat or boiler – for 1 hour, or until dough has doubled in size.
9. Knead salt and fruit into the risen dough.
10. Form the dough into 10 very flat rounds and put on a large, greased baking sheet.
11. Leave in a warm place for 15 minutes, or until swollen.
12. Preheat oven to hot, 450 deg F or gas 8 (230 deg C).
13. Bake in the centre of the preheated oven for 15 minutes, or until golden.
14. Leave to cool. Eat the same day.

SALLY LUNNS
Gives 8 portions

12oz (300gm) plain flour
½ level teaspoon salt
½oz (12gm) fresh yeast
⅜ pint (188ml) tepid milk plus 1 tablespoon cold milk
2oz (50gm) margarine, melted
1 standard egg, beaten
2 level teaspoons caster sugar

1. Sift the flour and salt into a bowl.
2. Cream the yeast with a little of the tepid milk.
3. Make a well in the flour and add the yeast liquid.
4. Mix margarine with rest of tepid milk and beaten egg.
5. Add to flour and beat well.
6. Knead the dough until smooth and elastic.
7. Divide dough into two and shape into neat rounds.
8. Put each round in a 5-inch (13cm) cake tin.
9. Grease or oil the inside of a large polythene bag.
10. Slip the tins into the bag.
11. Leave in a warm place – not near direct heat or boiler – for 1–1½ hours, or until dough has risen to top of tins.
12. Preheat oven to moderately hot, 400 deg F or gas 6 (200 deg C).
13. Bake the rounds in the centre of preheated oven for 15–20 minutes, or until golden. Remove from oven. Leave oven on.
14. Mix the cold milk with sugar and brush on top of rounds.
15. Put in oven for 3 minutes.
16. Leave to cool, and eat the same day.

SWEET BREAD
Gives about 10 portions

1lb (½ kilo) plain flour
1oz (25gm) fresh yeast
½ pint (250ml) plus 5 tablespoons tepid water
1 level teaspoon salt
1½oz (37gm) margarine
1oz (25gm) caster sugar

1. Sift the flour into a bowl.
2. Cream the yeast with a little tepid water then stir in rest.
3. Make a well in centre of flour. Add yeast liquid and mix well.
4. Knead dough until smooth and elastic.
5. Lightly grease or oil the inside of a large polythene bag.
6. Slip the bowl of dough inside the bag and leave in a warm place – not near direct heat or boiler – for 1–2 hours, or until dough has doubled in size.
7. Knead dough again, then knead in the salt.
8. Form dough into a large, flattish round about ½ inch thick.
9. Put on a greased baking sheet.
10. Cut the margarine into small pieces and dot over top of dough.
11. Leave in a warm place for 20 minutes.
12. Sprinkle sugar over dough.
13. Preheat oven to hot, 425 deg F or gas 7 (220 deg C).
14. Bake bread in centre of preheated oven for 25 minutes, or until cooked.

LEMON SPLITS
Makes 16

1lb (½ kilo) plain flour
2oz (50gm) margarine
1oz (25gm) fresh yeast
8 tablespoons tepid milk
8 tablespoons tepid water
2 small eggs, beaten
3oz (75gm) caster sugar
½ level teaspoon salt
small sachet powdered creamy topping
milk to mix
4 heaped tablespoons lemon curd

1. Sift flour into a mixing bowl.
2. Rub in the margarine.
3. Cream the yeast with a little tepid milk, then stir in rest of tepid liquids and egg.
4. Make a well in the centre of the flour and add the yeast liquid. Mix well. Knead until smooth and elastic.
5. Lightly oil or grease the inside of a large polythene bag.
6. Slip the bowl of dough inside the bag.
7. Leave in a warm place – not near direct heat or boiler – for 1 hour, or until dough has risen to twice its size.
8. Knead sugar and salt into risen dough and knead well.
9. Grease two baking sheets.
10. Shape the dough into 16 rounds.
11. Put the rounds on the baking sheets.
12. Leave in a warm place for 20 minutes.
13. Preheat oven to hot, 425 deg F or gas 7 (220 deg C).
14. Bake the buns in the centre of the preheated oven for 20–25 minutes, or until golden.
15. Leave the buns to cool, then make a deep cut in the centre of the top of each bun.
16. Make up the topping with milk, following directions on packet.
17. Fill centre of buns with the topping and lemon curd.

Index